D1554029

A FAILED VISION OF EMPIRE

DANIEL J. BURGE

A Failed Vision of
EMPIRE

The Collapse of Manifest Destiny,
1845–1872

University of Nebraska Press | LINCOLN

© 2022 by the Board of Regents of the University of Nebraska

All rights reserved

The University of Nebraska Press is part of a land-grant institution with campuses and programs on the past, present, and future homelands of the Pawnee, Ponca, Otoe-Missouria, Omaha, Dakota, Lakota, Kaw, Cheyenne, and Arapaho Peoples, as well as those of the relocated Ho-Chunk, Sac and Fox, and Iowa Peoples.

Library of Congress Cataloging-in-Publication Data
Names: Burge, Daniel J., author.
Title: A failed vision of empire : the collapse of Manifest Destiny, 1845–1872 / Daniel J. Burge.
Description: Lincoln : University of Nebraska Press, [2022] | Includes bibliographical references and index. |
Identifiers: LCCN 2021035852
ISBN 9781496228079 (hardback)
ISBN 9781496231666 (epub)
ISBN 9781496231673 (pdf)
Subjects: LCSH: Manifest Destiny. | United States—Territorial expansion. | United States—History—1849–1877. | United States—Politics and government—1849–1877. | BISAC: HISTORY / United States / 19th Century | POLITICAL SCIENCE / American Government / General
Classification: LCC E179.5 .B94 2022 | DDC 973.5—dc23
LC record available at https://lccn.loc.gov/2021035852

Set in Adobe Caslon Pro by Laura Buis.

To Louann, for everything

CONTENTS

ILLUSTRATIONS

ACKNOWLEDGMENTS

It is one of the few joys of working on a book that there is a section set aside to acknowledge those who contributed to its publication. A few pages are hardly enough to adequately recompense those who have had to tolerate my discussions of manifest destiny, or who have provided support when I was ready to abandon the project. What follows is certainly an incomplete list of those who have in some way contributed to this book, but hopefully it acknowledges those who have made it possible. I am grateful to each and every one of you.

This journey began at the University of Maryland, Baltimore County, where I came across scholars who helped push me toward a career in history. Marjoleine Kars never failed to encourage me in my pursuit of writing excellence and provided me with my first academic job, as a writing coach in one of her upper-level classes. Marjoleine is not merely a gifted writer herself; she is also an unfailingly kind scholar. Her generosity, patience, and kindness taught me much about what an academic career should resemble. In a similar fashion, Anne Sarah Rubin showed me that being a brilliant scholar does not prohibit a person from being genial. Not only did Anne read my rough drafts, but she also helped guide me toward the doctoral degree. Finally, Terry Bouton served as my academic advisor at UMBC, but he was much more than that. Terry tore into drafts and critiqued them, in a manner that would have made Edgar Allan Poe quite proud. While serving as a critic, Terry provided encouragement. Without his support I certainly would not be writing this.

It was while I was at UMBC that I learned the value of friendships that had little to do with the study of history. A special thanks to Jenness Hall for hiring me as the writing advisor for the Office of Graduate Student Life. I look back on my days working at UMBC as being one of the highlights of my career. This is probably because of the friendships I made. There are so many names I could mention, but especial thanks to Rachel Sturge and Nandadevi Cortes Rodriguez. Both of you modeled academic excellence and showed me how to conduct myself as a graduate student. But you also made graduate school fun. A similar thanks to Manica Ramos, who taught me much about graduate school. For our lengthy talks at Panera and for your long phone calls providing support after I moved to Alabama, I am always grateful.

At the University of Alabama, I was fortunate to have George Rable as my academic advisor. Mere words on the page can never express what George has done for me, both as a scholar and as a person. Gracious, curious, funny, and longsuffering, George is everything that I aspire to be as a scholar. From the minute I approached him with this project, George has supported it. George is the only one who has read every word of this manuscript in multiple drafts, and he has dissected it as efficiently as Joe Burrow cut through the Alabama defense on that unfortunate November evening a few years ago. I would add more, but as George has pointed out to me on several occasions, I have a tendency toward wordiness.

While working with George at the University of Alabama, I was supported by a network of incredible colleagues. Adam Petty's prolific ability to publish inspired me and showed me what a scholar could achieve. His humble demeanor and friendship as we navigated the academic job market taught me that not everything has to be a competition. Friendships run deeper. Kari Boyd toured battlefields with me, got me to attend a handful of social events, usually through the bribe of an apple pie, and generally helped me get through graduate school. A final thanks to Katie Deale, who remained a constant friend. Katie talked me through the dissertation process, taught me an appreciation of Alabama football, and remained a bedrock of support.

During my time in Alabama, Katie also helped me secure a position as an academic tutor. I am grateful to Brittany Price for hiring me. In my four years working at the Bill Battle Academic Center, I was beyond fortunate to tutor young men who left a deep impression on my own life. While I was ostensibly tutoring them, they each taught me much about the values of hard work, dedication to a craft, and a commitment to excellence. Wherever they have ended up, I am immensely proud of the men that they have become. Although this list is incomplete, I am grateful to Trevon, Chadarius, Christopher, De'Marquise, Irv, Pierce, Tanner, Darrian, Tua, Chris, Brian, Trey, Malachi, LaBryan, Jarez, Marcus, Byron, Cam, and Skyler. It was a pleasure to work with you all.

A book such as this is not possible without ample resources to conduct research and visit archives. Special thanks to John McClure for hosting me for a week at the Virginia Museum of History & Culture on a Mellon Research Fellowship. Thanks to Stephanie Lang at the Kentucky Historical Society for enabling me to spend a lovely week in Frankfort on a Scholarly Research Fellowship. Anyone who has conducted research at the Massachusetts Historical Society knows what a pleasure it is to spend time on Boylston Street. The Mellon research fellowship provided the funds, but I am especially grateful to Katheryn Viens, Conrad Wright, and Alexis Buckley for welcoming Louann and myself with incredible hospitality. Spending a month in Boston helped me reshape and reformulate my ideas for this book.

Other institutions and fellowships provided me time to research and write. Thanks to the North Caroliniana Society for providing me with an Archie K. Davis Fellowship to conduct research at the State Archives of North Carolina and the University of North Carolina. At Chapel Hill I was fortunate to have Jason Tomberlin help me track down several sources and provide me with the opportunity to present on my research. Shortly thereafter, I spent time at the Ulysses S. Grant Presidential Library, where John Marszalek and Ryan Semmes welcomed me. Thanks to the Ulysses S. Grant Association for funding this travel and for John's and Ryan's expertise, which helped me rethink Grant's approach to Santo Domingo. A trip to the Charles Redd Center for Western Studies at Brigham Young University helped me broaden my approach to manifest destiny by focusing more attention on the West. Special thanks to Brenden Rensick, Jay H. Buckley, and Amy Carlin for helping turn this into a most productive, yet congenial, research trip.

I am also appreciative of the New England Research Fellowship Consortium for supporting my longest research trip. At the Connecticut Historical Society, I am grateful to Natalie Belanger and Sierra Dixon for making me feel at home. The Mystic Seaport Museum provided an ideal location to conduct research. Maribeth Quinlan handled my many research requests with dexterity and patience. The New Hampshire Historical Society also provided a warm home for research. Sarah E. Galligan introduced me to several important collections. Korrena Cowing was an invaluable resource, as she tracked down collections and pointed my research in new directions. Morgan Swan provided similar assistance at the Rauner Special Collections Library at Dartmouth College, tracking down requests and helping me navigate the Webster papers. Although I was unable to use the Archibald Hanna Jr. Fellowship in American History as I planned, I am thankful for the gracious support of those at the Beinecke Library at Yale University who emailed me pertinent documents. Matthew Rowe quickly responded to my requests and tracked down everything I was unfortunately unable to view in person.

Research fellowships provided me with time to write, but I am also grateful for those scholars who helped me refine my ideas once I put them on paper. Joshua Rothman guided me at each stage of the writing process, but more importantly he taught me how to defend my arguments, both verbally and in print. As I look back at my time at Alabama, I realize how fortunate I was to have Josh as a mentor. Bob May has watched this project develop from its earliest stages and has commented at length on various editions of this manuscript. On a more personal level, Bob has helped me navigate the academic publishing world and has championed this project from the beginning. I am forever grateful for his kindness, knowledge, and wisdom. Rachel St. John, David Rich Lewis, and Jimmy Bryan Jr. have all provided encouragement and support. All three have generously provided me with advice and have encouraged me to publish. At the University of Nebraska Press, Bridget Barry has been everything I could ask for in an editor. She has responded to countless questions, helped me refine my prose and argument, and generally made this book possible. Thank you for believing in this book. A similar thanks to Emily Wendell, who has answered all of my many questions and helped this first-time author navigate the publishing process.

The Kentucky Historical Society has provided a hospitable academic home for me as I wrapped up the final stages of this manuscript. Moving in the midst of a pandemic is never easy, but I am grateful to Scott Alvey, Jessica Stavros, Jodi Lewis, Keith Jackson, Bill Burchfield, and Claire Gwaltney for their hospitality and kindness. At KHS I have been blessed to work with incredible colleagues who engage in public history on a regular basis. Chuck Welsko has welcomed my wife and me with open arms and helped introduce us to Kentucky. Chuck's stewardship of the Civil War Governors of Kentucky project, as well as his own research, has helped model to me what a career in public history should resemble. Stuart Sanders has similarly provided much-needed encouragement and support throughout the writing process. I am also thankful to Rebecca Wishnevski who brought me into several schools in Kentucky through the Host a Historian Program. Although I am not entirely sure the students appreciated my attempts to teach them about manifest destiny, I enjoyed trying. Rebecca's enthusiasm and remarkable patience with students reminded me how fun it can be to teach.

Outside of academia, I have had the unstinting support of family. While working on this project, I have been blessed to have gained a family in San Diego. They have supported me at every step of the way. My mother-in-law, Donna Calhoun, has welcomed me as a son, provided me with support, and navigated me safely through one of the scariest mountain roads I have traveled on in my life. In a similar manner, Craig Calhoun has been incredibly supportive. I have enjoyed our time watching sporting events and have come to appreciate the passionate intensity that folks in San Diego feel toward the Chargers. Dominic Sabatini has been the consummate host, offering a place to stay and absolutely incredible food. I never thought I would get a father-in-law who could teach me how to appreciate fine cuisine, but I am quite appreciative that I did. It would take too long to thank everyone who has made me feel at home in San

Diego, but thanks especially to Vera and Victor Moore, Debbie and Anthony Sabatini, Mari Jo and Nikol Sabatini, the Cerny-Bloom family, Amber and Vincent Winter, Emma and Eva Rodriguez, the Storniolo family, the Madruga family, Brandon Reese, Eddie Alves, and, of course, Aldina Alves.

On the opposite coast, I have watched my family grow and my brothers raise families of their own. Even though he entered into a career in finance, Josh has always loved history and, I am sure, will communicate that love, along with his fierce pitching ability, to Kylee, Carter, and Kinsley. As a younger brother, Kenny has had to deal with quite a bit, but he has taken it all with an unfailing sense of humor. I am grateful for our friendship, countless hours of Smash Bros., and getting to spend time with Vera and Kimmy. Steven, Mike, and Major have all helped me get my mind off of this project at various points and I consider myself lucky to count them as brothers. Although I never had sisters growing up, I am now blessed to have three incredible sisters-in-law: Margaret, Becca, and Sydney. I am thankful for each one of you. My grandparents have been there for me from the beginning. Returning to Maryland for the crab feasts and holiday dinners took my mind off work and reminded me why Maryland is such a special place. I love you all. I am only sorry that Nana was not able to see the completion of this book.

At the most personal level, this book would never have been possible without the support of my parents. My mom has not only been a teacher, but she has also enkindled in me a love of learning that has only increased over time. More than anyone else, she has encouraged me to write, taught me how, and cheered me up when I was convinced this project would not be published. My dad has played a similar role in my life. His dedication to teaching and writing, coupled with his remarkable sense of humor, have had an indelible impact on my own career. I appreciate the many phone calls of support and the steadfast love that you have shown.

Finally, none of this would have been possible without the support of my wife. Louann has been there for me since I first considered publishing a book. She has driven with me on research trips across the country, including one from Vermont to San Diego, put up with my complaints, helped me practice presentations, and served as my sharpest critic. She has left me alone to write on countless weekends and long evenings. More importantly, she has reminded me that a vibrant world exists outside of academia, one with good food, friends, and family. For all of these things, I am beyond grateful, and this is why I dedicate this book to her.

A FAILED VISION OF EMPIRE

Introduction

The Myth of Manifest Destiny

In March 1870 the *Courier-Journal*, a newspaper in Louisville, Kentucky, provided an overview of the history of manifest destiny. "The time was when Democratic Fourth of July orators talked earnestly of the 'manifest destiny' of our Republic to enfold the whole continent," the author explained, "and Democratic statesmen were sincere in their belief that under our then noble and benign system of government, State after State, and province after province, could be added safely . . . until 'the whole boundless continent should be ours.'"[1] Defining manifest destiny as the belief that the United States would expand over the entire continent of North America, this anonymous author saw the ideology as less than successful. Yet he or she was not saddened by manifest destiny's failure. "What may have been possible and desirable a decade ago," the author concluded, "may be the most absurd proposition on earth now."[2] In the mind of this writer, it was wise to let the idea of manifest destiny slowly fade away.

The *Courier-Journal*'s take on manifest destiny is informative for two specific reasons. First, the *Courier-Journal* defined manifest destiny as the belief that it was the destiny of the United States "to enfold the whole continent." It analyzed the acquisitions of Louisiana, Florida, Texas, and California, but it did not see obtaining California as fulfilling manifest destiny. Indeed, it specifically noted that manifest destiny entailed the absorption of the continent. Second, although the *Courier-Journal* did not see manifest destiny as a successful ideology, it certainly did not see it as an idea that pertained to the past. Writing in 1870, in the midst of President Ulysses S. Grant's first term, the *Courier-Journal* saw manifest destiny as a living, relevant idea. In the 1870s Americans were still debating manifest destiny and pondering whether future events would ever bring about its fulfillment.

The assessment provided by the *Courier-Journal* stands in stark contrast to that dispensed by subsequent academic historians. The *Courier-Journal* advanced a simple definition of manifest destiny, alleging it was the idea that the United States was to "enfold the whole continent." Historians have concluded that manifest destiny "never received a precise definition" and that it "did not belong exclusively to any one group or have one precise meaning."[3] Whereas the *Courier-Journal* saw the ideology as unfulfilled, historians have tended to view it as accomplished. In their work *Manifest Destiny*, historians David Heidler and Jeanne Heidler argued that "[James K.] Polk's presidency fulfilled what newspaper writer John L. O'Sullivan described as the United States' 'Manifest Destiny' to expand to the Pacific Ocean."[4] The *Courier-Journal* did not think that manifest destiny was overly popular, noting that most Americans were uninterested in acquiring Canada, Cuba, or Mexico. Historian David Reynolds, in contrast, wrote, "'Manifest destiny' was a slogan that captured the public imagination, signifying America's God-given right as the instrument of liberty and progress to occupy all the land from the Atlantic to the Pacific."[5]

These conflicting takes demonstrate the wide divergence between those who wrote about manifest destiny in the nineteenth century and those who have examined it in the early twenty-first. But what explains these vastly different interpretations? The simple answer is that the definition of manifest destiny evolved over time. In the nineteenth century Americans defined manifest destiny as the idea that the United States was destined to absorb the continent of North America, along with Cuba. Movements to acquire Canada, Mexico, and Cuba were unsuccessful, so most observers saw manifest destiny as a failure. Nearly fifty years later, academic historians began to reexamine the ideology, creating, in the process, a myth of manifest destiny. This myth redefined manifest destiny as the idea that the United States was destined to acquire the Pacific Coast. Working through this revised understanding, academic historians portrayed manifest destiny as a popular ideology that peaked in the 1840s under James K. Polk. Over time, this myth would nearly efface the earlier understanding of manifest destiny, obscuring, in the process, the contested nature of U.S. empire.

To understand the dramatic redefinition that occurred in the twentieth century, it is first necessary to examine the origins of manifest destiny. The phrase "manifest destiny" first appeared in 1845, in the *United States Magazine, and Democratic Review*.[6] Because the phrase was used in an unsigned article, historians have debated whether it was coined by John L. O'Sullivan or Jane McManus Storm Cazneau.[7] Regardless, the author in the *Democratic Review* made it clear that manifest destiny was the idea that the entire continent had been set aside for the United States. He or she argued that foreign powers were trying to limit "the fulfillment of our manifest destiny to overspread the continent allotted by Providence for the free development of our yearly multiplying millions."[8] The author believed that the United States needed to annex Texas as part of a larger historical process that would absorb the continent.

As time passed, the *Democratic Review* did not change its definition of manifest destiny.[9] "During the past four years," it groaned in 1852, "the Whig Administration has never lost a public opportunity of protesting against annexation. . . . All the world knows and says, that it is the manifest destiny of our political system to extend itself until it embraces the entire North American Continent."[10] In 1856 the magazine taunted the British and declared North America off limits for the British empire: "Looking nearer home, we see that it is the manifest destiny of North-Americans to colonize and control this continent."[11] In article after article, the *Democratic Review* looked to the future for the fulfillment of manifest destiny, which it continued to view as the idea that the United States would annex Mexico, Canada, and Cuba.[12]

Nor did the *Democratic Review* ever abandon its belief in manifest destiny. In 1859 the magazine pushed for the United States to embrace a "Continental policy" and demanded that it annex Cuba. The magazine boasted that it had "from its birth until the present moment, advocated the 'manifest destiny' of the American Republic."[13] In that same year, on the eve of the election of 1860, the *Democratic Review* again demanded that the United States conquer the continent. "We hope to witness, in the campaign of '60," it observed, "the organization of the Democratic party, upon a basis that will fully realize and recognize the non-intervention policy in respect to this continent . . . Let the 'manifest destiny' of this continent choose its own road in the great march of empire."[14] The *Democratic Review* folded shortly after the publication of this article. Yet from 1845 until 1859, the magazine, which openly bragged about being manifest destiny's greatest defender, always defined it as the expansion of the United States over the entire continent of North America, including the annexation of Canada, Mexico, and Cuba. In 1859 that destiny was still unfulfilled.

In the nineteenth century Americans shared the *Democratic Review*'s understanding of manifest destiny. Take, for example, the *New York Times*, which started in 1851 and quickly gained a national reputation. In 1852 the *New York Times* published "The Science of Manifest Destiny," an article that began: "Cuba, Mexico, Hawaii. Whichever of our wide windows we look through there lies a fresh prize for ambition; a new field for the experiment of republican theories."[15] Like the *Democratic Review*, the *New York Times* perceived manifest destiny as something yet to be accomplished.[16] In 1853 it examined recent events in Cuba, Canada, and Mexico.[17] It concluded that all three nations were wending their way to U.S. control, observing, "The limits of the Republic will, on every side be defined by the ocean shore."[18] U.S. expansion had only just begun.[19]

The *New York Times* not only trumpeted manifest destiny but also attacked papers that doubted its fulfillment. "While conservatives moralize on the evils of expansion," it opined in 1854, "and argue earnestly that we ought to shut down the gates, remain at home, and take care of the territory already acquired by the Anglo-American race, an irresistible power . . . is working out a great destiny on the continents. . . . Not only Westward does the empire tend; but South, Southwest, and more Westward than the Continent of America itself."[20] The *New York Times* dismissed those who warned of the dangers of expansion. For example, on July 8, 1858, the *New York Tribune*, a rival paper, derided manifest destiny.[21] The *New York Times* responded two days later. "The New-York *Tribune* is sorely grieved by the prevalent desire for increase of territory," the *Times* sarcastically noted.[22] It then further mocked the *Tribune* for protesting against the increase of territory and argued that if the United States had pursued the *Tribune's* policy then it would not have expanded past the original thirteen colonies. "The doctrines which that paper promulgates are obsolete," the *New York Times* concluded. "It is now half a century since the policy of acquisition received the practical approval of our Government and people."[23]

The dream of manifest destiny continued through the Civil War.[24] In the midst of Reconstruction, the *New York Times* returned to the refrain that Mexico had proved incapable of running itself, stressing that it would soon be time for the United States to intervene.[25] "The experience of Mexico has been most trying for forty years," the paper wailed in 1870, "and the future contains but very little hope of any improvement, apart from an incorporation into the United States."[26] Two years later, the paper ran a nearly identical article. "Mexico must first be Americanized by the introduction of our own population," this article conjectured, "with their arts and industries, and then we may safely trust to the natural desire that will arise in her breast to cast her lot with Uncle Sam."[27] For over two decades, then, the *New York Times* championed manifest destiny and eagerly awaited its fulfillment.

Both the *New York Times* and *Democratic Review* defined manifest destiny as the theory that the United States would acquire the continent of North America and the island of Cuba.[28] Because nineteenth-century Americans saw manifest destiny as the conquest of the continent, they increasingly lost faith in the ideology by the 1870s.[29] "But in fact," one paper noted in 1877, "there was never among the American people so little of the spirit of 'manifest destiny' at work in the direction of Mexico as now."[30] Another paper asserted in 1877, "The doctrine of 'Manifest Destiny,' as interpreted by President Polk, has lost much of its old power, because of events of more recent occurrence. The most thoughtful minds of this country are averse to the absorption of Mexico by conquest or wholesale annexation."[31]

As the decades passed, however, a curious transformation began to take place. Historians and writers who reflected back on the era of the 1840s and 1850s began to redefine manifest destiny. James G. Blaine, a prominent Republican politician after the Civil War, recalled in his memoirs that politician Stephen Douglas "was injured by his partial committal to what was known as the doctrine of 'manifest destiny,'—the indefinite acquisition of territory southward, especially in the direction of the West Indies."[32] Blaine, a Pennsylvanian who lived most of his life in Maine, turned manifest destiny into a southern idea. Blaine seemingly forgot that proponents of manifest destiny had always targeted Canada in addition to Mexico. The *New York Times* did something similar in 1879. "Before the abolition of slavery," the paper told its readers, "there was a considerable element in the South which was active in advocating the annexation of Mexico. This sort of propagandism faded out with the apparent necessity for carving new slave States from territory to be annexed."[33] The *New York Times* conveniently forgot that it had advocated for the acquisition of Mexico from 1853 until 1870 and instead pinned the blame on hotheaded southerners who desired to spread slavery.

By the 1890s it was common to condemn southerners for all the expansion that had occurred prior to the Civil War.[34] The idea that slaveholders had been behind manifest destiny became so deeply entrenched that it took time to overcome. In 1886 Theodore Roosevelt, a historian and future president, wrote, "Recent historians . . . always speak as if our grasping after territory in the Southwest was due solely to the desire of the Southerners to acquire lands out of which to carve new slave-holding states."[35] Roosevelt then explained that westerners, not southerners, were behind antebellum expansion: "Westerners honestly believed themselves to be indeed created the heirs of the earth, or at least of so much of it as was known by the name of North America, and were prepared to struggle stoutly for the immediate possession of their heritage."[36] Throughout his career as a historian, Roosevelt would continue to emphasize the role that westerners played in expanding the borders of the United States.

By the turn of the twentieth century, academic historians followed Roosevelt's lead and increasingly linked manifest destiny to western expansion.[37] For these historians, manifest destiny signified the acquisition of the Pacific Coast. Frederick Jackson Turner copied Roosevelt's argument in an article he published in the *Atlantic Monthly*.[38] Turner argued, "The Western man believed in the manifest destiny of his country."[39] Turner saw the West, not the South, as behind antebellum expansion. "It was the Western demands that brought about the purchase of Louisiana," Turner declared, "and turned the scale in favor of declaring the War of 1812. . . . The West caught the vision of the nation's continental destiny."[40] Gone, in Turner's interpretation, were the demands for Mexico, Cuba, and Canada. Turner helped turn manifest destiny into a synonym for western expansion.[41]

Soon historians began to expand Turner's argument. Undoubtedly, the most significant work on manifest destiny was completed by Ephraim Douglass Adams, a professor of history at Stanford University. In 1913 Adams published *The Power of Ideals in American History*, which included a chapter on manifest destiny.[42] Like Turner, Adams considered manifest destiny to be synonymous with western expansion. "We of the present age rightly regard as heroic the American migration from East to West," Adams wrote, "and exalt the personal virtues of the men who led."[43] Adams defined manifest destiny as the popular and pervasive idea that the United States was destined to expand from coast to coast to spread democracy.[44]

Adams believed there were two sides to the idea of manifest destiny, "the earlier expressing merely the conviction of superiority in [the U.S.] form of government . . . while the later phase carried with this belief the desire for new territory."[45] In other words, manifest destiny could mean territorial expansion, but it could also mean a belief in the superiority of U.S. institutions.[46] This broadened definition enabled Adams to argue that the ideology was almost impossible for Americans to resist.[47] He went on to contend that only the Civil War had ended Americans' passion for territorial expansion.[48] "It was a fever in the blood that steadily rose," he concluded, "and was allayed only by the letting of blood."[49]

Adams's study on manifest destiny directly contributed to the latter's reconceptualization. I call this reconceptualization the "myth of manifest destiny," as it completely effaced the earlier understanding of the ideology. Proponents of the emerging myth of manifest destiny argued that manifest destiny inflamed the popular imagination like a potent virus and drove white Americans to expand the boundaries of the nation until they reached the Pacific Coast. By the end of the 1920s this myth was widely accepted by academic historians.[50] In 1927, for example, Carl Russell Fish, a professor of history at the University of Wisconsin, published *The Rise of the Common Man, 1830–1850*, which included a chapter on manifest destiny.[51] Fish wrote that "not only did the new president, Polk, believe in Manifest Destiny but he believed it was the finger of God that pointed it out."[52] In Fish's synthetic overview, manifest destiny secured the election of Polk, brought on the U.S.-Mexican War, and sowed the seeds of discord that led to the Civil War.[53] In the conclusion of his work, Fish listed the "realization of manifest destiny" as one of the nation's most significant accomplishments.[54]

Over the ensuing decades, historians added elements to this burgeoning myth. Julius W. Pratt rescued John L. O'Sullivan from complete obscurity. In 1927 Pratt argued that O'Sullivan had created the phrase "manifest destiny."[55] A few years later, Pratt wrote a short biography of O'Sullivan.[56] Here, Pratt told the story of O'Sullivan's childhood, his friendship with Nathaniel Hawthorne, and his involvement with the Democratic Party. Pratt sought not only to illuminate O'Sullivan's life but also to give his subject a newfound historical importance. "But it was in the realm of politics," Pratt concluded, "that O'Sullivan's temperament peculiarly fitted him to be the spokesman of his party and his time."[57] Pratt sought to turn O'Sullivan from an unknown figure to the veritable voice of his generation.[58]

By introducing O'Sullivan to the historical profession, Pratt contributed more than any other historian to the myth of manifest destiny. But Albert K. Weinberg surpassed him only two years later with the publication of his formidable *Manifest Destiny: A Study of Nationalist Expansionism in American History*. In this lengthy volume, which stretched to well over five hundred pages, Weinberg sought to write a comprehensive history of expansion by focusing on what he termed "its motley body of justificatory doctrines."[59] In each chapter, Weinberg examined one justification for expansion. Unlike Adams, however, Weinberg had a generally low opinion of these doctrines and believed it was fortunate that the idea of territorial expansionism eventually went away.

In spite of his prodigious research, Weinberg's book was similar to previous ones on the subject. For instance, Weinberg defined manifest destiny in its broadest sense. As hinted at in his title, Weinberg equated national expansion with manifest destiny and lumped every "justificatory" doctrine under the latter concept. In a book with "manifest destiny" in the title, not a single chapter deals with manifest destiny as a doctrine in its own right. Furthermore, in seeking to define his terms, Weinberg relied heavily on Adams. Weinberg wrote, "This is the philosophy of manifest destiny—in essence the doctrine that one nation has a preeminent social worth, a distinctively lofty mission, and consequently unique rights in the application of moral principles."[60]

Weinberg also focused all his attention on the proponents of expansion. Although this is not surprising given that the book was a study of expansion, Weinberg reified the idea that manifest destiny was powerful and pervasive. Weinberg referred to the decade of the 1840s as "the roaring forties" and later observed that "because the idealism of the expansionist of this period was rooted in egoism, it had sincerity and an intensity which later expansionists never fully attained."[61] Weinberg's study would become the definitive study and contributed directly to the myth of manifest destiny. By leaving out opposition to the ideology, by presenting a single side of the argument, and by defining manifest destiny in an incredibly broad sense, Weinberg made it appear that expansionists were dominant until they chose to give up their desire for additional land.

As time passed, historians added to Weinberg's work by examining additional reasons why Americans believed in manifest destiny.[62] Increasingly, scholars focused on the religious connotations of the phrase. Ernest Lee Tuveson first stressed the linkage between Christianity and manifest destiny in *Redeemer Nation: The Idea of America's Millennial Role* (1968), observing, "[The] element most neglected hitherto in the many studies of the subject [manifest destiny] is the conception of the 'chosen people' with a millennial mission. . . . The idea that the United States has been called to be a chief means of world-wide redemption."[63] Tuveson's investigation led him to conclude that manifest destiny, which he defined as the idea that the United States had a redemptive mission to perform, had "developed, like millennialism itself, out of the Protestant theology."[64] Tuveson's *Redeemer Nation* led to an outpouring of works that traced the idea of manifest destiny back to Puritans in seventeenth-century New England.[65] According to these historians, a large portion of white Americans firmly believed they were a chosen people with a redemptive mission. This belief led them to assail their neighbors in the name of manifest destiny, as evidenced most clearly in the U.S.-Mexican War.[66] Manifest destiny was potent because it appeared in the guise of a religious mission.[67] In the 1840s, it became an article of faith for most Protestant Americans.[68]

Nonetheless, some historians remained skeptical that religious beliefs alone contributed to the broad appeal of manifest destiny. In 1981 Reginald Horsman published *Race and Manifest Destiny: The Origins of Racial Anglo-Saxonism*.[69] Horsman traced the growth as well as the origins of racial Anglo-Saxonism and argued that its rise coincided with the 1830s and 1840s. He wrote, "In these years American politicians and the American population were overwhelmed by a variety of influences . . . which inspired a belief that the American Anglo-Saxons were destined to dominate or penetrate the American continents and large areas of the world."[70] Horsman's work influenced a generation of historians who focused on the racial dynamics of western expansion and who argued that manifest destiny was popular because it appealed to white Americans' belief in their own racial superiority.[71]

As some scholars focused on the religious and racial aspects of manifest destiny, others turned to gender. In 1998 Amy Kaplan called for scholars to reexamine women's role in shaping U.S. foreign policy.[72] Three years later, historian Lynnea Ruth Magnuson answered Kaplan's call, in a dissertation that explored women's role as agents of manifest destiny. Magnuson argued that women played as pivotal a role as men in helping the nation obtain its manifest destiny.[73] Others agreed with Magnuson's assessment.[74] In 2005 Adrienne Caughfield examined women who moved to Texas and concluded that women "were no less players in the drama of manifest destiny than were men."[75] That same year, Amy Greenberg argued that gender influenced how Americans received manifest destiny.[76] Together, Magnuson, Caughfield, and Greenberg demonstrated that gendered notions of masculinity and femininity contributed to the rise and popularity of manifest destiny. As Caughfield argued, "The achievement of manifest destiny required all its proponents to play a role."[77]

Understanding the role that "all its proponents" played in manifest destiny led scholars to also focus on literature. In his tone-setting *The Age of Jackson* (1945), Arthur M. Schlesinger Jr. emphasized the role that journalists and writers played in pushing forth the ideas of Jacksonian democracy, which included manifest destiny.[78] Schlesinger highlighted the career of John L. O'Sullivan, credited him with being "among the first to set down the tenets of the new faith," and called the *Democratic Review* "the liveliest journal of the day."[79] Edward Widmer followed Schlesinger's lead, contending that the creation of the *Democratic Review*, under the genius of O'Sullivan, "was the first blow in a cultural argument that raged throughout the antebellum era . . . it involved taking control of American culture from Boston, from the Whigs, and from old conservatives everywhere."[80] Downplaying the violent tendencies of Young America, and indeed of manifest destiny, these scholars emphasized the role that the *Democratic Review* played in fostering U.S. writers.[81] More importantly, perhaps, they depicted the *Democratic Review* as an overwhelmingly influential magazine that captured the national spirit.[82] Writers such as Herman Melville and Ralph Waldo Emerson, who spoke out against manifest destiny, struggled against the tide of popular opinion, disgruntled citizens of a nation intent upon expanding.[83]

By 2020, then, a common definition of manifest destiny had been established, which consisted of three overlapping ideas. First, in its territorial form, manifest destiny signified the expansion of the United States from coast to coast. Fueled by racial Anglo-Saxonism, martial views of manhood, antipathy toward Catholicism, and a burgeoning nationalist literature, Americans in the 1840s swarmed into the West, fulfilling manifest destiny.[84] Second, viewed as an ideal, manifest destiny was the belief that the American people were a chosen people who had a special mission to perform. This mission did not always entail territorial conquests, but it could speak more broadly to a restrained form of expansion that sought to spread democracy and send missionaries abroad.[85] Third, because manifest destiny signified a range of sometimes conflicting beliefs, it was extraordinarily popular in the 1840s and early 1850s.[86] As Steven Hahn summarized in 2016, "The notion of the country's 'manifest destiny to overspread and to possess the whole continent,' articulated famously by the Jacksonian journalist John L. O'Sullivan, was very deeply laid in the political culture and embraced virtually across the political spectrum."[87] Like "a potent virus," manifest destiny proved contagious in the 1840s and 1850s.[88] Only the outbreak of sectionalism and the Civil War squelched the flames of this ideology.[89]

A few historians, however, published works to challenge the rising consensus. In 1955 Norman Graebner, a historian of U.S. foreign policy, flatly rejected the prevailing view of manifest destiny, arguing, "The aims of manifest destiny, to the extent they were defined at all, went far beyond what the nation acquired."[90] Through an examination of an array of sources, Graebner disentangled the idea of manifest destiny from western expansion. This enabled Graebner to argue that manifest destiny was not fulfilled. Graebner wrote, "Manifest destiny persists as a popular term in American historical literature to explain the expansion of the United States to continent-wide dimensions in the 1840's [*sic*]. Like most broad generalizations, it does not bear close scrutiny."[91] Having rejected manifest destiny, Graebner posited that expansion occurred because politicians in both parties desired ports along the Pacific Coast. There was no need to blame this expansion upon the vague concept of manifest destiny.[92]

Graebner was not the only historian to puncture holes in the myth of manifest destiny. In 1963 Lois Bannister Merk and Frederick Merk published a revisionist study that contradicted most of the existing scholarship on the topic.[93] The Merks rejected the widely held assumption that manifest destiny referred to a host of expansionist ideas and instead defined manifest destiny as the belief that the United States would control the continent of North America.

"Manifest Destiny was continentalism," they concluded, "It meant absorption of North America."[94] Therefore, the Merks did not believe that manifest destiny had been successful. Just as importantly, they challenged the popularity of manifest destiny, observing that the ideology "lacked national, sectional, or party following commensurate with its bigness."[95] Although some Americans had believed in manifest destiny, the majority had not. Lacking adherents, manifest destiny eventually fizzled out.

The findings of Graebner and the Merks did little to shift the dominant narrative, as most scholars continued to portray manifest destiny as an irresistible ideology that propelled Americans westward. In 1985, however, another scholar challenged the traditional interpretation.[96] Thomas Hietala rejected the theory that manifest destiny played a role in the territorial expansion of the 1840s, arguing that it was the task of historians to "separate the amorphous ideas 'in the air' from the particular ideas that motivated the expansionists."[97] In chapter after chapter of his book, Hietala sought to pin down those specific motivations. He concluded that Democrats embraced "territorial and commercial expansion" largely owing to their "uneasiness about race relations, modernization, population growth, antislavery agitation, and international competition for colonies and trade."[98] Democrats did not become expansion-minded in the decade of the 1840s because of their belief in manifest destiny or from a romantic sense of nationalism. Rather, Hietala argued, they were fearful of the future and sought to solve the nation's problems by expanding its boundaries.

Increasingly, literary scholars also began to question the pervasiveness of manifest destiny. In 2002 Shelley Streeby challenged the notion that Americans tacitly accepted the U.S.-Mexican War and empire-building projects, writing that "assertions of American exceptionalism cannot always be taken at face value, but rather should often be seen as nervous attempts to manage the contradictions of ideologies of U.S. empire-building."[99] The mere existence of prowar literature did not demonstrate the unbridled popularity of manifest destiny, but rather spoke to the fears that many had about its implementation.[100] Two years later, Stephanie LeMenager proffered a similar argument.[101] LeMenager demonstrated that U.S. writers such as James Fenimore Cooper and Washington Irving did not share a common view as to what the West would become and instead "elaborated their own mythic and real counter-sites to contest the space in which they lived."[102] In other words, antebellum writers responded in a variety of ways to territorial expansion.[103] John L. O'Sullivan and the *Democratic Review* did not speak for everyone.

At the same time that literary scholars were probing the popularity of manifest destiny, more historians began to examine the ideology in a fresh way. In 2005 Andrés Reséndez demonstrated that abstract notions of manifest destiny played no discernible role in the United States' acquisition of Texas and New Mexico. "Against the background of a generally stagnant Mexican economy," Reséndez found, "the Far North inevitably gravitated toward the American economy as frontier residents' livelihoods came to depend on keeping the lines of communication with the United States wide open."[104] A common marketplace, fears of Mexican centralization, and malleable notions of national identity all contributed to the annexation of New Mexico and Texas by the United States.[105] As Hietala had done two decades before, Reséndez chided his fellow historians for relying upon the vague concept of manifest destiny to explain western expansion.[106] It was time, he believed, to abandon this "most ahistorical construct" and examine more fully "how this process of expansion occurred."[107]

Over the next decade, a group of historians built upon Reséndez's work and began to question the dominance of manifest destiny and its use by academic historians as an explanatory device.[108] Sarah K. M. Rodríguez examined Anglo-American immigration to Texas and uncovered that most migrants were fleeing from the United States and were genuinely interested in becoming citizens of Mexico. "Those who immigrated to Texas," Rodríguez argued, "had little intention of serving as the forbears of Manifest Destiny, nor was it evident to them that the United States would emerge as the most geopolitically dominant nation in the Northwestern Hemisphere."[109] Migrants to Texas were not seeking to expand the boundaries of the United States. "The case of thousands of disillusioned Americans renouncing their homeland for its neighbor to the south shows that the Jacksonian US was no stronger or more unified than Mexico," Rodríguez observed.[110] Studies such as this cast doubt upon the prevailing narrative of manifest destiny. If Americans were seeking to flee from the United States, then how could western expansion be a result of an overwhelming belief in manifest destiny? Rodríguez conclusively demonstrated that Americans moved into new territories for a variety of reasons.[111]

While Rodríguez studied Texas, a region that ultimately became a part of the United States, Rachel St. John focused her attention on a failed annexation project. St. John traced the career of William Gwin, a senator from California who attempted to carve out an empire for himself in northern Mexico in the midst of the Civil War. Like Rodríguez, St. John used a specific case to illustrate that the boundaries of the United States were not predetermined, arguing that "the national framework of 'manifest destiny' conceals the extent to which these schemers operated independently of the United States and often embraced conflicting visions of how territory, power, and people should be divided."[112] St. John called into question the idea of manifest destiny, noting that Americans in the nineteenth century were hardly unified on the question of expansion.[113] Americans such as Gwin had no trouble conceiving of a completely separate empire that included the Pacific Coast and northern Mexico.[114] Focusing on a failed annexation project enabled St. John to prove that nineteenth-century borders were fungible. There was no single view as to what the United States would eventually look like.

By 2017, then, a group of historians had begun to challenge the dominant narrative of manifest destiny. Their ideas were brought together in a special issue of the *Pacific Historical Review*. In the opening article Andrew Isenberg and Thomas Richards Jr. briefly sketched out the historiography of manifest destiny.[115] After analyzing recent studies, including those by Rodríguez and St. John, Isenberg and Richards argued that "weakness and division defined American expansion."[116] Because of this, both authors agreed that manifest destiny was an inadequate way to explain why Americans occupied what became the West. Echoing the advice given earlier by Graebner, Hietala, and Reséndez, Isenberg and Richards called for their fellow historians to abandon manifest destiny. "We long ago scrapped other concepts of nationalist historians from that period," they noted, "such as Frederick Jackson Turner's frontier thesis, or the Dunning School's embrace of racial segregation, both of which, like manifest destiny, papered over the complexities of the past and all its myriad contingencies."[117] If most historians no longer accepted Turner or the Dunning School, then why were so many still using manifest destiny to explain western expansion?

Three years after the publication of this article, Richards published his own study of nineteenth-century expansion. Richards focused on what he termed "breakaway Americas."[118] His panoptic work enabled him to demonstrate the wide variety of empire-building projects that were afoot in the Jacksonian era, leading him to conclude that "white Americans imagined a plethora of geopolitical possibilities, from a United States that spanned the entire continent, to a continent composed of three or four transcontinental republics . . . to the emergence of a Pacific republic on the West Coast."[119] Based on these case studies, Richards again called for historians to jettison their reliance on manifest destiny.[120]

Given that most of these critiques have been published within the last decade, it is still too soon to know whether they will overtake the dominant historical narrative.[121] I seek to build upon the aforementioned scholars who have challenged the pervasiveness of manifest destiny, while proffering a slightly different argument. Like Graebner and the Merks, I define manifest destiny as the belief that the United States was destined to acquire the continent of North America, along with the island of Cuba. Nineteenth-century Americans were quite clear in their definition. They did not use manifest destiny as a synonym for western expansion, nor did they define it as some sort of ephemeral belief in the superiority of U.S. institutions. Neither should we. In contrast to previous historians, however, I move my examination of manifest destiny past the 1840s, showing that manifest destiny remained a contentious subject for nearly three decades.[122] Manifest destiny was not fulfilled in 1848, but neither did it mysteriously vanish. Instead, Americans continued to debate it and ponder its possible realization.[123]

The fact that Americans vigorously disagreed over manifest destiny illustrates that conflicting visions of empire emerged in the mid-nineteenth century. Drawing upon the work of St. John, Richards, and Rodríguez, I argue that Americans did not agree on what the future boundaries of the nation would look like. Many Americans fiercely protested against acquiring New Mexico, California, Central America, Cuba, and the Dominican Republic. Within the United States, there was bitter disagreement over every territorial acquisition. Instead of seeing the middle of the nineteenth century as an era in which Americans shared a common vision of empire, we should view it as a time when multiple visions of empire clashed. Indeed, because Americans did not share the same beliefs, most of these dreams of empire failed. Although proponents of manifest destiny never doubted that the United States would acquire the continent of North America, they were unable to bring about that consummation. Manifest destiny, like so many other ideas of empire in the nineteenth century, proved in the end to be humbug.

To build this argument, I analyze debates over manifest destiny that occurred over the course of three decades. Chapter 1 traces the emergence of manifest destiny as an ideology. Looking at discussions that surfaced during the U.S.-Mexican War, this chapter shows that manifest destiny failed to sweep through the nation uncontested when it was introduced. Rather, opponents of manifest destiny quickly marshaled an array of arguments to challenge it. They turned to religion and called manifest destiny a false doctrine; they compared proponents of manifest destiny to robbers who were unwilling to pay for the land that they coveted; and they bandied about racial epithets and warned that the United States could not annex the "undesirable" people of Mexico. Although the opponents of manifest destiny were unable to prevent the United States from annexing a large chunk of Mexico in the Treaty of Guadalupe Hidalgo, they nonetheless managed to thwart the dreams of those who had advocated for the annexation of all of Mexico.

In 1848 the proponents of manifest destiny suffered another setback. In the same year that the United States ratified the Treaty of Guadalupe Hidalgo, a presidential election was held. Chapter 2 examines this election and the concomitant rise of Zachary Taylor. Although Taylor led U.S. forces for a good portion of the U.S.-Mexican War, he ran his campaign on the principle of nonexpansion, as Whigs openly boasted of their opposition to the Democratic doctrine of manifest destiny. In addition to pitching Taylor as the peace candidate, Whigs warned that Lewis Cass, the Democratic nominee, was a proponent of manifest destiny and hence a dangerous man to entrust with foreign policy. This chapter illustrates not only that debates over manifest destiny endured past the U.S.-Mexican War, but also that manifest destiny did not always prove to be a popular issue in national elections. Zachary Taylor, an open skeptic of manifest destiny, defeated Cass, one of the ideology's largest supporters. Once in office, Taylor helped to advance a less bellicose foreign policy, highlighted by the passage of the Clayton-Bulwer Treaty. This treaty explicitly stated that the United States would not annex or colonize Central America. It would stand for the next fifty years as the major roadblock in the path of manifest destiny.

In spite of his accomplishments, Taylor's presidency did not lead to the demise of manifest destiny. Beginning with the Round Island Expedition in 1849, filibusters began setting out from U.S. shores seeking to overthrow the Spanish government in Cuba. Chapter 3 examines filibustering, Cuba, and Franklin Pierce. With a Democrat in the White House, opponents of manifest destiny refocused their attention. They condemned Pierce for supporting filibustering and compared filibusters to robbers who had to steal what they could not buy. This particular argument gained in popularity and put pressure on expansionists to pay for territory that they desired. When Pierce's ministers in Europe released the Ostend Manifesto, a document that seemed to hint that the United States could conquer Cuba if Spain refused to sell, the public response was quick and condemnatory. Although there were certainly other factors involved in the demise of Pierce's plan to annex Cuba, opponents of manifest destiny had successfully convinced a large portion of the public that filibustering was an illegitimate means to acquire territory.

Pierce's inability to acquire Cuba did not deter devout believers in manifest destiny. In 1856 Democrats simply replaced Franklin

Pierce with James Buchanan, believing that Buchanan would have greater success in carrying out his foreign policy. Chapter 4 focuses on the rise of sectional opposition to manifest destiny. Triggered by the passage of the Kansas-Nebraska Act in 1854 and Pierce's attempts to procure Cuba, opponents of manifest destiny increasingly began to equate manifest destiny with enslavers. They argued that proponents of manifest destiny were only targeting regions that could be converted into slave territory and they denounced James Buchanan for being a pawn of enslavers. Buchanan's continual insistence that the United States needed to acquire Cuba and northern Mexico lent credence to this theory. Although abolitionists had argued for over a decade that enslavers, whom they called the "slave power," were behind U.S. expansion, this argument gained power when it was embraced by the rising Republican Party. Republicans increasingly pledged themselves to preventing the expansion of slavery and they promised to squash all attempts to acquire Cuba, northern Mexico, and Central America. This sectional critique of manifest destiny proved to be quite effective, as James Buchanan failed to ram through any of his plans to acquire northern Mexico and Cuba. Like Pierce, Buchanan proved to be a grave disappointment to expansionists.

The outbreak of the Civil War in 1861 led to a splintering of manifest destiny. It did not destroy the ideology, however. Chapter 5 traces the conflicting views of manifest destiny that grew and evolved in the midst of the Civil War. In 1860 proponents of manifest destiny, such as William Henry Seward, saw the rise of the Republican Party and the election of Lincoln as a sign that manifest destiny would soon come to fruition. Northern expansionists hoped that the removal of the issue of slavery would enable the United States to expand over the continent. Yet within the North a variety of views on manifest destiny existed. Some northerners blamed manifest destiny for causing the Civil War and hoped that the conflict would humble Americans in the future. Other northerners continued to blame southerners for all the expansion that occurred prior to the Civil War. Many northern Democrats hoped that the South could rejoin the North and that together the two could achieve a united manifest destiny. Similar contradictory opinions emerged within the Confederacy. A few southerners boasted that the Confederacy had its own manifest destiny to work out and that it would soon acquire Cuba, the Pacific Coast, and northern Mexico. More than a few southerners, however, gloated that the formation of the Confederacy had killed the idea of manifest destiny. As long as the Confederacy existed, it was impossible for a single nation to control the continent. From 1860 to 1865, northerners and southerners continued to debate the relative merits of manifest destiny. The idea of manifest destiny remained very much alive.

If anything, by removing the issue of slavery from discussions of expansion, the conclusion of the Civil War and the passage of the Thirteenth Amendment allowed expansionists to redouble their efforts to acquire territories that they had long coveted. Chapter 6 thus examines the political career of William Henry Seward and his attempts to fulfill manifest destiny after the Civil War. As a fierce proponent of the ideology, Seward in his role as secretary of state tried to purchase as much territory as possible. From 1867 to 1868, he negotiated treaties to purchase Alaska and the Danish West Indies. To challenge him, opponents of manifest destiny turned to environmental arguments. They averred that the United States already controlled the best land and that expansion was unnecessary. Focusing attention on the polar bears and ice of Alaska and the earthquakes and hurricanes of the Danish West Indies, opponents argued that Seward was trying to purchase worthless territories that added nothing to the economy. Opponents of expansion called Seward a failed real estate agent and alleged that he had developed an unhealthy passion for buying up unwanted parcels of land. These arguments proved to be quite effective. Seward successfully managed his Alaska treaty through the Senate, but his later treaty to purchase the Danish West Indies stalled. Whatever momentum expansionists had gained by acquiring Alaska was subsequently lost, as Americans showed little interest in adding territories to the national domain.

Yet manifest destiny had one last gasp. In 1868 Ulysses S. Grant captured the presidency. Chapter 7 examines the racial critique of manifest destiny that flourished in the aftermath of Grant's election. Because Grant was a war hero who had somewhat nebulous political opinions, many expansionists predicted that he would use his immense popularity and the Republican majority in Congress to expand the United States. Visions of Canada, Cuba, and Mexico danced before the eyes of those who had never abandoned the dream of manifest destiny. Grant did prove to be an expansionist, but he did not target Canada, Cuba, or Mexico. Instead, Grant attempted to annex the Dominican Republic. To challenge him, opponents of manifest destiny pulled upon a racial critique of manifest destiny. They argued that the United States did not need to expand because it could not grant voting rights and citizenship to nonwhites. Would Americans, they asked, be willing to see somebody from Santo Domingo sitting in the United States Senate? From 1870 onward, opponents of manifest destiny crafted racist jokes about Dominicans and argued that their incorporation into the United States would lead to the downfall of the republic. Racial animus toward nonwhites helped to thwart Grant's plan to annex the Dominican Republic. As the 1870s progressed, then, most Americans were more than willing to let the ideology of manifest destiny fade away.

Understanding this long and contested history of manifest destiny will transform the standard narrative of U.S. expansion. Historians have traditionally relegated the story of manifest destiny to the decade of the 1840s and have utilized it as a bridge to the sectional crisis and the onset of the Civil War.[124] Instead of seeing manifest destiny as an ideology that was fulfilled in 1848, historians will need to wrestle with the fact that its support ebbed and flowed over three decades. Peaks of manifest destiny enthusiasm occurred after the capture of Mexico City in 1847, upon the election of Franklin Pierce in 1852, and after the purchase of Alaska in 1867. In each of these cases, proponents eagerly anticipated the fulfillment of manifest destiny. These hopes, however, were soon dashed. Polk decided not to push for the annexation of all of Mexico, Pierce failed miserably in his attempts to acquire Cuba, and Seward's purchase of Alaska did not pressure Canada into joining the United States. Future histories of U.S. expansion will need to grapple more fully with these failures and reassess the importance of territorial expansion in decades other than the 1840s.

Apart from changing the traditional narrative, removing the myth of manifest destiny will enable us to more fully understand the history of U.S. empire. Americans living in the middle of the nineteenth century did not share a common view as to what the future held. There was no fever in the blood that convinced Americans to annex the Pacific Coast or that prodded them to covet Mexico, Canada, and Cuba. From 1845 to 1872, Americans vigorously disagreed over the wisdom of expanding the boundaries of the nation. Visions of empire clashed. Expansionists like Jane McManus Storm Cazneau, William Henry Seward, and Stephen Douglas envisioned a nation that would spread over the continent and include a variety of islands. Opponents of manifest destiny thought that the boundaries of the nation were sufficient in 1845 and they fought to exclude New Mexico, California, Canada, Cuba, the Dominican Republic, and Central America. Policymakers, the press, and ordinary Americans questioned the wisdom and necessity of each territorial acquisition. Although the myth of manifest destiny has simplified the story of expansion, it has concealed the bitter disagreements that lay beneath the surface. It is only by jettisoning the myth of manifest destiny that we will be able to more fully understand the contingent and contested nature of U.S. empire.

1

Delaying Destiny

The U.S.-Mexican War and the Postponement of Manifest Destiny

On January 3, 1846, Robert Winthrop, a Whig from Massachusetts who would become Speaker of the House of Representatives the following year, rose to speak on "the Oregon Question." Congress had been debating whether or not the United States had a right to claim the Oregon territory and whether it was worth risking a conflict with Britain. Winthrop's speech on Oregon would not have gained lasting fame had he not decided to bring up a new subject: manifest destiny.[1] Winthrop observed that he had recently come across the phrase "in a leading Administration journal."[2] Winthrop poked fun at the ideology and asked incredulously if anyone could be foolish enough to believe in such an idea.[3] Perhaps, he told his audience, Adam had left a will leaving the continent of North America to the United States. "I have no doubt that, if due search is made," Winthrop joked, "a copy of this primeval instrument, with a clause giving us the whole of Oregon, can be somewhere hunted up."[4] Winthrop introduced the phrase "manifest destiny" into Congress to mock it.

Winthrop was not alone in denouncing manifest destiny.[5] During the U.S.-Mexican War, opposition to manifest destiny was widespread as Whigs, abolitionists, ministers, and editors across the United States spoke out against it. Over time, opponents of manifest destiny developed several standard arguments. Opponents critiqued manifest destiny as a blasphemous new religion and denounced proponents as false prophets. They alleged that manifest destiny contradicted George Washington's Farewell Address, in which Washington had advised Americans to stay on friendly terms with all nations. They called it a "robber's doctrine" and postulated that the fulfillment of manifest destiny would stir up sectional tension. Many southerners feared that the expansion of the United States would give northerners the preponderance of power in Congress. In contrast, many northerners feared that the acquisition of Mexican territory would enable slavery to spread and would empower southern slaveholders. Opponents of manifest destiny pointed out that the Southwest was an arid desert and maintained that annexing Mexicans would add a volatile population to the United States. Instead of quietly submitting to manifest destiny, individuals spoke out against it. In doing so, they successfully defeated the movement to acquire all of Mexico and forced proponents of manifest destiny to postpone their grandiose plan to acquire the continent.

In May 1846, the United States entered into a war with Mexico. The war was a direct result of aggressive U.S. maneuvering, as the United States had recently annexed Texas.[6] Within a year, President James K. Polk ordered U.S. troops to move into territory claimed by both Mexico and Texas, which resulted in Mexican troops firing upon U.S. soldiers.[7] Polk claimed that the United States was entering into a defensive war. But many Americans quickly realized that Polk hoped to use the conflict to expand the borders of the United States.[8] As the conflict intensified, it became evident that Polk and others were quite comfortable taking territory from Mexico.

Most Democrats backed President Polk in his quest to obtain land from Mexico, but they disagreed as to how much land should be taken. Moderate members of the party, including Polk, desired California and New Mexico.[9] Polk argued that this would be fair, as he blamed Mexico for starting the war.[10] More aggressive Democrats believed that the United States could seize all of Mexico and annex it to the United States. The *Democratic Review*, the highly partisan magazine that first printed the phrase "manifest destiny," fell into this category.[11] In October 1847 it observed, "Until every acre of the North American continent is occupied by citizens of the United States, the founding of the future empire will not have been laid."[12] Later that year, the magazine suggested turning Mexico into a dependency until the United States was able to "regenerate [Mexicans] in their habits and views, as to make them worthy of self-government."[13] Throughout the war, the magazine demanded that the United States seize land and scoffed at the notion that absorbing Mexico would lead to future difficulties.[14]

The *New York Herald* rivaled the *Democratic Review* in its zeal toward manifest destiny. Ostensibly a nonpartisan newspaper, the *New York Herald* boasted the largest circulation in the United States.[15] Edited by James Gordon Bennett, the paper supported Polk in 1844 and endorsed the U.S.-Mexican War.[16] Shortly after the outbreak of the war, the *Herald* declared, "It is the manifest destiny of the Anglo-Saxon race to people this vast continent."[17] Believing fully that manifest destiny would lead the United States to acquire the continent, the *Herald* pushed for the annexation of all of Mexico as the first step in that process.[18] In 1848, Bennett concluded, "The more attention and reflection we give to the annexation of the whole of Mexico to the United States, the more satisfied we are that the present prospect should not be allowed to escape."[19] For proponents of manifest destiny such as Bennett, the war seemed the perfect opportunity to acquire a large chunk of the continent.[20]

Opposition to manifest destiny largely came from members of the Whig Party, which formed in the 1830s to challenge Andrew Jackson. The Whigs managed to capture the White House for the first time in 1840 when they successfully ran William Henry Harrison.[21] In contrast to the Democrats, who championed aggressive territorial expansion, Whigs believed that the United States needed to expand gradually, if at all.[22] In 1844, the party nominated for president Henry Clay, who opposed the annexation of Texas. Clay, like many Whigs, believed that annexing Texas would lead the United States directly into a war with Mexico.[23] Not surprisingly, upon the outbreak of the war, Clay and other members of the Whig Party denounced Polk's machinations and mobilized to oppose manifest destiny.[24]

Over the course of the U.S.-Mexican War, Whigs developed several arguments to challenge manifest destiny. One of the earliest critiques that Whigs turned to was religious in nature. Congressman Jacob Miller, a New Jersey Whig, argued that manifest destiny "was a temptation in the form of the Spirit of evil, which whispered 'All these, if you will worship the god Conquest, I will give you.'"[25] Whigs frequently argued that the devil was enticing the United States with Mexico. William Duer, a New York Whig, asked fellow members of the House of Representatives to do "away with this mawkish morality! With this desecration of religion! With this cant about 'manifest destiny,' a Divine Mission, a warrant from the Most High."[26] It was one thing to wage war with Mexico, these critics argued, but it was another to state that the United States was fighting a holy war that had been sanctioned by the recently revealed gospel of manifest destiny. For Whigs, resisting manifest destiny became tantamount to resisting any other form of temptation.[27]

This religious critique of manifest destiny led many Whigs to draw comparisons between the U.S.-Mexican War and the Crusades. In doing so, they often pointed to the ill-fated Peter the Hermit. Peter the Hermit was a French priest who played a key role in organizing and leading French peasants during the First Crusade. To Protestants in the nineteenth century, Peter the Hermit came to symbolize the dangers of religious extremism. The *Richmond Republican* hoped that the people would not be duped by "some modern Peter the Hermit" who wanted to "extirpate error by the sword, and carry out the designs of the Prince of Peace by the bayonet and the cannon!"[28] Senator Joseph Underwood, a Kentucky Whig, noted that the peasants who followed Peter the Hermit were as deluded as those who were subjugating Mexico under the belief that they had a mission from God to civilize it. Underwood joked that no angel had appeared to tell him to conquer Mexico.[29]

By focusing on a character such as Peter the Hermit, Whigs crafted a weighty rebuttal to the idea of manifest destiny. Nowhere is this better seen than in a splenetic attack published by the *National Intelligencer*. The *National Intelligencer* was one of the most prominent Whig newspapers in the United States and frequently critiqued manifest destiny.[30] In this article, the author drew a direct parallel between the U.S.-Mexican War and the Crusades. "The Crusades were for the 'recovery' of what Europe had never possessed," the author noted, "and had not title to; the war was made for the 're-annexation' of that which we had never possessed." The author then compared Peter the Hermit to proslavery politicians, noting, "A hermit, mad and shallow, preached the one; overzealous theorists of slavery the other." If manifest destiny were a new and a false revelation, then it was up to the American people to recognize this; "If, in short, any such message of Fate has come to us, who shall assure us that it is not of the devil's fetching, like that other in Peter Hermit's time?"[31]

Whigs contended that following such a false revelation would lead to a swift punishment. In article after article Whigs warned about the looming wrath of God, which, they argued, would be kindled if the United States stole land from Mexico.[32] The *Richmond Whig* provided historical examples of God punishing nations. One author looked at five world empires: Assyria, Babylon, Egypt, Macedon, and Rome. In each case the story was the same. The empire of Syria rose to great heights, tried to dominate its neighbors, and was surpassed by Babylon. After Babylon had become a "heap," Macedon rose only to be overtaken by the Romans. Nobody could doubt the point of this story. "We should learn from this great moral lesson," the author intoned, "that the nation . . . may pursue that destiny with pleasure for awhile—may bear down all opposition . . . but having once entered on the career of her destiny, she must pursue it to the end. And what is that end? Let Assyria, let Egypt, let Macedon, let Rome, let all history answer."[33]

Many of the arguments against manifest destiny contained warnings of providential wrath. Unless the United States humbled itself, doom was inevitable. A letter to the *Raleigh Register, and North-Carolina Gazette* thought it "impious presumption" to try to figure out what God planned for the United States and then declared, "I repeat sir, that this plea [manifest destiny] sounds to me impious, and even blasphemous, and I have been astonished to hear it proclaimed from so many quarters."[34] This author hoped that the United States would forsake this "crusade" before it met God's just "retribution."[35] Others agreed with this assessment. The editor of the *Richmond Whig* warned a boastful orator who had extolled the glories of manifest destiny that he might one day be rebuked "by One who punishes national pride and arrogance . . . by national judgments."[36]

Such admonitions became commonplace during the war. The nation must either forsake conquest or face the inevitable wrath of God.[37]

Religious individuals who did not necessarily identify with the Whig Party also deployed the religious critique of manifest destiny. A Baptist minister in Massachusetts named Miles Sanford preached a rousing Thanksgiving Day sermon in 1847 that discussed the theme of "national greatness."[38] He called out those who claimed that the United States was somehow blessed because it was easily defeating Mexico. "What, though the star-spangled banner now waves in triumph over the Halls of the Montezumas," he observed, "God's curse will be written over against us for our wicked disregard of that Gospel that breathes 'peace on earth, and good will to men.'"[39] Sanford worried that Americans had forsaken the path of righteousness; drunkenness, desecration of the Sabbath, and a lust for conquest were all signs of this apostasy.[40] "Unless we repent," he warned, "our 'manifest destiny' will be recorded on the page of the future historian, as having terminated in the pitchy gloom and the heavy darkness of political night."[41] Sanford believed the United States had a role to play in world affairs, but that it needed to abandon its love of conquest and stop its iniquitous war with Mexico.

Other ministers warned that manifest destiny was leading the United States down the path of unrighteousness. Congregational minister Milton P. Braman delivered a blistering sermon on the U.S.-Mexican War that was quickly reprinted for national circulation.[42] Braman explicitly condemned the notion that a mysterious destiny compelled the United States to conquer its neighbors. "Where then is the destiny of our country revealed?" he asked his auditors. "It is announced by no living prophet. It is not recorded in the pages of the Bible, nor written upon the earth, nor figured in the constellations of the skies."[43] Like many others, Braman saw the idea of manifest destiny as a flagrant assault upon the Word of God, an apocryphal revelation that deceived the credulous. God did control the world but his providential workings remained a mystery. God would punish the nation that transgressed his eternal mandates. "If injustice, aggression and a disposition to trample on human rights," Braman thundered, "shall become the permanent and collective character of our government and people, there is no doubt about our destiny, we shall fall as fell Carthage and Rome. . . . We shall perish in our own corruption, and be swept away by Him who sits on the Throne of Eternal Justice."[44] For ministers such as Braman, there was still time for the United States to repent.[45]

Other critiques reinforced the vibrant religious opposition to manifest destiny that emerged over the course of the U.S.-Mexican War.[46] As the war progressed, Whigs increasingly argued that the United States was abandoning the advice of George Washington, who had admonished Americans to live at peace with all nations.[47] Referring to Washington's Farewell Address, a New Hampshire editor noted, "[The] present successor of Washington has set at nought this solemn counsel."[48] Washington had warned his fellow Americans not to meddle in the affairs of others and to "cultivate peace and harmony with all." It was therefore up to the Whig Party to restore the vision of Washington, so the United States could live in peace. "In this spirit," the author continued, "the Whigs take their stand against the Mexican war as being unnecessary, unjust, and unconstitutional. And in doing this, they plant themselves upon the counsels of Washington."

Southern Whigs, like northern Whigs, turned the words of the first president against Polk. The *Fayetteville Observer* chided Democrats for ignoring Washington's counsel in their dealings with the government of Mexico, arguing that invading Mexico contradicted Washington's advice to avoid becoming entangled with foreign nations.[49] In a similar manner, a Georgian wrote to the *National Intelligencer* chastising Polk for his aggressive war and noting, "The people are perfectly satiated with blood." He concluded the letter by suggesting that Polk should reacquaint himself with the Farewell Address and learn from the example of Washington. If Polk had done so, he would not have blundered into the U.S.-Mexican War.[50]

Whigs frequently compared Polk unfavorably with George Washington. Nobody did this more effectively than George D. Prentice. Born in Connecticut, Prentice had graduated from Brown University and then moved to Kentucky to write a campaign biography of Henry Clay.[51] In November 1830, Prentice helped establish the *Lou-*

isville Journal. As a fierce proponent of Henry Clay and defender of the Whig Party, Prentice gained a national reputation for his biting editorials. Throughout the U.S.-Mexican War, he denounced Polk and the idea of manifest destiny.[52] "The true policy of the Government," Prentice wrote in an editorial in 1847, "as asserted by the illustrious Washington in that monument of his wisdom and patriotism, his farewell address, is altogether inconsistent with the notions of the annexationists."[53] Prentice fervently disagreed with those who wanted to gobble up Mexican territory, believing that this conquest would endanger the stability of the United States. Prentice noted that Washington himself had warned Americans "to steer clear of entangling alliances with foreign Governments." Democrats angling for Mexican territory were therefore ignoring Washington's advice and were demonstrating their own "fearful degeneracy."

In March 1848 Prentice published a particularly scathing article under the title "The Wisdom of Washington and the Folly of Polk."[54] Prentice noted that the nation's first president had foreseen the danger of a man like Polk occupying the White House and that his departing words "could not have spoken with more appropriateness to the condition of the country." Had Polk heeded Washington's advice, he would not have dragged the United States into a sanguinary conflict with its southern neighbor. The actions of Polk and his fellow expansionists showed how far the nation had removed itself from the founding generation. "The manifest destiny men of the day," Prentice inveighed, "those men who assert that it is our mission to invade and lay waste neighboring States in order that we may occupy them, have no regard for the wisdom of the fathers of our Republic." If the United States continued conquering its neighbors, Prentice concluded, it would ultimately meet the same fate as Babylon or Rome.

Although Prentice frequently juxtaposed the names of Polk and Washington, he drew other comparisons. In March 1848 he discussed how U.S. soldiers in Mexico had stolen the belongings of a Mexican general as war trophies.[55] As he did so often, Prentice drew upon this small example to develop his argument. He noted that Polk had received a stolen cane as a gift. Prentice then hit his major point:

"The manifest destiny men, the class of philosophers to which Mr. Polk has annexed himself teach that it is of the very essence of virtue to steal Mexican property. We do not think that Mr. Polk will make any serious objections to the cane on account of its having been stolen." If Americans had a right to steal Mexican land, then who could expect them not to pilfer smaller items? In this illustration, Prentice reduced the president of the United States to the status of petty thief.

Whigs often compared manifest destiny to robbery.[56] A writer for the *Whig Review* used the following example. "A Mexican is travelling on the highway, with his own company of retainers," the story begins, "bearing certain valuables . . . when he is met by a band of industrious fellows, living on the road, whose chevalier chief claims to be his creditor."[57] An obvious parable on the behavior of Polk toward Mexico, the story continues with the "creditor" demanding immediate payment. When this payment is not provided, the creditor whips out his saber and pistol in order to convince the Mexican to part with his valuables. The moral is that the United States has been acting the part of the highwayman by forcing Mexico to give up its territory.[58] The editor of the *Richmond Whig* did not merely write a parable, but instead frankly admitted, "[A] strong power, in the neighborhood of a weak one, is but too apt to persuade itself, that it is its 'manifest destiny' to overwhelm it, as the robber thinks it his 'manifest destiny' to plunder all who want the spirit or the strength to defend their own."[59]

Some Whigs tied in this critique of manifest destiny with a concurrent attack on Anglo-Saxonism. Throughout the war, proponents of expansion boasted that Anglo-Saxons had been an expansive people for centuries.[60] Many expansionists gloried in their reputed Anglo-Saxon ancestry and saw the conquest of Mexico as one step in the great march of Anglo-Saxon civilization.[61] Critics of manifest destiny, however, blasted this theory.[62] Papers such as the *Richmond Whig*, which embraced a decidedly racist stance toward Mexico, continually enjoined its readers to spurn the violent heritage of the Anglo-Saxon past and to reject manifest destiny.[63] Congressman Joseph Root of Ohio was even more direct: "Did anybody ever hear of the Government of a great nation putting itself in such a position before," he asked his listeners, "Did any one ever hear of a nation boasting of being the descendants of the Anglo-Saxons—for we excuse and make a merit of our land robberies by saying we have Anglo-Saxon blood in our veins; our ancestors were land robbers, and we cannot help it."[64] In this speech, Root did not question the idea of Anglo-Saxon superiority, but he firmly rejected the notion that Anglo-Saxons were compelled by their natural instincts to aggressively expand over contiguous lands.

Whigs were often able to accept some of the tenets of Anglo-Saxonism without embracing manifest destiny. The *Cincinnati Atlas* declared, "We are proud of our race for its pre-eminence in mental energy and enterprise . . . but as to its national morality there are some things that may be said with truth that are not the most creditable."[65] This paper viewed the conquest of Mexico as robbery. The *National Intelligencer* sarcastically boasted, "We are, it appears, of the 'Anglo-Saxon race'—of a lineage of 'land-stealers,' a progeny of plunderers! Oh, pious genealogy!"[66] Believing that Anglo-Saxonism, as expounded by supporters of manifest destiny, was "clap-trap," the author nonetheless argued that if individuals were going to become followers of this idea, then they should model themselves after slightly nobler representatives of the race. Whigs believed that Anglo-Saxons could take pride in their ancestors without subscribing to the fatalistic view that destiny was compelling them to take their neighbor's land.

Whig opponents of manifest destiny were as likely to hail from the southern regions of the country as they were to come from the North. Unlike their northern counterparts, however, many southern Whigs worried that acquiring land from Mexico would threaten the institution of slavery. These fears peaked after David Wilmot, a Democrat from Pennsylvania, introduced his famous resolution in Congress.[67] The Wilmot Proviso stipulated that all lands taken from Mexico would remain free territory.[68] Although the resolution was not adopted, many southern Whigs perceived its introduction as evidence that the North stood to gain the most from acquiring Mexican territory. The *Richmond Whig* grumbled that because slavery was already illegal in Mexico, there was only a small chance "that slave labor" would "ever be introduced into such portions of her territory as may be ceded to or purchased by" the United States.[69] Because Mexico had outlawed slavery, many southerners questioned whether the South stood to benefit from the cession of Mexican lands.

To challenge the Wilmot Proviso, southern Whigs helped to craft the "no-territory" platform. In February 1847 Senator John M. Berrien of Georgia introduced an amendment that stated, "It is hereby declared to be the true intent and meaning of Congress in making this appropriation, that the war with Mexico ought not to be prosecuted by this Government with any view to the dismemberment of that republic, or to the acquisition by conquest of any portion of her territory."[70] Berrien's amendment, like the Wilmot Proviso, never passed, but Whigs rallied around the idea that the United States could win the conflict without acquiring territory from Mexico. In putting forth his no-territory amendment, Berrien made it clear that he was acting as a southerner. "I say, in my humble judgment, and speaking as a southern Senator representing a southern State," Berrien argued, "that the duty of the South—the interests of the South—the safety of the South—demands that we should oppose ourselves to any and to every acquisition of territory." If the United States seized Mexican lands, then the North and South would soon find themselves at odds, and Berrien did not believe that the South would necessarily emerge as the victor.[71]

Berrien was not alone in believing that the conflict stood to harm the South.[72] In November 1847 Henry Clay delivered a lengthy antiwar address. Born in Virginia in 1777, Clay rose to national prominence in Kentucky.[73] Few politicians have ever boasted as impressive a resume as Clay, who served as Speaker of the House of Representatives, as a U.S. senator, and as secretary of state, and who ran for president three times. In spite of his defeats, Clay remained a dominant figure in the Whig Party and in November he decided to break his silence on the conflict, delivering a speech in Lexington, Kentucky.[74] Clay derided Polk's unconstitutional actions while pointing to the impossibility of incorporating a large chunk of Mexico into the United States.[75]

As a slaveholder, Clay hardly ignored the slavery question. He argued that southerners needed to "disavow" the annexation of "any foreign territory whatever, for the purpose of introducing slavery into it." Clay noted that many had charged the "Slave States" with seeking to use the conflict to expand the institution of slavery, and he wanted no part of that. He had supported gradual abolition in Kentucky and hoped that slavery would one day fade away. At the conclusion of his speech, he put forth several resolutions specifically outlining his reasons for opposing taking territory from Mexico. The sixth of these stated, "That it seems to me that it is the duty of our country, as well on the score of moderation and magnanimity, as with the view of avoiding discord and discontent at home, to abstain from seeking to conquer and annex to the United States, Mexico or any part of it; and, especially, to disabuse the public mind in any quarter of the Union of the impression . . . that a desire for conquest is cherished for the purpose of propagating or extending slavery." Like his fellow southern Whigs, Clay saw no benefit to be gained from trying to spread the institution of slavery into Mexican territory.[76]

Northern Whigs also embraced the no-territory platform but did so for different reasons. Shortly after Berrien introduced his resolution, Daniel Webster, a Massachusetts senator, expressed his approval. In his speech Webster noted that the Whig Party was unified on the question of expansion, but he criticized northern Democrats for supporting expansion under the auspices of the Wilmot Proviso. "Every member of the Senate belonging to the party in the northern States," Webster observed, speaking of northern Democrats, "however warmly they may have declared themselves against new slave States, yet refused to vote against all territorial acquisitions—a measure proposed and offered to them as a perfect security against more slave States."[77] Webster tabulated the votes and faulted his northern brethren for opening the door to the possibility of new slave states. Northerners, Webster argued, could prevent the addition of slave states by accepting Berrien's amendment.[78] Webster and many of his northern colleagues supported Berrien's amendment because they opposed the spread of slavery.

Northern Whigs also predicted that taking Mexican land would lead to conflict between the North and the South. In February 1847 Senator Thomas Corwin of Ohio delivered a speech that rivaled Clay's in importance.[79] Corwin directly attacked manifest destiny and predicted that it could lead to the downfall of the republic. Near the conclusion of his speech, Corwin observed that states such as "New York, Pennsylvania, and Ohio" were sending delegates to Congress who were opposed to the spread of slavery, but southerners were hoping to add additional slave states. "Can it be expected," Corwin asked, "that they should expend in common, their blood and their treasure, in the acquisition of immense territory, and then willingly forego the right to carry thither their slaves, and inhabit the conquered country if they please to do so?" As did his southern peers, Corwin predicted that annexation would inevitably lead to a civil war. "Should we prosecute this war another moment," he argued, "or expend one dollar in the purchase or conquest of a single acre of Mexican land, the North and the South are brought into collision on a point where neither will yield. Who can foresee or foretell the result?" Northern Whigs opposed territorial expansion because they believed that doing so was the only way to avoid sectional tension and guarantee that the institution of slavery would be contained.[80]

Whether they hailed from the North or the South, Whigs rejected manifest destiny and embraced the no-territory platform, believing that northerners and southerners could not equally divide the spoils taken from Mexico. But they also relied upon other arguments that did not revolve around the question of slavery. Many Whigs leveled an environmental critique at manifest destiny, claiming that the United States already controlled the best land on the continent of North America. In his speech at Lexington, Henry Clay boasted of the natural fecundity of the United States, a land "capable of almost all the produce of the earth, except tea and coffee and the spices" and which included "every variety of climate, which the heart could wish or desire."[81] Clay rejected the idea that the United States would benefit from adding territory.[82] Daniel Webster would have undoubtedly agreed, had he been in Lexington that day. In his own speech on the U.S.-Mexican War, Webster avouched, "We want no accession of new States. The country is already large enough."[83] Clay and Webster firmly believed that the United States would gain few material benefits from seizing Mexican land.

Other Whigs argued that California and New Mexico were of little value. In March 1848 Congressman Truman Smith of Connecticut delivered a lengthy oration examining the lands of northern Mexico. Smith first looked at Chihuahua, Sonora, and Lower California, concluding that these regions were "filled with vast and usually impassable mountains . . . alternating with extensive deserts."[84] The lack of water and "impassable mountains" made it almost impossible to cultivate crops. Smith found New Mexico to be even more worthless. "All the country from this range to the boundary of the United States," he declared, "comprising, probably, three-fifths of the whole territory, cannot be occupied by civilized men, for the reason that it is destitute of wood and timber, and is very scantily supplied with water."[85] Smith buttressed each point with lengthy quotations from explorers and scientists, lending an air of scientific certainty to his conclusions.

Smith concluded by examining Upper California. Admitting that San Francisco and San Diego might be valuable ports, he doubted the wisdom of taking the rest of the territory. In his view, California could "sustain only a limited population, probably at most not over 200,000."[86] Why would the United States spend money to acquire a desert, mountains, and a region that was to be permanently cut off from the rest of the United States? Smith saw nothing to be gained from the cession and predicted that Polk would mislead Americans about the value of various lands.[87] "I shall not be surprised," Smith warned, "if the deserts of the Colorado and the 'howling desolation' of the Great Basin should all at once become a vast domain of luxuriance, filled with extensive forests and ever-smiling prairies that alternate with each other, garnished with beautiful lakes and extensive rivers, and teeming with numberless buffalo, deer, and other forms of animal life."[88] Smith remained convinced that Polk had not only carried out an unjust war but had also sent troops into harm's way for a worthless desert.

Truman Smith provided the most detailed assessment of northern Mexico, but he was hardly alone in his valuation of New Mexico and California. As soon as it became apparent that Polk was trying to obtain northern Mexico, Whigs questioned its value. Like Smith,

Roger S. Baldwin, a Connecticut Whig, saw New Mexico as a barren desert unsuited to "agricultural purposes." San Francisco and Sacramento might be valuable, but the rest of California was "worthless." "It is called a desert," Baldwin observed, speaking of California, "and, from what I saw of it, sterility may be said to be its prominent characteristic. It is peopled but miserably and sparsely. Humanity is there in its lowest form." Daniel Webster agreed, pronouncing that New Mexico and California were "not to be worth a dollar."[89] Whigs argued that nothing valuable could ever be produced in these regions.

Whigs were particularly incensed when they realized that the United States was offering to pay Mexico for such territory. John Van Dyke, a congressman from New Jersey, could not believe that the United States would be willing to purchase a desert. "This miserable territory . . . of mountains, rocks, deserts, and sands," he grumbled, "two-thirds of which are absolutely worthless, and the other third already owned by private claimants, is the whole of our indemnity for the past, and for this we pay in money much more than it is worth."[90] Van Dyke, like so many other Whigs, unfavorably compared northern Mexico with past territorial acquisitions, including Louisiana, Oregon, and even Texas. "Why not keep our money," Van Dyke concluded, "and let her [Mexico] keep her land? We have more land now than we know what to do with. We have millions on millions of acres of the best quality that we cannot get ten shillings an acre for."[91]

To protests about the value of the territory, Whigs added a racial critique of manifest destiny. In almost every speech and editorial delivered from 1846 to 1848, Whigs dismissed those living in northern Mexico as being unworthy of U.S. citizenship. Truman Smith's carefully crafted speech against expansion included numerous racist remarks. He doubted that any American would want to move to New Mexico and added, "A more degraded, ignorant, vicious, or brutal people, does not exist on the face of the earth."[92] Whig William L. Dayton of New Jersey shared an equally low opinion of New Mexicans. "It is a mongrel, piebald race," he told his Senate colleagues, "of every grade and hue, from the white man down to the negro—very few of the former—a degraded race, and must continue to be degraded."[93] Dayton could not imagine why anyone would wish to annex such a territory and he pondered whether his southern colleagues would welcome new senators from New Mexico. "Our southern friends are not likely to admit representatives of this piebald race with great haste at least on this floor," Dayton observed.

Whigs consistently harped on the defective character of those living in Mexican territory. Maryland senator James Pearce "wanted no partnership with outside barbarians. . . . He considered the Mexican people to be . . . a mixed, mongrel race; and he wanted no partnership with them."[94] John M. Berrien, who had introduced the no-territory amendment into the Senate, made a similar appeal: "Are you willing to put your birthright in the keeping of the mongrel races who inhabit these territories by incorporating them into the Federal Union?"[95] James Pollock, a Whig from Pennsylvania, considered the inhabitants of California and New Mexico "morally and physically degraded—of every complexion and color, from the deep ebony of the negro to the sickly white of the mulatto."[96] Whigs made it clear that they did not want to annex the peoples of northern Mexico.

Racial opposition to manifest destiny cut across sectional and partisan lines. John C. Calhoun, a prominent Democratic senator from South Carolina, hesitated to grab Mexican territory.[97] "If we annex the land," he told his colleagues, "we must take the population along with it. And shall we . . . by an act of Congress, convert the black, white, red, mongrel, miserable population of Mexico . . . into free and enlightened American citizens, entitled to all the privileges which we enjoy?"[98] John M. Niles, a Connecticut Democrat, asked his colleagues, "Will you unite Mexico, as States, with this Confederacy, with her mixed, mongrel, and degraded population?"[99] Washington Hunt, a New York Whig, regarded Mexicans as a "medley of mixed races."[100] Whether they hailed from South Carolina or New York, these men attempted to counter the appeal of manifest destiny by catering to racial fears.

Opponents who relied upon the racial arguments highlighted citizenship questions. Would the inhabitants of northern Mexico become citizens of the United States and would they have representatives in Congress? One paper dubbed New Mexican men "ignorant, dishonest, [and] treacherous."[101] The implications of annexation were frightening: "The people, if citizens, must be represented in Congress. If they elect a delegate—and we have now here candidates feeling that way—will you give him a seat? Will you let him speak?"[102] Whigs asked whether or not these new territories would be allowed to send darker-hued representatives to Congress. Papers such as the *National Intelligencer* hoped such would not be the case: "No more Mexican amalgamation—no more Mexican American Senators, either brown or black."[103] It was better to foreswear annexation than to accept "amalgamation."

Those who were opposed to taking land from Mexico did not do so because of their concern over Native American sovereignty. Whether they belonged to the Whig or the Democratic Party, these critics largely ignored the Native Americans who resided in the lands stretching from California to Texas.[104] Some Whigs did oppose the conflict because they believed it was unjust for the United States to wage a war with a "sister republic," but they seemingly did not share the same compunction over seizing Indigenous land.[105] Whigs, like their expansionist counterparts, recognized Mexican dominion and repeated the refrain that the United States was stealing land from Mexico. The thought that this would be stealing land from Native Americans did not trouble these critics, as Mexican claims to the region were never seriously questioned.

Over the course of the war, critics of manifest destiny marshaled an array of arguments against the ideology that echoed well beyond the halls of Congress. Humorists also mocked the men who claimed that manifest destiny would soon give the United States sway over the entire continent. Indeed, in the midst of the conflict, the United States' most famous humorist turned his attention to manifest destiny. In the early 1830s Seba Smith, the editor of the *Portland Courier*, created the character of Jack Downing.[106] Downing first appears as a simple farm lad from the fictional city of Downingville who travels to the state capital seeking to sell his wares. Young Jack gets wrapped up in the whirl of politics and soon becomes the confidant of presidents and men of affairs.[107] Smith, in the guise of Downing, wrote letters for the *Portland Courier* that recounted the adventures of the doltish Downing and his loveable relatives. What made these letters so amusing was that Downing and his relatives were all dyed-in-the-wool Democrats. Using these characters allowed Smith to poke some good-natured fun at the Democratic Party. From 1830 to 1833 Smith wrote fifty fictional letters, jesting about small-town life in Maine and taking shots at President Andrew Jackson and his policies.[108]

In 1833, Smith abruptly stopped penning fictional letters from Downing, as he turned his attention to new literary projects. Readers were doubtlessly surprised, then, to pick up their copy of the *National Intelligencer* in July 1847 to find the following note: "We were thrown quite into a flutter yesterday by receiving in our bag from the Post Office the following Letter from the Public's old friend *Major Jack Downing*, who seems to have written it to us for the purpose of communicating to the Public, in his plain way, some views of President Polk."[109] Choosing to send his letters to one of the most widely read Whig newspapers was certainly not a coincidence, as it provided Smith with a larger national audience than the *Portland Courier* could reach. It also showed that Smith's humor was of a highly partisan nature.[110] He intended to use Major Jack Downing to mock and malign Democrats.

To caricature Democrats, Smith turned Major Jack Downing into a manifest destiny man. After meeting with President Polk, Downing departs for Mexico City to participate in the U.S.-Mexican War. Once in Mexico, Downing becomes an exuberant proponent of annexation. "If we keep on annexin' as fast as we have done a year or two past," Downing writes to Polk, "it wouldn't take much more than half a dozen years to get clear down to t'other end of South America, clear to Cape Horn, which would be a very good stopping place."[111] Shortly thereafter, Downing envisions an empire spanning from North America to South America. Downing addresses his seventh letter "To James K. Polk, President of the United States of America, Mexico, &c," and his ensuing letter "To James K. Polk, President of the United States, and nearly half of Mexico certain, with a pretty tolerable fair chance yet for the whole."[112] In letter after letter, Downing expounds with rustic elegance on the prospect of the United States controlling the continents of North and South America.

The humor in Downing's letters derives from his naive approach to politics. Downing brings up weighty political questions and casually brushes them aside, often offering ridiculous solutions to complicated problems. In one letter Downing writes, "I hope there an't no truth in the story that was buzz'd about here in the army, a day or two ago, that Mr. Polk had an idea, when we get through annexin' down this way, of trying his hand at it over in Europe and Africa, and round there." Downing finds this problematic because Polk planned "to run the Missouri Compromise line over there, and cut Europe up into Free States and Africa into Slave States."[113] Juxtaposed to Smith's pointed satire was the very real problem of what would be done with the lands acquired by the United States. Would they become free or slave territories? Although Downing deals in hypothetical examples, he confronts a serious issue discussed throughout the United States.

Smith managed to work in other critiques of manifest destiny. In one letter Downing addresses those who doubt the value of filching Mexican territory: "Some think the business isn't profitable," Downing writes, "but it's only because they haven't ciphered into it fur enough to understand it."[114] Downing then explains how the annexation of Mexico would add to the glory of the United States because it would boost the population. "Some find fault with the *quality* of the people we get in this country," Downing notes, "jest as if that had anything to do with the merits of the case." He then concludes, "They ought to remember that in a Government like ours, where the people is used for voting, and where every nose counts one, it is the *number* that we are to stan' about in annexin', and not the quality, by no means."[115] With these jokes, Smith found a way to work in the racial and environmental critiques of manifest destiny. Downing can provide no logical reason for the United States to take all of Mexico, except for the fact that it will add Democratic voters to keep his party in power.

Smith wrote his most powerful critique of manifest destiny in October 1847 in the form of a dream sequence. Major Jack Downing tells readers that he had an "Annexation Dream" in which the United States "got through annexin' all North and South America."[116] Downing dreamed that the "whole country was turned into a

THE MAJOR'S ANNEXATION DREAM.

1. Major Jack Downing illustrated the absurdities of manifest destiny while pointing to its dangers. In his dream, the United States is turned into a ship of war seeking to conquer both North and South America. Seba Smith, "The Major's Annexation Dream," *My Thirty Years Out of the Senate* (New York: Derby and Jackson, 1860), 281.

monstrous great ship of war, and Cape Horn was the bowsprit, and Mr. Polk the captain."[117] With Captain Polk at the helm, the United States set out to conquer Europe, Asia, and the West India Islands. But the ship ran into a hurricane and faced immediate destruction. "The whole crew was in a mutiny," Downing remembers, "and the ship was so large, and the crew was such a mixed up mess of different sorts of folks that there was twenty different mutinies all at once, in different parts of the vessel."[118] The ship then crashed into the rocks and sank, claiming the lives of all of those onboard. Humor aside, the moral of Downing's "Annexation Dream" was evident. If the United States fulfilled its manifest destiny and conquered North and South America, there would be too many factions within the United States.

People would not speak the same language, they would not share the same interests, and they would inevitably try to form their own governments. The republic would sink and disappear. Through the character of Downing, Smith showed that the fulfillment of manifest destiny would trigger the downfall of the United States.

Over the course of the U.S.-Mexican War, the opponents of manifest destiny constructed an array of arguments to challenge the ideology. Nonetheless, early in 1848, Nicholas Trist, the envoy sent out by President Polk, negotiated the Treaty of Guadalupe Hidalgo.[119] When the treaty made its way into the U.S. Senate, a vibrant debate erupted between those who wanted more land and those who desired less.[120] Whigs vehemently protested against the treaty, maintaining their argument that the United States did not need additional land.[121] Some Democrats, including a rising young star in the party, Stephen Douglas of Illinois, denounced the treaty because it did not fulfill their expansive desires for the United States. In the end enough members of both parties decided that the Treaty of Guadalupe Hidalgo was a fair compromise. It was ratified by a Senate vote of 38–14.[122]

The passage of the Treaty of Guadalupe Hidalgo brings up two important questions. Did the opponents of manifest destiny fail? And did the acquisition of the Pacific Coast fulfill manifest destiny? The answer to these questions is no, because the land ceded in the Treaty of Guadalupe Hidalgo did not turn over all of Mexico to the United States. Believers in manifest destiny held it as an undeniable fact that the United States would annex the continent of North America.[123] As a paper in Alabama explained in 1847, "Many sneers have been uttered in regard to the talk kept up in some quarters . . . concerning the 'manifest destiny' of the Anglo-American Race. But if any thing is distinctly written in the book of fate, it is that this same race shall inevitably and speedily assume the control of the whole North American continent . . . the coming result is as certain as tomorrow's sunrise."[124] True believers never doubted this fact.

Opponents of manifest destiny understood that the ideology demanded the annexation of all of Mexico. George D. Prentice well described the supporters of manifest destiny in his *Louisville Journal*: "A portion of them . . . are in favor of civilizing, christianizing, and democratizing the people of Mexico. . . . They are the manifest destiny men proper, and believe it is our mission to annex Mexico for the benefit of the Mexicans."[125] Others defined manifest destiny in the exact same way.[126] When Kentuckian T. F. Marshall delivered a bellicose speech demanding that the United States annex Mexico, the *Richmond Whig* concluded, "He now belongs to the 'Manifest Destiny' party."[127] Another paper critiqued a prowar sermon by declaring that the minister was "among the most enthusiastic of the 'Manifest Destiny' party."[128] Saying that a person belonged to the "manifest destiny party" or was a "manifest destiny man" was one way of describing someone who supported absorbing all of Mexico. Opponents quite simply did not use the phrase to refer to somebody who advocated for the acquisition of New Mexico and California.

The Treaty of Guadalupe Hidalgo hardly fulfilled manifest destiny. True believers in manifest destiny, such as Stephen Douglas and the anonymous writers for the *Democratic Review*, denounced the treaty.[129] A decade after ratification, it still aroused strong emotions among expansionists. The *Democratic Review* whined in 1858, "Once we had all of Mexico. Then we should have kept it."[130] The U.S.-Mexican War should not be seen as the end of the era of manifest destiny, but rather as the first in a series of conflicts over the ideology. From 1846 to 1848 proponents of manifest destiny boasted that the United States would soon control the continent and proclaimed that the annexation of all of Mexico was to be the first step in that process. In contrast, opponents called manifest destiny blasphemous, said that it violated the precepts of Washington, and compared it to robbery on a national level. Opponents warned of sectional tension resulting from annexation, mocked the value of the territory in question, and hurled racial epithets at Mexicans. In the end neither side won this particular argument, as the Treaty of Guadalupe Hidalgo represented a compromise between those who wanted all of Mexico and those who wanted none of it. Over the next thirty years, both sides would continue to debate the merits of manifest destiny. But if the U.S.-Mexican War had taught the opponents of manifest destiny one thing, it was how to construct effective arguments. And they would use each of these arguments over the next three decades.

2

Promises of Peace

Washington's Farewell and the Election of 1848

In June 1848, a mere month after Mexico ratified the Treaty of Guadalupe Hidalgo, an article began to circulate in Whig newspapers. Called "Several of the Candidates," it lampooned the policy positions of Lewis Cass, the Democratic nominee for president. The article began by labeling John P. Hale of New Hampshire as the "Abolition Candidate" for president, but then ran through ten subsequent categories, listing Cass underneath each one. It cataloged Cass as the "Slave-Extension Candidate," the "Anti-Harbor Candidate," the "Old Hunker's Candidate," the "Aristocracy Candidate," and the "Northern Doughface Candidate." All of these highlighted Cass's shifting political views and would have resonated with a northern Whig audience opposed to extending slavery into the territories taken from Mexico. The sixth label that the paper applied to Lewis Cass was perhaps the most interesting of all: "'Manifest Destiny' Candidate—General Cass, of Michigan."[1]

As such political rhetoric demonstrated, the ratification of the Treaty of Guadalupe Hidalgo hardly ended disputes over manifest destiny. Indeed, shortly after the conclusion of the U.S.-Mexican War, the United States entered a presidential election in which the two major parties put forth candidates who strongly disagreed on the issue. In 1848 Lewis Cass had favored the annexation of all of Mexico, and he seemed likely to build on the expansionist policies of James K. Polk. Throughout the campaign, Whigs frequently dubbed Cass the candidate of manifest destiny. In contrast, the Whig candidate, Zachary Taylor, promised in a public letter not to seek territorial expansion and pledged that he would follow the principles of George Washington in foreign policy. The election of 1848 thus proved to be a turning point, as the election of Taylor ushered in a period of four years where the executive branch actively sought to thwart the fulfillment of manifest destiny.

On the surface, Zachary Taylor seemed to be an odd choice to head the Whig ticket. The vast majority of Whigs had fervently opposed the U.S.-Mexican War, but Taylor had led U.S. forces into northern Mexico and gained national fame through victories at Resaca de la Palma, Palo Alto, and Monterey. After Taylor's forces captured Monterey, President Polk and Secretary of War William Marcy became openly critical of Taylor's leadership.[2] Polk decided to give Gen. Winfield Scott command of an expedition to take Mexico City. Polk's plan to deprive Taylor of additional military glory soon backfired. In February 1847 General Santa Anna attacked Taylor's army, which had remained in Mexico. Facing a Mexican army that was three times larger than his own, Taylor refused to surrender. The ensuing Battle of Buena Vista would not result in a decisive victory for either side, but Americans saw it as a great triumph.[3] More than any event, the Battle of Buena Vista cemented Taylor's reputation as a military hero and added luster to the growing legend of "Old Rough and Ready."

At the same moment that Zachary Taylor was riding into the national spotlight and out of the good graces of President Polk, Whigs were searching for a presidential candidate. Henry Clay was the undisputed leader of the party, but his defeat in 1844 convinced many Whigs that he could never capture the White House.[4] As early as the summer of 1846, John J. Crittenden, a senator from Kentucky, turned to Zachary Taylor as a suitable candidate for the Whig nomination.[5] After the Battle of Buena Vista, the momentum for Taylor grew, as did the rumors that he was amenable to the Whig Party.[6] Over the course of 1847, however, Taylor refused to commit himself to a presidential run, declined to declare his political affiliation, and refused to take a firm stand on the controversial Wilmot Proviso.[7] As the war drew to a close, the momentum for a potential Taylor candidacy slowed.

This changed in April 1848 when Taylor released a public letter written to his brother-in-law, Capt. J. S. Allison, which would become known as the Allison letter. "My opinions have so often been misconceived and misrepresented," Taylor began, "that I deem it due to myself, if not to my friends, to make a brief exposition of them upon the topics to which you have called my attention."[8] Taylor first affirmed that he was a Whig. Taylor then promised that he would rarely use his veto power and that he favored allowing Congress to craft legislation regarding tariffs and internal improvements. He stipulated that "the will of the people, as expressed through their representatives in Congress, ought to be respected and carried out by the Executive."[9] All of these points aligned with Whig doctrine and were carefully crafted to appeal to northern and southern Whigs.

Taylor waited until his fourth point to explain his views on the U.S.-Mexican War. Taylor observed, "The principles of our government, as well as its true policy are opposed to the subjugation of other nations, and the dismemberment of other countries by conquest." He followed up this critique of Polk with a verbal masterstroke that aligned himself with the critics of manifest destiny: "In the language of the great Washington, 'Why should we quit our own to stand on foreign ground?'"[10] Whigs had critiqued Polk for not following Washington's example and now Taylor was promising that, if he were elected, he would be sure to do so. He would restore the standing of the United States in the international community and cultivate peace with all nations, just as Washington had hoped his successors would.

Less than two months later, Whigs met in Baltimore and nominated Zachary Taylor for president. Because of sectional tension and concerns over whether slavery would spread into the territories acquired from Mexico, the Whig Party did not draft a platform. Nonetheless, Whigs throughout the campaign referred to the Allison letter as "Taylor's platform."[11] The *Cleveland Herald* responded to the complaint in a Democratic newspaper that Taylor had no platform: "We much fear our neighbor has of late given Whig papers but a cursory reading. We invite his attention to the following Taylor Whig Platform, which since last April has appeared in most if not all of the Whig papers of the Union." The article concluded by reprinting the Allison letter with the signature "Z. Taylor."[12] Whigs regularly deployed the Allison letter as evidence that Taylor had his own platform.[13]

Taylor's letter helped advance a Whiggish approach to foreign policy. In May 1848 the Democratic Party convened at Baltimore and nominated Lewis Cass.[14] Unlike Taylor, who had never held a political office, Cass was a longtime politician, having served as territorial governor of Michigan, secretary of war, minister to France, and U.S. senator. And unlike Taylor, Cass was an unabashed expansionist. "If we should swallow Mexico to-morrow," Cass declared in the midst of the U.S.-Mexican War, "I do not believe it would kill us."[15] He would later tell his colleagues, "I am by no means satisfied that the day will not come in which the whole of the vast country around us will form one of the most magnificent empires that the world has yet seen."[16] Throughout his political career, Cass argued that expansion was beneficial and that there was nothing to fear from it.[17] Cass and Taylor could not have stood farther apart in their respective views of foreign policy.

Whigs did not downplay these foreign-policy differences. In articles, speeches, and campaign biographies, Whigs focused on manifest destiny and compared Zachary Taylor to Lewis Cass. One Whig paper ran excerpts from the Allison letter to show that Taylor opposed territorial expansion and agreed with Washington that the United States needed to avoid conquering others.[18] Across the page, that same paper printed the headline "In Favor of Conquest and Dismemberment" and quoted Cass to show that the Democratic candidate favored subjugating and annexing all of Mexico.[19] One frequently reprinted article likewise compared the two candidates.[20] This article quoted from Taylor's Allison letter to show that the Whig candidate opposed conquest; two quotes from Cass proved that the Democratic candidate desired war and the absorption of Mexico. After juxtaposing quotes from the two candidates, the anonymous author enjoined the reader, "Determine for yourself which utters the most Christian-like, human and patriotic language."[21] For Whigs, the choice seemed obvious.

Whigs also sought to draw parallels between Zachary Taylor and George Washington that extended beyond their mutual opposition to foreign entanglements.[22] One biographer noted that Taylor's sudden rise to fame in the midst of war was similar to Washington's.[23] Ben: Perley Poore[24] made a similar case for Taylor. After reviewing the general's battlefield exploits, Poore observed that Taylor had always emulated Washington in both his military conduct and his private behavior. "Like Washington," Poore noted of Taylor, "he had been trained to arms. Like Washington, he is a man of lofty patriotism, of mathematical integrity, and of stainless virtue."[25] Shortly after drawing this comparison, Poore directly quoted the Allison letter. Another campaign biography was even more direct, as it included an entire three-page section under the heading "His Position before the Country—His Resemblance to Washington."[26]

To solidify this connection, Whigs continually stressed the word "peace" in their political appeals. Taylor "[is] emphatically a man of peace," one campaign biography noted, "and there are none, whatever their prejudices, more averse to war, or more anxious to hold in check that lust of dominion and love of human slaughter."[27] A North Carolina newspaper dubbed Taylor the "peace candidate." "What a noble spectacle is here?" its editor panegyrized. "Another Cincinnatus returns to his Plough, and in the language of the Father of Our Country, counsels his Countrymen against the dangerous tendencies of war and conquest."[28] Because Taylor had led troops into battle, Whigs argued, he would refuse to needlessly plunge his country into another armed conflict. Electing Taylor would guarantee four years of sustained peace.

By way of contrast, Whigs stressed the bellicose character of Taylor's opponent. If Taylor was the peace candidate, Cass was the war candidate.[29] This was the tactic pursued by Truman Smith, a prominent Whig member of the House of Representatives who had become a leader in the Taylor campaign. In June 1848 Smith penned a public letter that played upon the traditional Whig theme of peace, noting that a Taylor administration would "consecrate all its faculties to the preservation of the peace of the country." He then turned his attention to Cass. "I desire to say nothing disrespectful of Gen. Cass," Smith began, before doing just that. "War! War!" Smith noted, "has been incessantly on his lips for years past. . . . What if war again should follow from it—the annexation of Cuba or indefinite extension on the side of Mexico?" Smith's point here was simple. A vote for Taylor would guarantee peace; a vote for Cass meant war.[30]

Throughout the summer and fall, Whigs harped upon the theme of war and peace. Many pointed with alarm to a prospective Cass administration. The *Boston Daily Atlas* warned its readers that if Cass were elected he would try to conquer Mexico, Cuba, and Jamaica.[31] Caleb B. Smith, another prominent Whig politician, asserted: "[Cass] stands forth the champion of increased territory from any and every quarter, no matter what amount of blood and treasure shall be wasted in its acquisition."[32] Whigs tried to paint an apocalyptic portrait of a future Cass administration. Should the Michigander win in 1848, they warned, the United States would immediately become embroiled in a conflict with either Britain or Spain and troops would be dispatched from Mexico to Cuba.

Whigs tried to make manifest destiny a central theme of the election. On numerous occasions Whigs identified Cass as the candidate of manifest destiny. The *Boston Atlas* warned its readers about Cass's dangerous views on expansion. "To your manifest-destiny-man," it admonished, "the rights of other nations . . . are as nothing—reason, religion, right, are of no avail against manifest destiny."[33] Could the United States trust a man who wanted to enlarge the United States past its current boundaries? Many did not. A letter appearing in the *Daily Banner* of Wisconsin described Cass as a risky candidate, the "manifest destiny Senator" who would support the annexation of Yucatán and Cuba and lead the United States into another war. Taylor seemed like the safer candidate because he promised peace for four years.[34] Unless one wanted "perpetual war," one should vote for Taylor.

Whatever doubts some Whigs had about Taylor, they could enthusiastically vote against Cass. Daniel Webster took this approach throughout the campaign season. Webster had represented Massachusetts in the U.S. Senate from 1827 to 1841, served as secretary of state under Presidents William Henry Harrison and John Tyler, and then returned to the Senate. As one of the most powerful members of the Whig Party, Webster had hoped to secure the nomination for himself in 1848 and was deeply disappointed to be overtaken by Taylor. Webster begrudgingly supported Taylor's candidacy, but only because of his hatred and fear of Cass. As Webster wrote to Edward Everett, "I regard Genl Cass as the most likely man in the Country to embroil us with foreign nations. He loves war, & commotion: &, besides, he utterly hates England."[35] Webster genuinely feared a Cass administration and so he delivered several campaign speeches on behalf of Taylor, hoping to sway New Englanders to vote against Cass.

In two speeches that received wide attention, Webster offered only tepid support for Taylor, going so far as to note that Taylor was a military man and that it was not wise to nominate military men for president.[36] But Webster saved his ammunition for blasting Cass. "I hold him, I confess," Webster told his New England audience, "in the present state of the country, to be the most dangerous man in whom the powers of the executive Chief Magistracy could well be placed."[37] Webster later observed, "[Cass] believes in the doctrine of American destiny; and that that destiny is to go through wars, and invasions, and maintain vast armies, to establish a great, powerful, domineering government over all this continent." Speaking a month later, Webster asked his audience whether they wanted a candidate who would retain peaceful relations with foreign powers or a man who believed in manifest destiny. Webster did not believe that Cass could keep the United States from war.[38]

Horace Greeley's *New York Tribune* adopted this same line of reasoning. The *Tribune*, especially in its widely circulated weekly edition, was one of the most popular newspapers in the United States and exerted a great deal of influence over Whig voters.[39] Greeley remained a committed Whig, but like many others, he had hoped that Henry Clay would secure the nomination.[40] After the party nominated Taylor, Greeley agreed to back his candidacy, but his support was lukewarm. As one article in the *Tribune* forthrightly stated, "That we should greatly prefer to Gen. Taylor as President Mr. Clay, Mr. Webster, or almost any prominent Whig Statesman, we shall no more disguise henceforth than heretofore."[41] Yet Greeley threw his halting support behind Zachary Taylor, mainly because he feared a Cass presidency: "We believe he [Taylor] will be more hostile to War, more solicitous for Peace, more favorable to simplicity in the Government and utility in its expenditures than Gen Cass would be."[42] Whatever his reservations about Taylor, Greeley thought him much less likely than Cass to involve the country in another costly war.

Whigs differed in their level of enthusiasm for Taylor but remained horrified at the thought of a believer in manifest destiny occupying the White House. "We do not want Canada, or Cuba, or the West Indies, or Yucatan, or the projected republic of Sierra Madre to be annexed to the United States," a writer for the *American Review* remarked on the eve of the election.[43] Whigs repeated what they had said throughout the U.S-Mexican War; the United States was large enough and there was no need to increase sectional tension by adding new states. "'Democracy' is now engaged in earnest efforts to make Gen. Cass President," one Whig journal warned, "with undefined objects of war, conquest, and territorial extension floating before his eager vision."[44] If Americans voted for Cass, they would immediately face the prospect of a war with either Britain or Spain.

The *National Intelligencer* asked its readers directly whether they were in favor of war or peace.[45] In a lengthy article that ran in October 1848, the most influential Whig newspaper reminded its readers that Cass endorsed Polk's war against Mexico. Not only did Cass believe the conquest of Mexico just, but he also desired more land than Polk. A Cass administration, in short, would likely involve the United States in another war of conquest. After discussing Cass's lust for land, the author provided an excerpt from Taylor's Allison letter, proving that Taylor abhorred war and would seek to keep the United States out of conflicts with its neighbors. As a committed Whig, Taylor would defer to the power of the legislative branch and would not seek to usurp its authority. As did most Whigs, this author concluded the article by briefly comparing Taylor to Washington.[46]

Seba Smith took arguments about Cass's bellicosity and transformed them into humorous material. In a letter written in the summer of 1848, Major Jack Downing remarks, "There isn't agoing to be

THE MODERN GILPINS. LOVE'S LABOR LOST.

2. Prominent members of the Democratic Party are seen here heading toward an electoral defeat. Cass is holding the sword of annexation, shouting about manifest destiny, a clear reference to his aggressive foreign policy. John L. Magee, "The Modern Gilpins. Love's Labor Lost" (New York: James Baillie, 1848). From Library of Congress Prints and Photographs Online Catalog, https://www.loc.gov/pictures/item/2008661478/.

no more annexin' till Mr. Cass comes in President."[47] In that same letter, Downing worries about the growing popularity of Taylor and the likelihood that he will defeat Cass. "I don't know, after all," Downing laments, "but this annexin' Mexico will turn out to be an unlucky blow to the party; for what will it profit the Democratic party if they gain the whole world and lose the Presidency?"[48] As an office-seeker, Downing is less concerned about the fate of the United States than he is about a patronage appointment if the Whigs return to power. But he continues to stump for Cass, albeit in a decidedly humorous fashion. "I made a roarin' speech for Cass," Downing reports to Polk in a subsequent letter, "told 'em what a great statesman and great warrior he was; and how he had proved the former by offering to swallow all Mexico, and how he had proved the latter by breakin' his

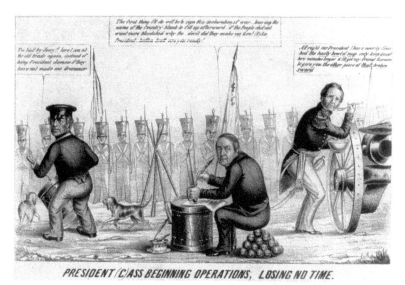

PRESIDENT (C)ASS BEGINNING OPERATIONS, LOSING NO TIME.

3. Depicting Cass as a warmonger became a common theme throughout the election of 1848, as seen in this image. "President (C)ass Beginning Operations, Losing No Time" (New York: H. R. Robinson, 1848). From Library of Congress Prints and Photographs Online Catalog, https://www.loc.gov/item/2008661480/.

sword in a passion." Smith's satire remained sharp and Major Jack Downing continually reminded his readers that Cass was a committed annexationist who would likely provoke a war.[49]

The Whig portrayal of Cass as a sword-wielding fanatic passed into popular culture. This is most clearly seen in the humor of Elbridge Gerry Paige, who wrote under the name Dow, Jr. During the 1840s Paige gained immense popularity for his "short patent sermons," which appeared in the pages of the *Sunday Mercury*, a New York newspaper. Modeled upon popular sermons, each patent sermon began with a short quotation and then contained commentary and advice, typically of a farcical nature. In 1848 Paige penned a column analyzing the conduct and principles of the three leading contenders for the presidency: Zachary Taylor, Martin Van Buren, and Lewis Cass.[50] Using the guise of Dow, Jr., Paige mocked all of them. He labeled Martin Van Buren a shady opportunist who was seeking "revenge" on the Democratic Party for overlooking him in 1844,

4. Cass's bellicose qualities are on full display here. He calls out new territories to conquer as he wields the bloody sword of manifest destiny. "A War President: Progressive Democracy" (New York: Peter Smith, June 6, 1848). From Library of Congress Prints and Photographs Online Catalog, https://www.loc.gov/pictures/item/2003674553/.

and he dubbed Zachary Taylor a nincompoop who lacked political principles.

Paige reserved his most scathing comments for Cass and warned that his election would spell disaster for the United States. "We have no idea of having a man in the White House who would involve the country in a war with the Sandwich Islands in less than twenty-four hours after his inauguration," the fictional exhorter warns. Paige prophesied that Cass would seek to conquer his neighbors and bring them under the control of the United States. To drive home his point, Paige turned to the ludicrous. "Ere the dog-days were over," he preached, "he [Cass] would send an invading army to march through the white sands of Coney Island—there to capture All the unoffending clams, because one of their race once had the audacity to disagree with (the stomach of) a discharged midshipman . . . and occupy the enemy's country till two-thirds of the poor conquered clams consented to be roasted alive, and one half of their territory for ever annexed." Paige clearly did not believe that Van Buren, Taylor, or Cass were presidential material, but he seemed to have particular animosity toward Cass. He concluded his section on Cass with an acerbic comment: "We can have no such a ferocious monster as Cass."[51]

Paige's fictional sermon evinces the fact that manifest destiny was a focal point of the election of 1848. This is not to argue that expansionism was the paramount issue, nor that it necessarily swayed the majority of voters.[52] As historian Joseph Rayback demonstrated, the issue of the Wilmot Proviso and what to do with the lands acquired from Mexico emerged as a significant issue.[53] In many southern states, Zachary Taylor was aided by the fact that he was an enslaver.[54] Southerners felt him a safer choice than Cass on the pivotal issue of slavery. Moreover, as historian Joel Silbey has shown, Whigs and Democrats relied upon their traditional voting bases in 1848 and few voters shifted their allegiance from the previous presidential campaign.[55] However, the question of manifest destiny should not be overlooked as one of the more significant issues of the election. Drawing from Washington's Farewell Address allowed Taylor to promise the American people peace for the next four years. It also enabled Taylor and his supporters to paint an apocalyptic view of what manifest destiny would bring in its wake: war with Britain, Spain, and perhaps Mexico, and invasions of far-off islands. Would the nation rather side with Washington or embrace the new idea of manifest destiny? This was a theme that the Whigs reiterated to great effect over the course of the campaign.[56]

Taylor's victory led some Whigs to celebrate the defeat of manifest destiny. The *National Intelligencer* applauded the people for their wisdom in voting Taylor into the highest office in the land. "They have shown," its editor exulted, "that their virtue can resist the seductive but fatal visions of conquest, territorial aggrandizement, 'manifest destiny,' 'Anglo-Saxon supremacy,' &c, with which they have been tempted; that their intelligence can distinguish between names and things."[57] According to this way of thinking, manifest destiny was a tempting ideology that appealed to the baser instincts of the American public, but the American people had demonstrated that they were wise enough to reject it. The *New York Courier and Enquirer* summed this up best by reading the election as a repudiation of manifest destiny and a vindication of the principles of George Washington. The results appeared decisive: "The manifest destiny doctrine, which under the direction of Mr. Cass was to lead us all over this continent, to spread Anglo-Saxon institutions . . . is silenced. We shall be content, as General Taylor, borrowing the language of General Washington, has said, 'to stand upon our own soil.'"[58]

Other editors breathed a sigh of relief that the United States had been saved from Cass. Shortly before Taylor's inauguration, the *New York Express* drove this point home: "Our 'manifest destiny,' we were told, over and over again, was to rob foreign countries, and to plunder their people; and General Cass was the candidate of our manifest destiny men." As a "manifest destiny man," Cass was particularly dangerous. If he had managed to capture the White House, Cuba, Canada, and Yucatán would have been targeted and the United States would have found itself in at least one war. "The success of General Cass would have entailed upon us the wars common to all such dynasties, and to all such chieftains, who know of no National Progress but what is won by destroying and robbing our fellow men," the paper concluded. Fortunately, the triumph of Zachary Taylor had ensured that the United States would embark upon four years of peace.[59]

The election brought Taylor to the White House, but doubts remained about what policy he would pursue.[60] After all, Taylor had never held elective office and the frequent Democratic refrain had been that he lacked political principles. Taylor dispelled that particular canard in his inaugural address.[61] Despite the brevity of his speech, Taylor included multiple references to George Washington. "To the example of those illustrious patriots I shall always defer with reverence," he noted, "and especially to his example who was by so many titles 'the Father of his Country.'" Taylor observed that he sympathized with people striving for liberty throughout the world, but that the wisest course for the United States to pursue was to adhere to the advice given by Washington and to maintain strict neutrality. Taylor then made a somewhat veiled reference to the U.S.-Mexican

War, noting that he hoped all international problems could be solved diplomatically and that his administration would always "exhaust every resort of honorable diplomacy before appealing to arms."[62] To contemporaries, Taylor's meaning was clear.[63] The archexpansionist *New York Herald* groused, "For four years to come, at least, no annexation scheme will be indulged in by the government."[64]

Whereas proponents of manifest destiny complained, Whigs approved of Taylor's message and especially his commitment to a foreign policy styled after Washington.[65] One paper appreciated that the address was "modest and liberal in tone, and entirely free from the blustering, 'fifty-four-forty' style in which Mr. Polk had the bad taste to assume the Presidential station."[66] An Ohio paper rejoiced, "[Taylor] repudiates the Gunpowder theory, and relies on negotiation."[67] Not surprisingly, some Whigs complimented Taylor by comparing his inaugural to Washington's.[68] Whigs were not disappointed by Taylor and agreed that he had solidified his reputation as a legitimate member of the party. Indeed, mere months after Taylor delivered his address, the *National Intelligencer* declared, "We may say that the Inaugural Address of President Taylor embodies . . . the doctrines which we have always upheld." It went on to explain that in foreign policy this meant that Whigs relied upon Washington's Farewell Address and firmly rejected "Manifest Destiny."[69]

Taylor soon had the opportunity to put his foreign policy principles to work. In 1848 President Polk had dispatched Elijah Hise to Central America. Polk tasked Hise with negotiating treaties to gain U.S. control over a possible interoceanic canal route. Hise successfully completed his diplomatic mission, as he not only secured treaties of commerce and friendship with Nicaragua and Honduras but also negotiated a separate treaty with Nicaragua that provided the United States with the concessions necessary for the construction of a canal.[70] The Hise Treaty, signed in June of 1849, stipulated that the United States would provide protection to Nicaragua from hostile nations. The Senate, however, never had a chance to vote on the treaty. Seeing Hise as a Polk loyalist, Taylor recalled him, replaced him with Ephraim G. Squier, and never considered submitting the Hise Treaty for Senate ratification. Taylor preferred working with Great Britain to soothe over tensions regarding Central America.[71]

Taylor viewed readjusting the relationship with Great Britain as critical. Great Britain had laid claim to British Honduras, what would later be known as Belize, in the eighteenth century.[72] Far more problematic to many Americans was Britain's activities during the U.S.-Mexican War. Since the eighteenth century the British had been involved with the Miskito Kingdom, who claimed sovereignty along the coasts of what became Nicaragua and Honduras. Resisting all attempts at incorporation into the Spanish empire, the Miskito Kingdom increasingly turned to Britain for protection. By the eighteenth century Britain had taken to the practice of crowning a King of the Miskito Kingdom, typically in British Honduras, and recognizing his authority. In 1847 Britain decided to take its relationship with the Miskito Kingdom a step further, officially announcing that it recognized the claims of the Miskito Kingdom to the coast. In 1848 Britain sent several ships and seized the port of San Juan. Nicaragua tried and failed on several occasions to recapture the port city.[73]

Zachary Taylor entered office hoping to stem British influence and to secure a stake for the United States in a possible canal through Central America. To help him obtain this goal, Taylor appointed John Clayton, a prominent Delaware Whig, as secretary of state.[74] Affable, gregarious, and well liked by his peers, Clayton had firmly opposed Polk's aggressive foreign policy and had spoken out against the U.S.-Mexican War and the "all-Mexico" movement.[75] Taylor tasked Clayton with negotiating a treaty with Britain that would solve the canal issue and limit Britain's role in Central America. Negotiations began in earnest when the British dispatched Sir Henry Bulwer to Washington DC in December of 1849 to discuss a possible treaty.[76] It still took almost four months for Clayton and Bulwer to reach an agreement, but on April 19, 1850, both parties signed what became known as the Clayton-Bulwer Treaty.[77]

The Clayton-Bulwer Treaty marked a reasonable compromise between the two governments. Both Great Britain and the United States had been seeking economic power in Central America and were interested in controlling a potential canal.[78] Article one of the treaty stipulated, "The governments of the United States and Great Britain hereby declare, that neither the one nor the other will ever obtain or maintain for itself any exclusive control over the said ship canal."[79] Arguably, another stipulation was of even greater importance: "Neither will [Great Britain and the United States] ever erect or maintain any fortifications commanding the same . . . or occupy, or fortify, or colonize, or assume or exercise any dominion over Nicaragua, Costa Rica, the Mosquito coast, or any part of Central America."[80] Up until 1850, the United States had pursued an aggressive foreign policy, expanding from a string of states along the coast to a nation that spanned a continent. Believers in manifest destiny expected this growth to continue until the United States sprawled over the entire continent. The Clayton-Bulwer Treaty struck at the heart of this theory by proclaiming that the United States would never colonize Central America.

Senators in the United States were thus presented with a treaty that directly contradicted manifest destiny, a fact that Zachary Taylor did not seek to disguise. In a message that was sent to the Senate along with the official treaty, Taylor observed that upon entering office he had found Great Britain "in possession of nearly half of Central America."[81] He believed that the Clayton-Bulwer Treaty limited British influence. But he also believed that it would prevent the United States from seeking to exercise control over Central America. His message stated directly, "If there be any who would desire to seize and annex any portion of the territories of these weak sister republics . . . or to extend our dominion over them, I do not concur in their policy."[82] The central point of this treaty was clear; the United States had renounced annexation and colonization in Central America.

Unlike the Treaty of Guadalupe Hidalgo, the Clayton-Bulwer Treaty did not cause much stir in the Senate. The treaty was signed on April 19, sent to the U.S. Senate on April 22, and reported out of committee, without amendment, on May 15.[83] Shortly after the treaty had been signed in April, newspapers across the United States began to report on it. The *New York Herald*, which was one of the first papers to break the news, reported favorably, observing, "The terms of this treaty are represented as being very satisfactory to the United States."[84] The *National Intelligencer* and *Louisville Courier* believed that the treaty would glide through the Senate.[85] These prognosticators proved to be correct as the Senate ratified the Clayton-Bulwer Treaty on May 22 by an overwhelming majority. The final tally stood at forty-two in favor of the treaty with a mere eleven votes in opposition. In spite of the Senate being controlled by the Democratic Party, Clayton-Bulwer was never in serious danger of being rejected.[86]

The debate in the Senate was held behind closed doors and no speeches were recorded. A quick glance at those who voted against the treaty, however, is quite revealing. All eleven votes in opposition came from Democrats. These included two extreme expansionists who had voted against the Treaty of Guadalupe Hidalgo: Stephen Douglas of Illinois and David Atchison of Missouri. Five no votes were registered by men who had voted for the Treaty of Guadalupe Hidalgo but who were well-known expansionists: Daniel Dickinson of New York, Jesse Bright of Indiana, Jefferson Davis of Mississippi, Hopkins Turney of Tennessee, and David Yulee of Florida.[87] The final four men had been recently elected: Isaac P. Walker of Wisconsin, James Whitcomb of Indiana, Solon Borland of Arkansas, and Jeremiah Clemens of Alabama. Although these men hailed from different regions and had varying levels of political experience, they were all outspoken expansionists.

Most Democrats who opposed the treaty believed that it thwarted the fulfillment of manifest destiny. One Democratic paper grumbled, "We did not deem it possible that any administration would pledge our government, by a treaty with Great Britain or any foreign power, never to annex any portion of Central America to the United States."[88] This paper did not worry about the interoceanic canal, but was disturbed by the nonannexation clause. "We are one of those who have looked forward with hope to the period when the whole of North America, embracing the States of the Isthmus," the article continued, "would constitute but one great federal republic. . . . But now, it seems, we have bound ourselves, by solemn treaty with Great Britain." How could manifest destiny be fulfilled if the United States pledged never to annex Central America?

This argument soon found its way into the pages of the Washington *Union*, the paper that had functioned as the official organ of the Polk administration. In May 1850 the paper attacked Clayton: "He has in that treaty permitted Great Britain, our formidable maritime and commercial rival, to fix our boundaries for us; in short, to apply the Monroe principle to ourselves. Does he imagine he can, by any pretext or sophism, reconcile the American people to this mortifying and disgraceful surrender of their rights and honor?" In this lengthy article the author never once examined the canal issue, but instead analyzed the wording of the clause regarding annexation and compared it with the language used in the Treaty of Guadalupe Hidalgo. Like so many others, this author saw the ban on annexation as the overarching flaw in the Clayton-Bulwer Treaty. If ratified, it would prevent the United States from carrying out its manifest destiny.[89]

Other Democrats privately expressed reservations about the terms of the treaty. James Buchanan, who had recently served as secretary of state in the Polk administration, opposed it. Buchanan lobbied his friends to block its passage, writing to John Alexander McClernand, a member of the House of Representatives from Illinois.[90] In his letter to McClernand, Buchanan lashed out at the treaty and derided its provisions on annexation. "They are neither more nor less than a solemn stipulation on the part of the United States to Great Britain," he expostulated, "that at no future period, shall we ever annex to our Country, under any circumstances, any portion of the vast country of Central America." For Buchanan, the canal question was clearly secondary to the issue of territorial expansion. "Let us enter into a similar stipulation with Great Britain in regard to Mexico," he continued, "and our limits are forever bounded by the Rio Grande, for such would be the true purport and meaning of our engagement with that over-reaching power."

As a congressman, McClernand had no power to block the Clayton-Bulwer Treaty, and so Buchanan turned his persuasive powers upon William R. King, a senator from Alabama and close friend, who chaired the Committee on Foreign Relations. Buchanan urged King to oppose the treaty and was undoubtedly surprised when King calmly explained why he was voting to ratify.[91] In a second letter Buchanan reiterated his objections and attacked the stipulations regarding the canal, arguing that the United States would have been better off doing nothing. "But this is a very small affair," he explained, "compared with the right which has been assumed by Great Britain & yielded by us to limit our progress on this continent *throughout all future time.*" Although he decided to drop the subject after realizing that King's mind was made up, Buchanan made it clear in his correspondence that he opposed Clayton-Bulwer primarily because it blocked the possibility of annexing the various republics of Central America.[92]

Such opposition to the Clayton-Bulwer Treaty, however, did not run very deep. Senator King dismissed Buchanan's concerns and brusquely told him that he was "decidedly opposed to any further acquisition of Territory at this time in any quarter."[93] Other senators agreed with King. Whig newspapers gleefully reported that most Democrats were in favor of the treaty.[94] The *New York Courier and Enquirer* thanked the *Union* for its arguments and sharply observed that the vote revealed the *Union*'s limited political influence.[95] The *Natchez Courier* ran an even more biting article under the mock headline "We Are Sold to the British." "Such was the indignant ejaculation of the Washington Union," this article ran, "when it heard that Mr. Clayton had negotiated the Nicaragua treaty!" It then observed, "What will be the outpourings of its grief when it learns that Gen. Cass and Mr. Foote, Messrs. Mason and Hunter, Butler and Dodge, Downs and Soule, King and Shields, Houston and Sturgeon, and several other democrats, all 'good men and true'—not merely witnessed the bill of sale, but themselves assisted in fixing the seals upon the instrument." With the vote overwhelmingly in their favor, Whigs happily ridiculed expansionist Democrats for failing to mount much opposition to the treaty.[96]

Zachary Taylor had little time to celebrate the passage of the Clayton-Bulwer Treaty.[97] The exchange of ratifications took place on July 4, 1850, the very day Zachary Taylor fell ill after attending Fourth of July festivities in Washington DC.[98] Taylor managed to sign the treaty on July 5, but he died on July 9, leaving Millard Fillmore as president of the United States. The ratification of the Clayton-

Bulwer Treaty would be Taylor's most significant achievement during his brief term in office.

In spite of the short duration of his presidency, Taylor did reshape U.S. foreign policy. This is partially because his triumph in 1848 kept Lewis Cass from becoming commander in chief. Over the ensuing decade, only Stephen Douglas and William Henry Seward would have their names more closely associated with manifest destiny than Lewis Cass.[99] Even voters who were skeptical of Taylor in 1848 expressed relief at the defeat of Cass.[100] Horace Mann, for example, who refused to support the Whig Party in 1848 because of its stance on slavery, nevertheless privately wrote to a friend that he was grateful for Taylor's victory, as it had prevented slavery from spreading into the Southwest and blocked the potential annexation of Cuba.[101] At the very least, the election of Taylor ensured that Cass would not be controlling foreign policy.

Taylor's influence was not merely negative, however. Once elected, he fulfilled his campaign pledge to avoid war. Taylor's willingness to negotiate with Britain and refusal to considering annexing Central American nations represented a clear break with the policies of James K. Polk. With the help of his astute secretary of state, Taylor crafted a treaty that repudiated the idea of manifest destiny.[102] Proponents of manifest destiny quickly recognized that Clayton-Bulwer undercut their beloved ideology and they spent the next decade railing against it and demanding its abrogation.[103] Stephen Douglas, to cite the most famous example, fought for the next ten years to abrogate the treaty and never tired of boasting that he voted against it.[104] In a similar fashion, the *Democratic Review* denounced the treaty with regularity.[105] Taylor's election and subsequent ability to secure the Clayton-Bulwer Treaty shattered the dream of manifest destiny. The various republics of Central America seemed likely to escape the grasp of the United States.

3

Rejecting Robbery

Filibusters, Spain, and the Quest for Cuba, 1850–1855

W illiam Marcy was normally not a very passionate man. Considered to be one of the "Old Fogies," Marcy was a veteran Democratic politician who by 1855 had served as governor of New York, secretary of war, and now, secretary of state under Franklin Pierce. A quiet and affable man who enjoyed his books, Marcy was nonetheless irked as he penned a letter to his friend L. B. Shepherd. As secretary of state, Marcy had been dealing with the fallout over the Ostend Conference, a gathering in 1854 where three ministers declared that the United States could forcibly take Cuba if Spain refused to sell. For once, Marcy's passions got the best of him. "I am entirely opposed to getting up a war for the purpose of seizing Cuba," he fumed, "the conduct of Spain and the Cuban authorities has been exaggerated and even misrepresented." He then elaborated, "The robber doctrine I abhor, if carried out it would degrade us in our own estimation. . . . Cuba would be a very desirable possession if it came to us in the right way, but we cannot afford to get it by robbery or theft. . . . I do not believe the robber doctrine when calmly considered will be popular, or that a party can sustain itself upon it."[1]

Opponents of manifest destiny had developed the "robber doctrine" argument during the U.S.-Mexican War, but it had faded from use after the election of Zachary Taylor. Soon, however, armed groups of men known as filibusters were setting out from the United States with the express purpose of annexing Cuba. The election of Franklin Pierce, an avowed expansionist, revived Whig fears that Democrats would use the presidency to launch an aggressive program of territorial expansion. To challenge the rising tide of manifest destiny, Whigs resurrected the robber doctrine. Calling proponents of manifest destiny "robbers," "brigands," and "highwaymen," Whigs argued that the only way the United States should expand was by purchasing territory legally. By forcefully pushing this argument, Whigs drove a wedge between moderate Democrats, who wanted to buy territory, and radicals, who hoped that the United States could filibuster to claim Cuba. Lacking a coherent policy, the Democratic plan to acquire Cuba floundered. In spite of retaking the White House, Democrats were unable to push forward manifest destiny.

The death of Zachary Taylor placed Millard Fillmore in the White House. Hardly as popular as the war hero Taylor, Fillmore was a New Yorker who had been selected to provide sectional balance to the Whig ticket.[2] Taylor's sudden death left Fillmore with a host of problems. Foremost was the question of slavery in the territories recently acquired from Mexico. Even though he was an enslaver, Taylor had backed the admission of California as a free state, a view that rankled members of his own party, including Henry Clay.[3] In January 1850 Clay had introduced his own compromise measure.[4] Clay's proposal was meant to pacify southern members of Congress, who opposed adding two free states out of land taken from Mexico. What would have happened had Taylor lived remains a matter of some dispute, but his death paved the way for the passage of the Compromise of 1850.[5] Clay's omnibus measure failed, but broken into individual bills, and shepherded through by Stephen Douglas, the so-called Compromise of 1850 passed Congress in August and September of 1850. California became a free state, New Mexico and Utah became territories, a new fugitive slave law was passed, the boundary dispute between New Mexico and Texas was resolved, and the slave trade was banned in Washington DC.[6] The sectional crisis that many feared had seemingly been averted.[7]

Deciding what to do with the land taken from Mexico was not the only complex issue that Fillmore inherited. Fillmore also had to deal with filibusters.[8] A year before, several hundred men had gathered off the coast of Mississippi at Round Island.[9] Their goal was to land an armed force to "liberate" Cuba from Spain. As soon as

Taylor caught wind of this, he dispatched the United States Navy.[10] Surrounded and starving, the men of the Round Island Expedition eventually gave up and returned to their homes.[11] To discourage similar expeditions, Taylor issued a proclamation and declared such ventures to be in violation of U.S. law.[12]

Taylor's proclamation hardly deterred the more determined filibusters. Immediately after the failure of Round Island, a group of exiled Cubans, led by Narciso López, and sympathetic Americans established the Junta Promovedora de los Intereses Politicos de Cuba.[13] Ostensibly a political club, this organization planned another invasion of Cuba. Moreover, its members decided that Narciso López would lead the expedition. Born in Venezuela, López had become caught up in the wars of independence that had rippled through South America in the early nineteenth century.[14] López joined the Spanish military and spent the next decades of his life as a loyal Spanish soldier, slowly moving up the ranks to become a general.[15] López eventually settled in Cuba, where he failed in various business enterprises. In an unexpected move, López became wrapped up in revolutionary politics and fled to the United States. Once in the United States, López continued plotting against the Spanish government in Cuba.[16] As Congress grappled with the Compromise of 1850, López raised his revolutionary army.

The army was small, with not quite six hundred men.[17] In late April 1850 it departed from New Orleans. López expected his forces to be augmented by the people in Cuba, whom he believed would join his invading army.[18] On May 19, 1850, López and his army went ashore at Cárdenas, Cuba. The filibusters captured the Spanish garrison, along with the home of the lieutenant governor. But López was unpleasantly surprised when Cubans did not rally to his banner. He returned to his ship, hoping to launch a second invasion on Cuba's western coast, but once aboard his men held a vote and decided it was best to abandon the expedition. The filibusters sailed back to the United States and López's army dispersed.[19]

As word of López's invasion reached the United States, the public reaction divided along political lines. Many Democratic papers wished López success and hailed him as a liberator.[20] Whig papers,

5. Opponents of filibustering frequently equated filibusters to robbers. Here, López is shown fleeing with his loot. John L. Magee, "Genl. Lopez the Cuban Patriot Getting His Cash," 1850. From Library of Congress Prints and Photographs Online Catalog, https://www.loc.gov/item/2008661527/.

in contrast, denounced López and his followers.[21] A Vermont editor contended, "Their real purpose was neither more nor less than robbery. López and his men are simply a gang of buccaneering scoundrels."[22] The *Richmond Whig* observed, "[López] is a vagabond and adventurer. A band composed of such materials organize and invade a peaceful community—they burn houses, rob, and murder men, women, and children . . . if it does not constitute piracy, we do not know what piracy is."[23] The fact that López had fled from Cárdenas as soon as resistance appeared led his critics to charge him with cowardice. Surely, a liberator would not have run away when faced with opposition. "The expedition of Gen. Lopez is very generally indignantly denounced," the *North American and United States Gazette* explained. After discussing how López had only managed to steal money from Cárdenas, the paper concluded, "The judgment of mankind will pronounce this nothing less than robbery and murder."[24] Certainly, López had his admirers, but the Whig press readily dismissed him as a pirate and robber.[25]

However unsuccessful, the López fiasco caused Americans to ponder the value of Cuba. As they had during the U.S.-Mexican War, most Whigs maintained that adding territory to the United States would only stoke sectional tension. They discouraged all attempts to take Cuba, whether by purchase or by filibustering. Democrats, however, divided over the issue. Most Democrats saw Cuba as a desirable territory, but they could not agree how it was to be obtained. Aggressive sheets such as the *Democratic Review* supported filibustering and López's invasion, believing that a freed Cuba would ask to be annexed by the United States.[26] Shortly after the debacle at Cárdenas, a Mississippi editor came out strongly in favor of another filibuster invasion. "Cuba must be freed from Spanish tyranny," this editor proclaimed, "and we must aid in the work." The United States should provide weapons to the Cubans so they could fight back: "We have but to put arms in their hands, and they will fight to the last drop of their blood for their liberties."[27] Proponents of filibustering believed that the United States needed to take aggressive action to secure Cuba.

Many expansionists, however, saw filibustering as a hindrance to the cause of Cuban annexation. Richard Burleigh Kimball exemplified this viewpoint.[28] In 1850 Kimball published a book offering both a comprehensive overview of Cuban history and a plea for the acquisition of that island by the United States. In the ninth chapter Kimball turned his attention to the question "what is to become of Cuba." In his view Spain had lost the right to control the island by its indifference to the people's welfare.[29] Taking it for granted that Cuba would break from Spain within a year or so, the question, for Kimball, centered on which power would control the island. At this point Kimball raised the old bugbear of expansionists and warned that Great Britain was secretly plotting to take Cuba.[30] This was standard fare for expansionists, as was Kimball's claim that if revolution broke out in Cuba it might lead to a massive slave revolt.[31]

Kimball's arguments were hardly original, but the language of his concluding chapter was intriguing. In this chapter Kimball argued that the United States needed to purchase Cuba from Spain, as manifest destiny was "a poor excuse for the unlawful seizure of the territory of a friendly power."[32] Undoubtedly, Kimball had observed the many arguments equating robbery with manifest destiny, because he then continued, "For the same plea [manifest destiny] is as good in the mouth of the highwayman as in that of a power who shall take to the high road of nations, and, armed to the teeth, prey upon the weaker."[33] Kimball was an expansionist but he did not embrace filibustering or armed invasions. Kimball believed that legally purchasing Cuba was the only method the United States should use. Anything else was robbery.[34]

President Fillmore expressed no interest in acquiring Cuba, whether by purchase or armed invasion. When word reached the White House that López was plotting another expedition, Fillmore decided to issue his own proclamation. After using two paragraphs to explain the situation, Fillmore stated, "Such expeditions can only be regarded as adventures for plunder and robbery, and must meet the condemnation of the civilized world, whilst they are derogatory to the character of our country."[35] Fillmore not only condemned the expedition but he also warned that all those who participated would be prosecuted to the full extent of the law.

López paid no heed to Fillmore's proclamation. On July 4, 1851, a small band of rebels who had been in contact with López issued a declaration of independence from Spain and rumors began circulating that a revolution had begun in Cuba.[36] By August, the *New Orleans Picayune* confidently reported, "There is no longer question of a wide and apparently concerted rising of the people of the island against the Government."[37] Convinced that a genuine rebellion had begun, López set out for Cuba, slipping away from New Orleans with a filibuster crew of roughly five hundred men.[38] He and his men landed in Cuba, only to realize that they had been misled; no revolution was underway. Spanish troops captured López on August 28 and executed him a few days later.[39]

Upon hearing of the invasion, many Whigs again denounced the filibusters. "Whatever name may be given to Lopez and his followers," a Pittsburgh newspaper declared, "every well-informed man knows their real character. . . . They are engaged in one of the vilest attempts at robbery that ever disgraced humanity, and if there is any difference between them and common pirates, the latter can claim the advantage."[40] Even after the execution of López, Whigs remained convinced that most filibusters were motivated by pecuniary incentives. The *National Intelligencer* claimed that "of the prime movers of the desperate enterprise against Cuba, the greater part had probably no higher aim than their own personal advancement and interest."[41] After admitting that some men might have been motivated by patriotism, the paper still concluded that "no small number of them were enticed into the service more by the prospect of plunder than by the love of liberty." Filibusters, in short, were pirates.

Democrats, on other hand, criticized Fillmore's proclamation and deplored the executions (dubbed "massacres") of López and his men.[42] Many blamed Fillmore for exercising illegal authority in putting forth a proclamation.[43] "We do not hesitate to say," the *Democratic Review* thundered, "that the President of the United States stands at this moment responsible, not only for the butchery of his countrymen, but for the failure of the attempt to give liberty to Cuba."[44] Fillmore's proclamation gave Spanish authorities the right to treat the captured men as pirates. López's poor planning, they argued, had nothing to do with his defeat, as he "had to contend with the allied powers of Queen Isabella and President Fillmore, and it could not be expected that with a force of four hundred [*sic*] men, he could defeat both."[45] The Washington *Union* made responsibility for the tragic denouement clear.[46] The paper declared, "President Fillmore's proclamation is to the effect that anybody on earth might catch up at sea any American engaged in the Cuban enterprise, and drown, hang, or shoot him at pleasure, tried or untried, arrested or resisting."[47] Over the next year, Democrats continued to blame Fillmore for López's failure.

Yet expansionists remained of two minds. Supporters of filibustering demanded retribution for the death of López. "They are roused," one paper declared, speaking of the American people, "and demand vengeance for the gross insult she [Spain] has offered our flag, and for the butchery of our common brethren."[48] Public meetings were held in Savannah, New Orleans, New York, Nashville, and Philadelphia in which angry citizens demanded that the government exact revenge.[49] Others counseled patience. The *New York Herald* urged its readers to wait until the next presidential election, when the people could elect an expansionist who would work to secure Cuba through an "open and aboveboard purchase."[50] Although they grumbled about Fillmore, many expansionists were unwilling to back an armed invasion.

López's death in 1851 paved the way for a vibrant debate over Cuba, annexation, and the merits of filibustering. Whatever their disagreements on policy, both Whigs and Democrats realized that 1852 would be a pivotal election. Democrats could bewail Fillmore's proclamation and denigrate him as a murderer, but they could not push forward Cuban annexation without the White House. In a similar manner, Whigs realized that control of the White House enabled them to set the terms of debate. There was no threat of Cuban annexation as long as a Whig remained commander in chief. With this in mind Whigs met in Baltimore to select their next candidate. Millard Fillmore remained popular in the South, but most northern Whigs were unhappy with his stance on the Compromise of 1850 and refused to support him.[51] Jettisoning Fillmore, Whigs opted to nominate Winfield Scott, a hero of the U.S.-Mexican War who had been born in Virginia.[52]

Democrats had several contenders and so the nomination was hotly contested. In spite of his defeat in 1848, Lewis Cass remained the favorite. Both James Buchanan of Pennsylvania and William Marcy of New York, however, had lengthy careers in politics and were intent upon challenging Cass for the nomination. A fourth contender was the up-and-coming Stephen Douglas of Illinois. Born in Vermont, Douglas had moved to Illinois and taken up the practice of law, where he rapidly rose in the Democratic Party ranks.[53] He served two terms in Congress before taking his place in the U.S. Senate. There Douglas became known as a fervent expansionist, voting against both the Treaty of Guadalupe Hidalgo and the Clayton-Bulwer Treaty.[54] At a mere thirty-eight years old, Douglas represented the Democratic Party's future and stood as the candidate most committed to the principles of manifest destiny.[55]

Douglas was aided in his quest for the nomination by the *Democratic Review*. In 1851 a Kentucky-born journalist named George N. Sanders purchased the magazine.[56] From 1845 to 1851 the magazine had remained the firmest proponent of manifest destiny and so it was not altogether surprising that Sanders decided to throw the magazine's support behind Douglas.[57] What was unexpected, however, was the virulence of Sanders's attacks on other Democrats. In January 1852 the *Democratic Review* examined the upcoming presidential election. As was typical, Sanders decried the foreign policy of the Fillmore administration and accused the Whigs of truckling to the British in Central America and to the Spanish over Cuba.[58] After chastising Whigs for their feckless foreign policy, Sanders turned heavy fire on members of his own party. "Age is to be honored, but senility is pitiable," Sanders wrote, belittling older Democrats. By the end of the article, Sanders had managed to insult all the leaders of his own party, whom he considered to be too old to implement a vigorous foreign policy. He concluded that the party needed to nominate a younger man.[59] Without naming him, Sanders clearly supported Douglas.

Sanders's opening blast demonstrated the wide cleavage in the Democratic Party. The faction around Sanders and Douglas became known as Young America and its members relentlessly attacked their

LOCO FOCO CANDIDATES TRAVELLING.
ON THE CANAL SYSTEM.

6. A satire of the Democratic contenders in 1852, Stephen Douglas is noticeably shorter than the other candidates and is the only one fixated on fulfilling manifest destiny. J. Childs, "Loco Foco Candidates Travelling, on the Canal System," 1852. From Library of Congress Prints and Photographs Online Catalog, https://www.loc.gov/pictures/item/2008661545/.

opponents as "Old Fogies."[60] In contrast to the Old Fogies, who generally supported a cautious expansionism, the Young Americans were ardent proponents of manifest destiny.[61] Yet the exuberance of the Young Americans and their willingness to openly criticize more established members of the party undermined the faction's attempt to secure the nomination for Douglas.[62] When Democrats met in Baltimore in June, the Old Fogies were able to successfully thwart Douglas's candidacy.[63] It took forty-nine ballots before disgruntled delegates provided Franklin Pierce, a compromise candidate, the necessary two-thirds majority.[64] In a contest that included Buchanan, Marcy, and Douglas, Pierce was clearly the least experienced candidate. He had represented New Hampshire in the House and Senate and served in the U.S.-Mexican War. But he was hardly a distinguished legislator and his military service included an embarrassing incident in which he fell off his horse. Still, Pierce was forty-seven, handsome, and a fine orator. He seemed like an ideal compromise candidate. Young America and most expansionists ended up fully supporting Pierce's candidacy.[65]

Whigs, for their part, determined to assail Pierce as they had Cass. "We know, that, if Pierce be elected," George D. Prentice groaned in the *Louisville Journal*, "our countrymen will be allowed the fullest liberty to invade Cuba, and we believe in our hearts that such an invasion would lead to a more dreadful foreign war than we have ever yet been engaged in and to the destruction of our country's prosperity and good name if not to the destruction of the country itself."[66] Whigs had kept the United States out of war for four years, but Pierce would certainly follow in the footsteps of James K. Polk. Other Whigs quoted from the *Democratic Review* to show that Pierce would be dominated by the Young America faction.[67] A paper in Vermont asked its readers, "Is it better to have a Loco Foco land-stealing Administration, with strong filibuster or manifest destiny principles . . . thrust upon us, than a Whig Government that has already saved us from a foreign war and a world of domestic troubles growing out of this Cuban annexation mania?"[68] The answer, to Whigs at least, was that "it would be a calamity to have a Manifest Destiny man at the helm."[69]

Throughout the campaign, Whigs predicted that a Democratic victory would encourage filibustering. One concerned citizen wrote to the *Savannah Republican*, "It is a shame that any Whig should support Pierce and the platform adopted by the party who nominated him. I am as ardently a Whig as ever. . . . I am less disposed to trust the Democratic Party, composed as it is of Disunionists, Abolitionists, Fillibusters, Interventionists, and Democrats."[70] Pierce himself might not support filibustering, but he would surround himself with men who did. On the eve of the election, a paper in Vermont advised its readers, "The *fillibusters* are now secretly armed about New York, and in Southern cities, waiting only for a new Administration that shall encourage another foray upon Cuba, and other foreign territory."[71] Stephen Douglas and Pierre Soulé, a senator from Louisiana, were itching for war. "Under the name of 'our manifest destiny' and 'progressive democracy,'" the paper warned, "they are deliberately seeking personal and partisan advantages that will directly involve us in a disgraceful war."[72] If Pierce won the election, the filibusters were primed to strike.[73]

Unlike in 1848, few Americans heeded these alarms. When the votes were counted, Winfield Scott only captured Kentucky, Tennessee, Vermont, and Massachusetts, a disastrous showing that foreshadowed the demise of the Whig Party. Not surprisingly, Whigs read the election as evidence that filibusters would soon be setting off in the name of manifest destiny.[74] Making matters worse, expansionists unleashed a torrent of proexpansion rhetoric in the aftermath of Pierce's victory. The *Democratic Review* called the election of 1852 the "most important event in all history next to the war of Independence," and argued that foreign relations, rather than domestic issues, would dominate the new administration's agenda.[75] The *New York Herald* rejoiced at the overthrow of the conservative Whigs and the triumph of expansionism.[76] "It is now universally believed," the *Herald* gloated, "that the inauguration of General Pierce will be the inauguration of a new epoch in the history of the country, and of an entire revolution in the management of our foreign affairs."[77]

Questions remained, however, about the course that Pierce would pursue. Some Whigs bemoaned the likelihood that Pierce would embrace filibustering, yet careful observers realized that Democrats were unsure about how to proceed. To exploit these divisions, Seba Smith crafted a Jack Downing letter to Franklin Pierce, congratulating him on his victory.[78] Downing worries about the dangers of Democratic divisions. If Pierce nominates a member of Young America to his cabinet, Downing warns, the Old Fogies will revolt.[79] After discussing the factions within the party, Downing asks whether Pierce plans on launching a filibuster invasion of Cuba or if he is going to approach Spain about purchasing it. Downing then reminds Pierce of the sage advice of his uncle, who told him, "In nine cases out of ten it costs more to rob an orchard than it would to buy the apples."[80] Although written in the guise of a humorous letter, Downing's missive captured the paramount foreign policy question of Pierce's administration. Would Pierce rob the orchard or would he seek to buy it?[81]

Those closest to Pierce believed he would eschew filibustering. In December 1852 the Washington *Union* mocked Whigs for believing that the election of Pierce would lead to filibustering.[82] "A short time since," the editor wrote, "the whig press was in a panic at the thought that the approaching victory of the democratic party would give the country over to the sway of *filibustierism*. It is amusing to see how the result of the election has quieted all such apprehensions."[83] Of course, Pierce would seek more territory for the United States, but the Washington *Union* labeled the new president a "conservative" who would be careful how acquisitions were carried out. The Whigs had slandered Pierce as a "filibustier" and had made the election "hideous with their clamors against what they called the democratic spirit of rapine and robbery."[84] Pierce was not a filibuster. In putting forth this argument, the Washington *Union* made it clear that on the issue of expansion, Pierce was more likely to align himself with the Old Fogies than with the Young Americans.[85]

In March 1853 Pierce clarified his foreign policy views in his inaugural address. Pierce opened his section on foreign policy by rebuking his Whig predecessors. He boasted, "The policy of my Administration will not be controlled by any timid forebodings of evil from expansion. . . . Our attitude as a nation and our position on the globe render the acquisition of certain possessions not within our jurisdiction eminently important for our protection."[86] Pierce did not mention Cuba, but there was no doubt what he was talking about. The president then elaborated on how territory might be acquired, declaring that it would not be through a "grasping spirit, but with a view to obvious national interest and security, and in a manner entirely consistent with the strictest observance of national faith."[87] Pierce clarified that his foreign policy would "leave no blot upon" the country's "fair record."[88]

As seen in his inaugural, Pierce's views aligned with the more conservative expansionists.[89] This fact is further evidenced by a passionate newspaper battle waged by two powerful organs: the *National Intelligencer* and the Washington *Union*. Shortly after Pierce delivered his address, the *Intelligencer* concluded that Pierce had embraced manifest destiny, declaring, "Though the word be not mentioned in connexion [*sic*] with this purpose, it may be regarded as the first approach to recognition of the principle of MANIFEST DESTINY as a rule of action for this Government in the conduct of its relations with Foreign Powers."[90] In this article the *Intelligencer* briefly retraced the history of manifest destiny and explained how Pierce's embrace of the ideology spelled danger for the United States. Surely the nation was heading into rough waters if manifest destiny men controlled administration policy.

The rival Washington *Union* excoriated the *Intelligencer* for misreading the inaugural address. The editor noted that Pierce had never used the phrase "manifest destiny," yet nearly "three-quarters of the Intelligencer's article" was "devoted to the doctrine of the phrase of 'manifest destiny.'" Cuba was a possible target of the administration, but Pierce was neither a filibuster nor a believer in manifest destiny and it was wrong of the *Intelligencer* to accuse him of harboring such sentiments. Pierce did want to expand the nation but he would do so by scrupulous adherence to international law.[91]

This sharp rebuke struck a nerve with the *Intelligencer*. Instead of doubling down and declaring that Pierce was indeed a believer in manifest destiny, the *Intelligencer*, remarkably, conceded the point. "We must, in sheer justice," the editor now observed, "reject all suspicion of his [Pierce] being under the control of the Manifest-Destinarians, and merely regret that casual expressions in any phrase of the Inaugural, which seem at the first glance to lean to a favorite doctrine of that school, have given rise to apprehensions on that ground in any quarter."[92] As was typical for Whigs, the editor denounced manifest destiny, explaining why it seemed likely that Pierce would follow its dictates. But in the end, both the *Intelligencer* and the *Union* agreed that Pierce's inaugural did not endorse the idea of manifest destiny and that Pierce was most likely to pursue the policy of acquiring the island of Cuba through purchase.

Pierce soon proved the Washington *Union*'s interpretation correct. Once in office, Pierce took a middle-of-the-road path. Pierce chose William Marcy, the consummate "Old Fogy," as secretary of state.[93]

Pierce also named two strident expansionists to cabinet posts; Jefferson Davis became secretary of war and Caleb Cushing became attorney general.[94] Both of these men, however, were only loosely connected to the Young America movement.[95] Stephen Douglas did not receive a cabinet post, but Young America was represented with diplomatic appointments. Pierce sent John L. O'Sullivan to Portugal and Pierre Soulé to Spain.[96] Both of these men were aggressive expansionists and open proponents of filibustering.[97] In making these appointments, Pierce sought to placate the various factions within the Democratic Party.

Of all Pierce's appointments, the selection of Pierre Soulé was the most questionable. Soulé was a committed expansionist and something of a revolutionary. Born in France, Soulé was arrested for writing polemical tracts opposing King Charles X.[98] His brief confinement in a French jail did nothing to curb his enthusiasm for radical politics. Upon arriving in New Orleans in the 1820s, he remained a firebrand. In 1847 Soulé, comfortably married into the local aristocracy, entered the Senate. Throughout his time in office, Soulé stood out as an ardent opponent of monarchy and as an expansionist.[99] Soulé's diplomatic appointment appeased Young America, but most realistic observers pondered whether or not it was a wise selection. The *New York Herald*, a paper that was certainly not opposed to some old-fashioned expansion, wrote, "Mr. Soulé is the especial idol of Young America . . . and is believed to be ready at the tap of the drum to plunge forward to the extremest verge of filibusterism. He is believed by some to be almost fanatical . . . so that the ultimatum of 'manifest destiny' is obtained."[100] Such was the reputation of the man Pierce selected to negotiate for Cuba.

For this mission to succeed, Soulé had to ingratiate himself with the Spanish court, but he was ill suited for such a task. Soon after arriving in Spain, Soulé fought a duel with the French ambassador, the Marquis de Turgot.[101] Instead of recalling Soulé for this indiscretion, which had made him an outcast at the Spanish court, Pierce decided to change his approach.[102] In March 1854 Marcy issued new instructions, telling Soulé that the United States was willing to purchase Cuba and would offer as much as $100 million.[103] Before Soulé could submit a proposal to Spain, Marcy sent him another message, asking him to meet with James Buchanan, minister to Great Britain, and John Mason, minister to France. Marcy tasked the three men with formulating a Cuban policy.[104] The three ministers gathered at Ostend, Belgium, from October 9 to October 11 and reconvened the following week at Aix-La-Chappelle, Prussia.

In many respects, the indecision of the inexperienced Pierce led to the creation of what became known as the Ostend Manifesto. Instead of formulating his own foreign policy, Pierce asked his ministers for their advice. Over the course of several days, Buchanan, Soulé, and Mason drafted a document that explored the various reasons why the United States needed to acquire Cuba.[105] Included were statements such as "the Union can never enjoy repose, nor possess reliable security, as long as Cuba is not embraced within its boundaries."[106] The authors cataloged several catastrophic events that might occur if the United States failed to acquire Cuba. The African slave trade might be reopened, France or Britain might seize the island from Spain, or Cuban slaves might rise in revolt, leaving an "Africanized" Cuba.[107]

The ministers recommended purchasing Cuba, stating that the United States should pay a fair price for acquiring so valuable a territory. They boasted, "The United States have never acquired a foot of territory, except by fair purchase."[108] Had they stopped there, the document would have been unremarkable, but instead they added, "After we shall have offered Spain a price for Cuba, far beyond its present value, and this shall have been refused, it will then be time to consider the question, does Cuba in the possession of Spain seriously endanger our internal peace . . . should this question be answered in the affirmative, then, by every law human and Divine, we shall be justified in wresting it from Spain." The authors followed this dubious logic with an equally strained metaphor, writing that the United States could claim Cuba in the same way that it was permissible for a person to tear down his neighbor's "burning house," if it threatened to catch his own home on fire. The claim that the United States could simply seize Cuba would gain the most notoriety.

Because the document was a communication from Buchanan to Marcy and never meant to be public, several months elapsed before it was released. As early as November 1854, newspapers began reporting about a clandestine meeting of ministers at Ostend.[109] By December, the *North American and United States Gazette* observed, "There can be no doubt that the public mind of this country is very curious to learn the origin, purpose and proceedings of the alleged convention of American Ministers at Ostend."[110] The *New York Herald*, which seemed to have an insider's perspective, speculated that the cabinet was trying to suppress the documents pertaining to the meeting.[111] Even with this speculation, it still took over three months and mounting pressure before the full text of the document was released.

Outrage was immediate. Horace Greeley's *New York Tribune* led the charge. In a widely quoted editorial, the *Tribune* dubbed the document the "Manifesto of the Brigands."[112] The *Tribune* argued that Soulé and Buchanan were embracing robbery as an official policy. Using a mundane example to drive home the point, the editor declared, "If a man calls upon you in your parlor and insists upon having your chandelier or your carpet, because he is highly pleased with the patterns of these articles, it would seem to be quite enough for you to tell him that you decline the transaction. If he persists, you have nothing to do but to kick him out." The Ostend Manifesto was a convoluted justification for thievery, the *Tribune* argued: "Spain will not be cajoled or bullied into selling what belongs to her and thereupon Soule tells us she must be robbed and murdered. To this have we come! Even the solemn, measured, old-fashioned Buchanan condescends to sing such a penitentiary tune—the very ribaldry of robbers and cut-throats."

The *Tribune* soon supplemented outrage with ridicule. In a follow-up article aptly titled "The Buccaneering Embassy," the author observed, "The longer the reader reflects upon the developments of the Ostend Conference, the more pitiable and laughable it will appear . . . laughable, from the fact that the missile blows nobody to pieces but its authors, whose remains it scatters to the winds." At least the conference itself had been fortuitous, because it had sabotaged the efforts of Pierce to acquire Cuba. "So far as we can observe," the *Tribune* claimed, "nobody anywhere comes to the defense of this stupendous piece of moral brigandage."[113] Although this was something of an exaggeration, for there were those who defended the manifesto, the document proved to be a political lightning rod.[114]

Many newspapers agreed that the Ostend Manifesto exemplified the "robber's argument" for expansion. The New York correspondent for the *Milwaukee Daily Sentinel* commented, "The whole object of that conference, as the whole burden of that note, is Cuba, Cuba, Cuba, and as to how we shall possess ourselves of it, whether by an inordinate amount of purchase money, or by direct robbery."[115] The *Boston Daily Atlas* called it a "wholesale national robbery" and "ill-concealed piracy."[116] A letter to the editor of the *National Intelligencer* used similar language, calling the manifesto "the most barefaced official avowal of a highwayman's creed . . . ever yet been laid before the world."[117] Using words and phrases such as piracy, brigandage, highwayman's plea, and robbery linked the Ostend Manifesto to filibustering. It seemed as if Pierce had embraced the robber's argument for expansion.[118]

Astute observers realized that Pierce had been placed in a difficult situation. George D. Prentice, for example, noted the impossibility of purchasing Cuba. "If any idea is still entertained at Washington," Prentice wrote, in a lead editorial, "that Cuba can be bought, it might as well be abandoned at once as the most stupid folly."[119] Prentice briefly examined Soulé's attempts to purchase the island and concluded that Spain was not interested in selling. How could the United States buy an island when it was not for sale? "But . . . we believe, upon second thought," Prentice continued, "that even that foolish idea had better continue to be cherished at Washington, if the only alternative is to be the unleashing of the filibusters."[120] As president, Pierce had to decide whether he wanted to purchase Cuba or send a filibuster invasion. Tongue firmly in cheek, Prentice suggested that Pierce, having tried the former, should have a go at filibustering.

Prentice used this argument to illustrate a larger point; Franklin Pierce had no viable plan to acquire Cuba. After hinting that Pierce needed to unleash his filibuster forces, Prentice joked, "If 'manifest destiny,' as the Democratic organs have all along been telling us, is about to make Cuba a part of the United States, these organs had better prevail if possible upon their good friend manifest destiny to

THE "OSTEND DOCTRINE".

Practical Democrats carrying out the principle.

7. Many Americans enjoyed making fun of the Ostend Manifesto. Here, the language written by Buchanan is turned against him, as four muggers provide him with reasons for stealing his wardrobe. Nathaniel Currier, "The 'Ostend Doctrine'. Practical Democrats Carrying Out the Principle," 1856. From Library of Congress Prints and Photographs Online Catalog, http://www.loc.gov/pictures/item/2003656587/.

inform them how the thing is to be accomplished." For three years, Prentice had heard Democratic orators and editors proclaim that manifest destiny was about to bring Cuba into the fold of the United States. But they had made no progress toward achieving that goal. This led Prentice to remark, "However manifest the destiny may be, the way is about as far from being manifest as anything we ever heard of in our lives."[121]

The Ostend Manifesto quickly became the butt of jokes.[122] Seba Smith had Major Jack Downing develop a sudden interest in Cuba and find his way to Ostend, reporting back to Pierce: "I say, Gineral, I'll tell you what 'tis, them three S's (Sickles, Sanders, and Souley) are the three smartest chaps that ever growed in North America."[123] In this letter Smith highlighted the bizarre nature of the Ostend Conference and had Pierre Soulé spew forth ridiculous comments about coming "pesky near kindlin' the flame of Democracy from one end of Spain to t'other."[124] Instead of treating those gathered at Ostend as respectable men discussing an important topic, Smith portrayed them as buffoons whose hatred of monarchy led them to embrace absurd diplomatic positions.

Although Smith treated the Ostend Conference in a humorous fashion, he nonetheless coupled it with a serious warning. His next letter, which appeared, not coincidentally, in March 1855, featured Major Jack Downing aboard the "Fillibuster Schooner Two Pollies."[125] After attending the Ostend Conference, the impetuous Downing sails for Cuba to foment a revolution. "I've got my commission to go ahead from Mr. Buchanan, and Mr. Mason, and Mr. Souley," Downing writes to Pierce, "and the nub of the whole thing is, we've got to take Cuba."[126] The entire letter was a satirical commentary upon the immorality of the Ostend Manifesto. Downing tries to convince Pierce that the United States has the right to seize Cuba. "The upshot was, we concluded we would have Cuba by hook or by crook," Downing casually tells Pierce, "and that Mr. Souley should go right back to old Spain and tell the Queen so." Downing would return to the United States without launching an invasion, but the letter captured the central problem with the Ostend Manifesto. It seemed to justify the seizure of Cuba and it could possibly motivate Americans to filibuster and precipitate a conflict with Spain.

From 1850 to 1855 the language of robbery proved an effective counterargument to the logic of manifest destiny. In 1852 Franklin Pierce had the firm backing of Young America and expansionists saw him as the hope of manifest destiny. One Wisconsin paper declared on the eve of the election, "Without yielding much to imagination . . . the time is not far remote, when the United States will control not only all North America, but South America also. It is the manifest destiny of this country, and who that desires its future glory will not contribute to this grand result, by helping to elect Gen. Pierce."[127] Optimism abounded that the youthful Pierce would craft a bold foreign policy, one modeled upon Polk's.

Pierce, however, was no Polk. Unlike his Democratic predecessor, who had provoked a war with Mexico to obtain his territorial goals,

Pierce refused to deploy force. In January 1854, when Pierce heard that a filibuster invasion of Mexico was underway, he issued a proclamation against it.[128] Four months later, he issued a separate proclamation, targeting those who were seeking to raise a force to invade Cuba.[129] Both times, Pierce hoped to obtain additional territory through purchase, not through filibustering. Given that he refused to sanction filibustering or aggressive diplomacy, it is not altogether surprising that Pierce's expansive plans were largely unsuccessful. Pierce's minister to Mexico did manage to negotiate the Gadsden Treaty in 1853, which was ratified the following year. This treaty provided the United States with additional land that would become parts of the states of Arizona and New Mexico.[130] Yet this hardly fulfilled the hopes of expansionists. Pierce had entered office boasting that he would not be afraid of territorial expansion. He left office having added about twenty-nine thousand square miles to the nation.[131]

Pierce's conservative approach to foreign policy played a role in his unsuccessful attempts to acquire land, but so did Democratic infighting. In his single term of office, the inexperienced Pierce proved unable to placate the various factions within his own party. Trusting volatile personalities such as Soulé and O'Sullivan with delicate diplomatic assignments made little sense, given that both men openly supported filibustering. Having them work with William Marcy, who despised filibusters and Young America, proved to be a disastrous choice. Had Democrats agreed on how to acquire Cuba, or had Pierce simply decided on a straightforward course of action, the ministers would never have gathered at Ostend and the manifesto would not have been written. Factionalism thus directly contributed to the creation of a document that waffled between purchase and intervention and that only served to bring opprobrium upon Pierce.

Nonetheless, it was not merely Democratic infighting or presidential timidity that undermined Pierce's foreign policy. Opponents of manifest destiny successfully exploited the divisions in Democratic ranks and continually asked how expansionists planned on fulfilling manifest destiny. Did they dare support filibustering? Would they embrace the robber's doctrine and steal Cuba from Spain? In article after article, in speech after speech, opponents of manifest destiny drove home the point that the United States should not steal territory by invading it. This argument proved to be quite effective.[132] Democrats from Franklin Pierce to Lewis Cass distanced themselves from filibustering.[133] As William Marcy did in his letter of 1855, most moderate Democrats refused to embrace the "robber's doctrine."[134] With the leaders of the party dedicated to purchasing Cuba, there was little that proponents of manifest destiny could do, except hope that Spain would be willing to sell. Opponents of manifest destiny were more than willing to wait until that happened.

4

Stalling the Slave Power

The Sectional Critique of Manifest Destiny, 1855–1860

In January 1859 John P. Hale rose to address his Senate colleagues. Born in New Hampshire and a graduate of Bowdoin College, Hale had joined the ranks of the recently formed Republican Party. Known for his wit and biting oratory, Hale began his speech with a brief history of manifest destiny, reminding his listeners that believers in manifest destiny thought that the United States would acquire the continent of North America. He then launched into his critique, in a cleverly humorous speech that portrayed manifest destiny as a sentient being. Hale explained that he opposed manifest destiny because it "always traveled South. Although it was the mission of 'manifest destiny' to take in the whole continent, he never seemed to remember that there was a north side of it. He was always traveling South."[1] As laughter broke out, Hale continued by tracing the history of U.S. expansion, telling his auditors that the United States was willing to go to war for southern territory, but that it had always compromised elsewhere. If the United States truly wanted to fulfill its manifest destiny, it had to turn its eyes north.

Hale was being facetious, as he was not suggesting that his Republican colleagues invade Canada.[2] But Hale represented a larger shift that took place in the middle of the 1850s.[3] In the U.S.-Mexican War most opponents of manifest destiny were Whigs, and southerners within the party had led the no-territory movement. From 1846 to 1854 few individuals alleged that manifest destiny was a southern ideology. Yet Franklin Pierce's actions during his presidency helped to create a sectional critique of manifest destiny.[4] Pierce not only tried to purchase Cuba, but he also supported the Kansas-Nebraska Act. These events, which helped lead to the fracture of the Whig Party and the rise of the Republicans, engendered a belief that manifest destiny was a purely sectional ideology. Soon, Republicans and abolitionists sought to block all attempts to acquire territory. Instead of equating manifest destiny with robbery, or alleging that it violated the dictates of George Washington, opponents argued that manifest destiny was a southern ideology, created by enslavers to add slave territory.[5] From 1855 to 1860 this proved to be a remarkably successful argument.

In the same year that Franklin Pierce ordered his ministers to gather in Ostend, a debate brewed in Congress. At the beginning of 1854, Stephen Douglas introduced the Kansas-Nebraska Act.[6] This bill was designed to create the territory of Nebraska and the territory of Kansas out of lands that had been a part of the Louisiana Purchase.[7] Such bills were somewhat routine, as the United States had recently authorized the creation of the Minnesota Territory, the Utah Territory, and the New Mexico Territory. What was different about Douglas's bill, however, was that it overturned the Missouri Compromise line and stipulated that Kansas and Nebraska could choose for themselves whether to be slave or free. The Missouri Compromise, which had passed in 1820, had codified that all lands north of $36°30'$ that had been a part of the Louisiana Purchase were to be free.[8] Douglas's aims are still subject to debate, but he shepherded the bill through a reluctant Senate and saw it pass the House by a narrow margin.[9] On May 30, 1854, Franklin Pierce signed the Kansas-Nebraska Act into law.

The result was a political earthquake.[10] Although some northern Democrats had supported it, most northerners perceived the Kansas-Nebraska Act as a southern measure, as it opened the door for slavery in both Kansas and Nebraska.[11] Throughout the North, anti-Nebraska meetings denounced the measure. In June 1854 a group of congressmen and senators who were opposed to the Kansas-Nebraska Act met in Washington DC.[12] Solomon Foot, a Whig senator from Vermont, served as the chair, but the meeting's secretaries, Congressmen Daniel Mace of Indiana and Reuben E. Fenton of New York, were both Democrats. A committee subsequently appointed to draw up an address consisted of seven Democrats and six Whigs.[13]

The "Address to the People of the United States" explained how the United States had expanded and it looked at each sectional dispute that had occurred from the Louisiana Purchase to the Compromise of 1850. After outlining their opposition to the Kansas-Nebraska Act, the authors looked toward the future and predicted that the slave power would seek to obtain new territory.[14] The entire concluding paragraph went into detail about this vast and menacing plot.[15] "The object of the Administration, and of those who represent the slave States, is, as we believe, to prepare the way," the members noted, "for annexing Cuba at whatever cost, and a like annexation of half a dozen of the States of Mexico, to be admitted also as slave States." Not only was the slave power targeting Cuba and Mexico, but it wanted to swallow up all of South America: "Unmistakable indications appear . . . of a purpose to annex the eastern part of San Domingo, and so to subjugate the whole island. . . . And this is to be followed up by an alliance with Brazil, and the extension of slavery in the valley of the Amazon." These congressmen feared the slave power and saw expansion through a sectional lens.[16]

Such arguments extended far beyond the walls of Congress. A group of concerned citizens in Vermont produced a set of resolutions that denounced the bill.[17] Shortly after the meeting, Edward D. Barber penned an open letter to the *Middlebury Register*. "In my opinion," Barber wrote, "the slaveholders do not so much desire its passage, for the purpose of occupying those territories . . . as to establish a principle in American legislation." Like many other northerners, Barber saw Kansas-Nebraska as part of a larger plot to add slave territory to the United States: "It is hidden in the womb of time, if not written on the pages of that 'manifest destiny' of which we hear so much and which has so many disciples, that the warm and fertile plains of Cuba, and the inviting and salubrious regions of Mexico, will yet, and probably within the lives of the present generation, fall into the embrace of the Republic." Barber maintained that southerners had secured passage of Kansas-Nebraska in order to seize hold of the government. With the Missouri Compromise repealed, southerners could add Cuba, Mexico, and other regions, confident that they would become slave states.

The argument that enslavers were behind U.S. expansion was certainly not new. Abolitionists had firmly opposed the annexation of Texas and argued that enslavers desired Texas to expand the institution of slavery.[18] Abolitionists were equally disdainful of the phrase "manifest destiny." As early as 1853, *Frederick Douglass' Paper* had argued that enslavers were using manifest destiny as a cloak for the expansion of slavery over the western hemisphere.[19] Gradually, other abolitionists began to pick up this argument.[20] In an article published in 1854, the *National Era* casually noted, "The defenders and apologists of Slavery are fond of the popular phrase 'manifest destiny.'"[21] Like many abolitionist papers, the *National Era* saw the passage of Kansas-Nebraska and the ongoing attempts to purchase Cuba as evidence that manifest destiny had become a means to strengthen the slave power.[22] So, too, did William Lloyd Garrison, who denounced manifest destiny, Kansas-Nebraska, and Franklin Pierce in the pages of the *Liberator*.[23] For nearly a decade, abolitionists had depicted manifest destiny as an enslavers' ideology.

The passage of the Kansas-Nebraska Act, however, helped this argument gain a wider audience. More and more northerners began to portray expansionists as rapacious enslavers. Horace Greeley's influential *New York Tribune* denounced the Kansas-Nebraska Act before it even passed Congress. In one article Greeley snipped a portion from the *Southern Standard*, a South Carolina newspaper, to prove to his readers that the leaders of the Democratic Party were plotting to expand the institution of slavery. Greeley argued that the passage of Kansas-Nebraska would lead southerners "1. To take Cuba. 2. To conquer St. Domingo and reduce its inhabitants to Slavery. 3. To unite with Brazil and perform the same conquering and enslaving process on all the other West India Islands. 4. To then enter into an alliance with Brazil for the establishment and fortification of Slavery throughout South and North America."[24] Greeley had been a loyal Whig, but beginning in 1854 he increasingly presented manifest destiny as part of a larger southern ploy to expand the slave power.

Within a short space of time, congressmen heatedly denounced the slave power's expansive plans. Lewis D. Campbell was a representative from the state of Ohio who became a leader of the anti-Nebraska forces in the House. Campbell railed against expansion and the power of enslavers. "People in the slave States," he declared, "are seeking the acquisition of Cuba—they take our money to buy the Mesilla valley; the Sandwich Islands are demanded; and mysterious proceedings are going on at the proposed 'naval depot in St. Domingo.'"[25] Campbell noted that the repeal of the Missouri Compromise meant that enslavers could take their slaves into any territory acquired by the United States. And he was determined to make a stand against this principle. "Will the people of the free States submit?" he asked his audience rhetorically. "Upon the authority of their voice in the late elections, I answer, emphatically, No."[26] Instead of viewing expansion as a partisan measure, as Whigs had traditionally done, Campbell saw expansionism as being driven by southerners.[27]

More and more frequently, northerners denounced enslavers for being the driving force behind all antebellum expansion. Typical was an article published in an Ohio paper under the title "Southern Demands."[28] The author explained that the South was trying to acquire more territory for slavery. Papers such as this faulted northern Democrats for truckling to overbearing southerners. "Servile Democracy accedes at once to this piratical proposition," the paper concluded, "and vapors about 'manifest destiny' and the 'extension of the area of freedom.'" The *Fremont Weekly Journal* embraced a similar interpretation of history, informing its readers that northerners had surrendered to southern pressure over the annexation of Texas, the U.S.-Mexican War, and the Compromise of 1850.[29] Seemingly, all these events had strengthened the South. "And they are not going to stop now," the paper opined. "Cuba is to be obtained . . . St. Domingo, Porto Rico, and others of the West India Islands have already been selected by the Administration. . . . Then they say it is manifest destiny that we should control the whole of the Western Continent." Many northerners began to come around to the belief that something needed to be done to prevent the repeated aggression of the slave power.

As suspicions of a vast southern conspiracy began to grow, Franklin Pierce did little to allay such worries. Pierce signed off on Kansas-Nebraska a few months before the Ostend Conference made it clear that he was seeking to acquire Cuba. The realization that Pierce had been striving to acquire Cuba since his inauguration only confirmed many northerners in their belief that the government was now in the hands of the slave power. "Whoever sustains Pierce . . . and the doughfaces, really sustains their principles and acts," one northern paper declared.[30] At the beginning of his time in the White House, Pierce had frequently been labeled a Young American, but as his term progressed, he was more commonly denigrated as a feckless doughface.[31] That is, he was denounced as a northerner who catered to the whims of the South. Why was Pierce expending political capital to purchase Cuba and to open up the territories of Kansas and Nebraska to slavery? The only reason that made sense was that Pierce was doing the bidding of the slave power.

Cuba, Nebraska, and Kansas loomed before the northern public as the examples of a voracious slave power. Abolitionists led the charge and warned that enslavers had their sights set on dominating these regions.[32] The American Anti-Slavery Society believed that the acquisition of Texas had only whetted the appetite of the South and that it was preparing to chew up Nebraska, Kansas, Cuba, Haiti, and the Sandwich Islands.[33] Abolitionists portrayed both Kansas and Cuba as the battlefields upon which the forces of slavery and antislavery were to meet. Typical was an article penned by David Lee Child in 1855 titled "Kansas and Cuba." "Not content with the subjugation of Kansas to its hellish designs," Child noted, "the Slave Power, backed up by the whole strength of this indescribably wicked administration, is bent on the immediate conquest of Cuba! The plot has been long maturing, and its consummation is at hand."[34] Articles such as this cast expansion as a southern plot to expand slavery's hold on the nation. And they saw both Cuba and Kansas as targets of Pierce's "indescribably wicked administration."[35]

As abolitionists deplored the influence of the slave power, a new political party slowly formed that embraced the slave power thesis. Founded in 1854, the Republican Party gained adherents and picked up an assortment of anti-Nebraska Democrats, Whigs, temperance reformers, and Nativists. This coalition remained somewhat fluid in 1855, as Democrats, Whigs, Republicans, Know-Nothings, and various combinations of these parties competed for votes in the North.[36] As a political party, Republicans embraced many aspects of the Whig Party, including skepticism toward manifest destiny. Yet the Republicans were not merely former Whigs and their opposition to manifest destiny differed from that of the Whigs in certain noticeable ways. From 1846 to 1852 Whigs had conjured up a variety of arguments against manifest destiny, ranging from the racist to the religious. Republicans, and especially former Whigs, would use some of these critiques, but Republicans tended to focus on the slave power. Most Republicans came to embrace the idea that the United States could not expand until there was no threat of slavery moving into new territories.

By 1855 those who identified with the fledgling Republican Party were using their platform to denounce the slave power and manifest destiny. Congressman Richard Yates of Illinois had won election as a Whig but became a Republican after Kansas-Nebraska. In a congressional speech, Yates linked the repeal of the Missouri Compromise with attempts to expand slavery into the tropics. He caustically noted, "Slavery has its longing eye on California, on Utah, and New Mexico. She is calculating on four slave States in Texas. Cuba looms up in her vision. . . . Mexico and Central America are also in the prospect, and overstepping the barriers of the continent, her insatiate eye is regaling itself on the States of the southern continent."[37] As did many other Republicans, Yates saw the slave power as the motivating force behind the expansion of the United States. If northerners did not fight back, enslavers would soon gobble up Mexico, Central America, and Cuba, and their power would be unmatched.

Republicans not only denounced the slave power but they also crafted a version of history rooted in sectional conflict. In October 1855 Israel Washburn, a representative from Maine who quickly became a leader of the Republican Party, delivered a speech that outlined why a new party was necessary. Washburn built his argument by recounting the story of slavery's spread from the Missouri Compromise onward.[38] "The South demanded Texas," he asserted, and as soon as the U.S.-Mexican War was over it tried to seize New Mexico and Utah. The North protested but was unable to prevent the spread of slavery, the passage of the Fugitive Slave Law, and the repeal of the Missouri Compromise. In each of these instances, Washburn argued, the North had buckled to southern demands and, as a result, had strengthened the institution of slavery. It was time for a new party that could push back "when the South should seek to acquire Cuba, and San Domingo, and New Mexico." Washburn effectively advocated a political party to oppose southern oligarchs and prevent the spread of slavery.

Even expansionists within the new Republican Party embraced this vision of history. William Henry Seward was a Whig senator from New York who moved into the ranks of the Republican Party. In 1855 Seward delivered a speech in Albany, New York, entitled "The Advent of the Republican Party."[39] Seward argued that enslavers in the United States had become a "privileged class."[40] It was enslavers who were behind expansion, first using the Missouri Compromise to expand slavery into the Southwest and then abandoning the compromise when they needed more territory. "Canada, lying all along your northern borders," Seward told his New York audience, "must not even be looked upon, lest you may lust after it, while millions upon millions are lavished in war and diplomacy to annex and spread slavery over Louisiana, Florida, Texas, Mexico, Cuba, and Central America."[41] Seward was an expansionist who would go on to become one of the leading proponents of manifest destiny. In 1855 he was unwilling to expand the nation because he believed it would only redound to the benefit of enslavers.

Actions of leading Democrats only helped to convince Republicans that their analysis was correct. In June 1855 a man named William Walker landed with a filibuster force in Nicaragua.[42] Born in Tennessee, Walker graduated from the University of Pennsylvania, where he studied medicine.[43] An unimposing man who stood under 5 feet 5 inches tall and weighed less than 130 pounds, Walker eventually settled in California.[44] A short time after arriving in California, Walker decided to launch a filibuster attack into Mexico.[45] Walker and his forty-five men managed to seize a small town in Lower

California, leading Walker to create what he called the Republic of Lower California.[46] Walker never exercised any real authority, however, and his expedition quickly fell apart.[47] Walker and his men fled back to California, where he was tried for violating the Neutrality Act. He was acquitted by a sympathetic jury that took less than ten minutes to render a verdict.[48] Although his Republic of Lower California failed, Walker gained a reputation as a filibuster and he was soon invited by a group in Nicaragua to aid it in its own civil war.[49]

Once he landed, Walker gained a small following and increased his influence within Nicaragua.[50] In October Walker and his forces helped negotiate a treaty.[51] This treaty dissolved the Democratic and Legitimist governments and installed a new coalition under Patricio Rivas.[52] As an elder statesman, Rivas was named the provisional president of Nicaragua, with the stipulation that a new election would be held within fourteen months. Walker was named commander in chief of the army and was seen by many Americans as the real power within Nicaragua. In December of 1855 the Rivas government, ostensibly under orders from Walker, dispatched the Kentucky-born Parker H. French as its minister to the United States.[53] Franklin Pierce remained somewhat unsure of what to do with French and refused to recognize him.[54] Realizing that Pierce would never recognize Parker, Walker dispatched Fr. Augustin Vijil to the United States as the new representative. In May 1856 Franklin Pierce officially recognized Vijil as the legitimate representative of Nicaragua.

Walker's rapid ascent led to jubilation among the proponents of manifest destiny. Balls and parades were held in his honor.[55] The *New York Herald*, which had begun to grow somewhat skeptical about manifest destiny, suddenly rejoiced, "The late news from Nicaragua opens up a magnificent field of action for Gen. Walker, and a most glorious prospect for 'manifest destiny' throughout the Central American and Mexican States and the neighboring islands of the sea."[56] Public dinners were hosted to raise funds for General Walker at which speakers openly predicted the speedy fulfillment of manifest destiny.[57] Walker was merely the prototype, they argued, of the men who would eventually set out from the United States, settle, and colonize the rest of

Central America, until the entire region fell under U.S. sway.[58] An article in the *Democratic Review* declared, "Looking nearer home, we see that it is the manifest destiny of North-Americans to colonize and control this continent. We feel that the Isthmus of Panama especially is necessary to us, as the connecting link between our Atlantic and Pacific Empire."[59] Believers in manifest destiny were thrilled by Walker's actions and were even more pleased when he became the president of the Republic of Nicaragua in July 1856.

Republicans perceived Walker's rise to power as more evidence of slavery's tenacious hold upon the United States. The *New York Tribune* credited Walker for ingratiating himself into the Nicaraguan government, but it predicted that Walker would soon demand power for himself. "When the revolution is thoroughly legitimated by the recognition of several powers," the paper conjectured, "Walker will be ready to make himself nominally dictator, as he already is in reality, and to carry his great project another step towards its consummation." Once in power, Walker would seek to join his empire with slave states in the American South. The *Tribune* prophesied, "That project is briefly to fill the country with Americans, to introduce Slavery, and to procure the annexation of Nicaragua to the North American Union as a Slave State, with a prospect of a similar result for the adjoining countries."[60] Americans should then ponder this question: "What do the people of the Free States think of this new conspiracy to extend the power of the oligarchy by which they have so long been ruled and used?"[61]

In many ways, the events of May 1856 helped solidify Republican fears, as the battles in Nicaragua and the violence in Kansas dominated the news. It was in May that Franklin Pierce officially recognized the Rivas-Walker government, a move that many northerners condemned.[62] In that same month Senator Charles Sumner of Massachusetts delivered a lengthy address in the Senate entitled "The Crime against Kansas."[63] Outraged by the speech, Congressman Preston Brooks attacked Sumner in the Senate and brutally beat him with a cane. Meanwhile, in Kansas a group of proslavery settlers raided and burned the free-soil city of Lawrence, an event that would become known in the northern press as the "Sack of Law-

STALLING THE SLAVE POWER

rence."[64] Events in Nicaragua and Kansas were thus reported side by side, broadly linked to a proslavery conspiracy.[65]

Complicating matters further, 1856 was a presidential election year. Democrats convened in Cincinnati in early June to nominate a candidate. On the seventeenth ballot James Buchanan emerged as the winner. In addition to nominating a man who had helped pen the Ostend Manifesto, Democrats adopted an exceptionally belligerent platform.[66] The platform stated that the United States had a right to control "the great highway" that connected the "Atlantic and the Pacific Ocean," a resolution that seemed to call for the abrogation of the Clayton-Bulwer Treaty.[67] It continued, "In view of so commanding an interest, the people of the United States cannot but sympathize with the efforts which are being made by the people of Central America to regenerate that portion of the continent which covers the passage across the Interoceanic Isthmus."[68] Not only did the platform offer support to Walker's regime in Nicaragua, but it added, "The Democratic party will expect of the next Administration that every proper effort be made to insure [*sic*] our ascendency in the Gulf of Mexico."[69] In spite of the violence in Kansas, Democrats confidently looked to a future where the United States would spread over Central America and claim Cuba.

Later that month, Republicans gathered in Philadelphia and held their convention. Republicans had several prominent contenders, including Salmon Chase of Ohio, William Henry Seward of New York, and Supreme Court Justice John McLean.[70] Convinced that they needed a popular individual for their first candidate, Republicans eventually selected John C. Frémont, a man whose political experience consisted of a short stint as a senator from California. Nonetheless, he had great national appeal. Frémont had garnered the nickname "the Pathfinder" for leading four expeditions to the West Coast during the 1840s.[71] Frémont was well known and Republicans hoped that would boost their chances in a national contest. The Republicans' platform stood in stark contrast to the Democratic platform. Republicans had a plank that read, "That the highwayman's plea, that 'might makes right,' embodied in the Ostend Circular, was in every respect unworthy of American diplomacy, and would bring shame and dishonor upon any Government or people that gave it their sanction."[72] While Democrats focused on expansion, Republicans criticized the Ostend Manifesto, and by extension James Buchanan, refusing to allow Democrats to forget the failures of Pierce's Cuban policy.

In the 1856 campaign Republicans carved out several lines of attack against James Buchanan. Some Republicans portrayed Buchanan as the mindless minion of the slave power. "We say emphatically . . . that the 'democratic' party has become a mere proslavery party," one northern paper proclaimed, "and bound to obey the commands of the slave power."[73] It averred that Buchanan "must eat dirt with the rest of the northern candidates, and unhesitatingly swallow all he formerly said against admitting slavery into the territory made free by the Missouri Compromise." Editors warned that Buchanan would be unwilling to stand up to the demands of the South. "It ought to be understood at once," a Boston paper observed, "that no more than Franklin Pierce is Mr. Buchanan a man to resist the demands of party, or the blandishments of the South. He has been the mere creature of circumstances for sixty years; he will be the same creature to the end."[74] Throughout the campaign, Republican papers attacked James Buchanan as a doddering old man who had done the will of the slave power throughout his political life.[75]

Whatever their views on Buchanan, Republicans believed that Democrats had embraced filibustering. "The Cincinnati platform declares boldly in favor of an aggressive policy," a paper in Cleveland observed, "to wrest from neighboring States whatever territory we may covet. Never before was Fillibusterism established as part of a party creed."[76] In 1852 Whigs had charged that Franklin Pierce would filibuster for Cuba, but Republicans in 1856 had the added advantage of a Democratic platform that openly sympathized with William Walker. A paper in Vermont went point by point through the Democratic platform and showed how it supported filibustering for Nicaragua. It also pointed out that the phrase "ascendency in the Gulf of Mexico" signified "the annexation of Cuba, the other West India islands, and Mexico."[77] Democrats were not even trying to cloak their lust for slave territory. Even the *New York Herald* disapproved of the militancy of the Cincinnati platform, informing its readers, "The foreign policy of the democratic party, as proclaimed at Cincinnati, in the unmistakable language of the confident filli-buster, means nothing more nor less than Cuba, Mexico and Cen-tral America 'peaceably if we can, forcibly if we must.'"[78]

Republicans did not forget about Buchanan's role in the craft-ing of the Ostend Manifesto, and many attacked him on that score. The *New York Tribune* reminded its readers, "His name stands first among the signatures to the Ostend Manifesto—a paper of which it is hard to say whether the depravity or the folly is most conspicu-ous."[79] Republican papers delighted in deploying the term "Buchanier" to describe the partisans of Buchanan. "The doctrine of the Ostend manifesto is one of the cardinal points in the Buchanier platform," one paper jeered.[80] A Wisconsin paper included a column, "Nurs-ery Rhymes for Young Fremonters." This included as its first rhyme:

"Who goes there?"—
  "A Buchanier!"
"What d'ye want?"—
  "Cuba, dear!"
"What d'ye offer?"—
  "Ostend notes!"
"Get ye gone you'll get no votes."[81]

Reminding the electorate that James Buchanan was a determined expansionist who coveted Cuba remained a key point for Republicans.[82]

Republicans often combined these arguments to demonstrate how the slave power was poised to strike. John Allison, a Republican representing Pennsylvania in the House, delivered a lengthy address in Congress entitled "The Republican Party: Its Necessity and Its Mission."[83] In this speech Allison condemned Democrats for their embrace of the "highwayman's plea" and for nominating the man who wrote the Ostend Manifesto. Allison's speech dealt with the repeal of the Missouri Compromise and the ongoing disputes in Kansas, but he managed to weave Cuba into his argument. After detailing the growth of the slave power in the United States, Allison causti-cally observed, "The man who suggests the stealing of an island for

FORCING SLAVERY DOWN THE THROAT OF A FREESOILER

8. Democratic attempts to expand the institution of slavery are somewhat graphically depicted here. Noticeable are the references to Central America and Cuba on the Democratic platform, illustrating the international aspirations of the slave power. John L. Magee, "Forcing Slavery Down the Throat of a Freesoiler," 1856. From Library of Congress Prints and Photographs Online Catalog, http://www.loc.gov/pictures/item/2008661578/.

the purpose of adding to the slave power of the country, could not be expected to condemn the appropriation of Kansas to the same purpose." For representatives such as Allison, Cuba and Kansas were linked because both were sought by enslavers. Republicans had to unite to prevent slavery from gaining ascendency in either region.[84]

As Whigs had done with Taylor, Republicans assured the public that Frémont was the safer choice when it came to foreign policy. The *Bangor Daily Whig and Courier* drew the contrast in an article titled "This Side and That Side."[85] The author juxtaposed a paragraph from the Ostend Manifesto and a paragraph from Frémont denouncing the document. No commentary was provided. The *Boston Daily Atlas* was even more succinct, telling its readers, "A vote for John C. Fremont—is a vote to save the country from ruinous wars, which must inevitably result from carrying out the doctrines of the Ostend Manifesto."[86] This paper warned of the dangers of a Buchanan presidency. "We answer that the probability of war to obtain Cuba," its

9. Republicans frequently portrayed the slave power as dangerous both at home and abroad, as illustrated in this depiction of the Democratic platform. B. Thurston, "Democratic Platform Illustrated" (New York: James G. Varney, 1856). From Library of Congress Prints and Photographs Online Catalog, https://www.loc.gov/item/2008661581/.

editor observed, "in the event of Mr. Buchanan's election, is greater than the probability of a dissolution of the Union in consequence of the election of Col. Fremont. What misery and utter ruin, what wide spread suffering and dismay, war would bring in its train, it is not for us to paint."[87] Much as Whigs had done in 1848, Republicans in 1856 tried to paint a picture of what would occur if Buchanan were elected.

Despite Republican warnings about the slave power dominating any Democratic administration, Buchanan won the election over John C. Frémont and Millard Fillmore (the American Party candidate), picking up nearly 60 percent of the electoral votes. In contrast to Pierce in 1852, Buchanan had a long history of supporting expansion, from voting for the annexation of Texas to attempting to purchase Cuba.[88] In light of his extensive record on the issue, many observers predicted that Buchanan would act on these convictions. The *Richmond Whig* feared that Buchanan was possibly planning for "the admission of Kansas as a slave State—the practical enforcement of the Ostend manifesto with respect to Cuba—the keeping of his weather eye open to political movements in Nicaragua and Mexico— and a general compliance with the programme laid down by the filibusters, secessionists, and manifest destiny men of the South."[89]

And indeed, Buchanan proved to be an expansion-minded president.[90] The possibility of annexing Nicaragua, hinted at in the Democratic platform, quickly proved to be a chimera as Walker's regime crumbled. Hounded by a Central American coalition led by Costa Rica, Walker was engaged in skirmishes throughout most of the winter, and he was forced to flee from Nicaragua in May 1857.[91] With Nicaragua no longer in play, Buchanan turned his attention to Mexico, which he believed was ripe for annexation.[92] In 1857 Buchanan had his secretary of state, Lewis Cass, dispatch new instructions to John Forsyth, the minister to Mexico.[93] Cass's letter told Forsyth to "purchase from Mexico the province of Lower California, together with nearly all of Sonora, and that portion of Chihuahua . . . north of the parallel of thirty degrees."[94] He even laid out the price: "The sum stipulated to be paid for these is twelve millions of dollars, or eight millions of dollars [for] the Sonora and Chihuahua territory and four millions of Dollars for Lower California."[95] Cass's letter included a draft for a boundary treaty, consisting of seven articles.[96] These explicit instructions, and the fact that Buchanan sent along an entire draft of a treaty, demonstrate the extent to which Buchanan was committed to purchasing land from Mexico.[97]

Buchanan's Mexican gambit went nowhere. Much like Spain, Mexico refused to sell additional territory and so Buchanan was forced to use an indirect approach. In his second annual message, after brusquely dismissing agitation over Kansas, Buchanan turned his attention to foreign policy. He recommended that Congress provide funds for purchasing the island of Cuba, which he claimed was "of vast importance to the United States."[98] He then launched into a somewhat turgid explanation of Mexican history, claiming, "Mexico has been in a state of constant revolution almost ever since it achieved its independence."[99] Buchanan recommended that the United States quickly act to establish a "protectorate" over the northern Mexican states of Chihuahua and Sonora. "I can imagine no possible remedy for these evils and no mode of restoring law and order on the remote and unsettled frontier," he wrote, "but for the Government of the United States to assume a temporary protectorate over the northern portions of Chihuahua and Sonora and to establish military posts within the same."[100]

Congress refused to act. And so Buchanan sent a message asking for permission to use military force to protect U.S. citizens in Mexico. This time the Senate did bring up Buchanan's proposal for a vote, and it was defeated, 31–25.[101] The Senate appeared wary of issuing Buchanan a blank check. It was also a highly partisan vote. With the exception of a handful of Democratic senators, the negative votes were cast by Republicans and members of the American Party from the Midwest and Northeast. All the votes in favor of the measure came from Democrats. In the Thirty-Fifth Congress, Republicans remained a minority but their unity on such issues made it nearly impossible for Buchanan to make headway with schemes of territorial acquisition.

Buchanan's actions confirmed Republicans in their belief that he was indeed the tool of the slave power. In March 1858 the *New Hampshire Statesmen* urged citizens to go to the polls and vote Republican, so that the slave trade would not be reopened and Cuba would not be acquired.[102] Joshua Giddings, a Republican from Ohio, made the connection explicit in a speech in the House of Representatives, telling those gathered, "I would also warn the Spanish Crown and other continental Powers, that our present Executive is seeking, by all the various means and arts of diplomacy, to detach Cuba from its allegiance, to annex it to the United States in order to increase the influence of the slave power, and add strength to this American infidelity."[103] Henry Wilson, a senator from Massachusetts, delivered a similar speech in the Senate, in which he argued that the struggle over Kansas was only a small part of the larger contest between slavery and freedom. "The Administration," Wilson alleged, "is converting the American Democracy into a mere organization for the perpetuity, expansion, and dominion of human slavery on the North American continent."[104]

Increasingly, Republicans labeled manifest destiny an enslavers' ideology.[105] In January 1859 John P. Hale delivered a biting take-down of manifest destiny, which he lampooned as a southern ideology. "So wanting in fidelity to his mission was 'manifest destiny,'" he joked, "that was to overrun this whole continent, so engrossed was he in looking South, that whilst his mission had been proclaimed, and he was attending to southern interests, the Administration actually sold out a part of one of the northern States, the State of Maine."[106] Hale asked his fellow senators why believers in manifest destiny were always spending money to buy potential slave territories. A month later, Stephen Clark Foster, a Republican from Maine, delivered a similar speech in the House. "Sir, we have heard much of 'manifest destiny,'" Foster declared. "We are told that the people of the United States are destined to absorb and annex the whole continent of North America, if no more; but I am sorry that all efforts at annexation have hitherto been made in but one direction."[107] Foster reminded his listeners that the United States had recently acquired Louisiana, Florida, Texas, and California. He then asked them to "look in the direction of the north pole for once." Both Foster and Hale wondered why Buchanan was offering large sums for Mexico and Cuba, but nothing for Canada. Republicans hypothesized that it was because manifest destiny was a southern ideology.

In spite of Republican opposition, Buchanan pressed forward. Realizing it was impossible to push his protectorate scheme through a recalcitrant Senate, Buchanan shifted tactics and embraced what could be termed economic imperialism. After the resignation of John Forsyth as minister to Mexico, Buchanan appointed Robert McLane as minister plenipotentiary, with instructions to offer as much as $10 million dollars for the purchase of Lower California and Sonora. Mexico remained unwilling to sell any of its territory.[108] McLane did manage to negotiate a treaty with Mexico that satisfied Buchanan. What became known as the McLane-Ocampo Treaty stipulated that the United States would pay $4 million for a right of way across the

STALLING THE SLAVE POWER

Isthmus of Tehuantepec, which at the time was considered a possible canal route. Far more importantly for Buchanan, the treaty allowed the United States to transport military equipment and troops to the region and also permitted the United States to intervene in Mexico if U.S. lives or property were endangered.[109] Although this treaty did not provide Buchanan with the outright cession of land that he desired, he still submitted it to the Senate.

The treaty went down to an ignominious defeat. On May 31, 1860, the Senate rejected the McLane-Ocampo Treaty by a vote of 27–18. As with the protectorate scheme, not a single Republican voted in favor, while a handful of Democrats voted against the treaty.[110] Not surprisingly, many Republicans voted against the treaty because they feared it was part of a larger scheme to expand slave territory. The *Lansing State Republican*, for instance, reported, "The objects of the bill are to open Mexico as a hold for slavery, and to secure a Southern line for the Pacific Railway. . . . With those manifest objects, can it be doubted that every Republican vote in the Senate will be against it."[111] The *Vermont Phoenix*, another Republican organ, alleged that supporters of the treaty were no better than filibusters.[112] Perhaps the best summation of the Republican argument against the treaty came from the *New York Times*, a paper that supported the treaty and lobbied for its passage: "And how does the great Republican party receive this treaty? . . . They will have it that this treaty has been made by Mr. Buchanan acting as the agent of the slave power, and with the covert design of bringing on a war, seizing territory, running up the negro flag, and . . . securing two millions of money to be used in the next Presidential election!"[113] Determined and unified Republicans made it impossible for Buchanan to achieve his expansionist goals.

From 1855 to 1860 opponents of expansion efficiently deployed the sectional critique to stymie manifest destiny. This can be seen not only in newspapers and congressional debates, but more broadly in popular culture. In 1858 an antislavery festival took place in Concord, Massachusetts.[114] One of the highlights that was covered by a reporter from the *Liberator* was the production of two popular plays: *The Jacobite* and *Dr. Dilworth*. The morally minded citizens of Concord enjoyed the food and the doubtless nonalcoholic drinks, but their moral outrage was aroused by a prologue written specifically for the occasion. In the prologue the stage direction reads, "Enter Slavery in a clerical dress, with a bottle in his hand in the form of a Bible, MANIFEST DESTINY in the dress of a Western pioneer."[115] As on so many other occasions, opponents of manifest destiny decided to mock the ideology by personifying it as a living human being.

The dialogue reveals Manifest Destiny trying to appease the downtrodden figure of Slavery, who carries around a bottle. Slavery proclaims:

> Manifest Destiny, my brother dear,
> O let me pour my sorrows in your ear!

Slavery then proceeds to complain that he has had trouble properly using the Bible to back up his arguments. Being a good brother, Manifest Destiny consoles Slavery by pointing out that he himself has always used the Bible effectively. He then suggests that Slavery learn from his use of the Bible to make more effective arguments:

> But don't abuse the Bible! how it sounds
> When Cushing comments and black Ross expounds!
> Why, is not Walker, with his travelling sword,
> Another Gideon chosen of the Lord?

This dialogue drives home the point that slavery and manifest destiny are cut from the same cloth. They are, quite literally, brothers. Near the conclusion of the short prologue, Manifest Destiny advises his brother to look to new lands:

> But join with me by purchase or by war
> To gain fair Cuba and Nicaragua.
> Then shall your restless course be check'd no more.[116]

Within this prologue one can catch the culmination of an idea that had first cropped up in the early 1850s and only gained force over time; manifest destiny was no longer a national ideology that could appeal to all sections. It sounded good and promised unlimited expansion and national growth. But like the character in this play, manifest destiny favored the South and sprang from the same parent that had produced the proslavery defense. Over time, this led opponents of manifest destiny to view most attempts at expansion as mere devices through which the dying slave power sought to revive itself.[117]

Republicans proved to be remarkably successful at utilizing the sectional critique of manifest destiny to gain political power. Abolitionists had argued for over a decade that the slave power was anxious to add territory to buttress the institution of slavery, yet it was not until the middle of the 1850s that a rising political party firmly embraced this argument. A good example of this can be seen in the speeches of Thomas Corwin. Born in Kentucky, Corwin later moved to Ohio, where he would go on to have a prominent political career. In 1847, as a member of the Whig Party, Corwin had denounced the U.S-Mexican War as immoral and predicted that if the United States took land from Mexico, it would lead to divisions between northerners and southerners.[118] In 1859 Corwin delivered a speech to a Republican meeting at Xenia, Ohio, where he warned Republicans not to seek to acquire any additional territory. The passage of twelve years did change Corwin's reasons for opposing expansion, however, as he lectured his audience, "They say that it is manifest destiny, that we must expand: but manifest destiny always runs to the South."[119] It was only in the late 1850s that Corwin called out manifest destiny for being a southern idea.

Republican opponents of manifest destiny were not successful in capturing the White House in 1856, but they were able to thwart Buchanan's expansive plans for the nation. Republicans unified behind a common historical narrative that depicted the slave power as the driving force behind territorial expansion. The slave power, Republicans argued, had negotiated the Louisiana Purchase, managed the annexation of Texas, pushed the United States into war with Mexico, and filibustered for Cuba and Nicaragua. Manifest destiny, as Hale joked, looked only south. From 1855 to 1860 Republicans wielded the sectional argument to block manifest destiny. Until the threat of slavery was removed, many northerners were simply unwilling to risk adding territory to the national domain.

5

Controlling the Continent

Manifest Destiny in the Civil War

In November 1860 the *New York Herald* published a letter from John L. O'Sullivan to William Henry Seward. O'Sullivan boasted of the growth of the United States, telling Seward, "If we are now out of the swaddling clothes of our national infancy, we are still in the period of our national boyhood . . . whether as measured by years or by comparison with the manifest destiny of our sublime future." In spite of the growing sectionalism within the United States, O'Sullivan still believed that Americans would "occupy the whole continent," as soon as they felt they lacked sufficient "elbow room." As one of the founders of the *Democratic Review* and a frequent contributor to it during the 1850s, O'Sullivan never shied away from his belief that the United States would fulfill its manifest destiny. Yet, in November 1860 O'Sullivan did fear one thing: the possible election of Abraham Lincoln. After discussing the bright future of the United States, O'Sullivan lectured Seward on the dangers of northern radicalism and warned him that the election of a Republican would shatter the Union, as the South would be justified in seceding. O'Sullivan ended by urging his fellow New Yorkers to vote the Democratic ticket to save the nation from the radical Republican Party.[1]

In many regards, O'Sullivan's letter aptly captured the changing nature of manifest destiny in 1860. O'Sullivan firmly believed in manifest destiny, but he rejected the notion that Republicans could help fulfill that destiny.[2] As a fiercely partisan Democrat who had cheered the annexation of Texas and Cuban filibustering, O'Sullivan perceived the Democratic Party as the only national party and

109

the only party capable of expanding the United States. Fellow New Yorker William Henry Seward also embraced manifest destiny and would become one of its firmest proponents. Seward's vision, however, contrasted sharply with O'Sullivan's. Seward believed that the United States could only add territory once the threat of slavery was removed. The *New York Herald*, which printed the letter from O'Sullivan to Seward, remained a proexpansion newspaper, but it gradually moved from a Democratic viewpoint to a Sewardian vision. By the outbreak of the Civil War, the *Herald* would be petitioning Lincoln to conquer Canada and Mexico and bring about the completion of manifest destiny.

From 1860 to 1865 a variety of viewpoints emerged on manifest destiny. Some northerners, building on the arguments of a previous generation, blamed manifest destiny for causing the Civil War and hoped that Americans would humble themselves and reject an aggressive foreign policy in the future. Other northerners expressed few reservations about the ideology and continued to blame the South for all the expansion that occurred prior to the Civil War. The Civil War, in their opinion, was necessary to prevent the slave power from swallowing up Mexico and Central America. Southerners, in a manner similar to northerners, split into various camps as the Civil War unfolded. Initially, many hoped that the Confederacy could expand and annex Cuba and northern Mexico. As the Confederacy struggled for survival, many southerners created their own critique of manifest destiny. They labeled it a northern ideology and rejoiced that even if Yankees subdued the Confederacy, they would never rule the continent of North America. These divergent viewpoints clashed in the midst of the Civil War, as Americans continued to debate manifest destiny.

The failure of James Buchanan to acquire Cuba and northern Mexico did little to damage the dream of manifest destiny. Expansionists continued to run articles declaring that the United States would soon annex Mexico. "Let other nations say what they please," a paper in Philadelphia reported in 1860, "manifest destiny points clearly either to the entire redemption, or to the complete conquest of Mexico."[3] Papers typically narrated what was going on in Mexico and then declared that it was up to the United States to restore order and bring Mexico into the fold of the United States.[4] One editor supported taking over all of Mexico, arguing, "It may be premature to call for annexation, but it is manifest destiny, and our increasing population will fit us to sustain the task of regenerating Mexico."[5] Readers of papers in the early 1860s would not have been surprised to read the headline in a Kentucky newspaper that announced "Mexico to Be Invaded: Our Manifest Destiny."[6] Calls to invade Mexico, to establish a protectorate, or to annex the entire country frequently ran in Democratic papers.

As Democratic expansionists saw manifest destiny as an unstoppable force, they were seemingly not disheartened by the failures of the Pierce and Buchanan administrations. In January 1860 Illinois Democrats met in Springfield, nominated delegates to send to the national Democratic convention, and passed a series of resolutions. One read, "*Resolved*, That manifest destiny points to the acquisition of Cuba, and portions of Mexico as essential to our prosperity and security; and that we commend the foresight and patriotism of the President in his wise endeavors to obtain such acquisition by means in harmony with the friendly relations of nations."[7] Although praising Buchanan, some Democrats favored an even more aggressive foreign policy than he had pursued. One of the last articles that appeared in the *Democratic Review*, which folded in 1859, applauded Democrats for embracing an expansive foreign policy, but argued that they needed to beat their plowshares into swords. The author forcefully stated, "The diplomacy which we require . . . is the bold assertion and maintenance of the letter and spirit of the *Monroe Doctrine*, and the recognition and strict compliance of the *Ostend Conference Manifesto*."[8] The *Democratic Review* believed that a more aggressive course was needed.

Similar sentiments were advanced within the halls of Congress. In March 1860 Samuel Sullivan Cox, a Democratic congressman from Ohio, delivered a rousing speech in defense of manifest destiny. Cox told his audience that the United States would one day take Mexico and would turn it into an economic powerhouse. He then warned Britain, Spain, and France not to interfere with the course of U.S. progress. Cox declaimed, "Call it what you will . . . manifest destiny, territorial expansion, star of empire, *La Joven America*, and even filibusterism—it is here. We must make the best of it."[9] Like most believers in manifest destiny, Cox argued that the United States would be forced to claim the entire continent. He also seemed to be not fully aware of the fractures within his own party on the question of expansion, as he did not fear what would happen if the United States somehow acquired Mexico, Canada, and Cuba.

To some degree, Democratic optimism was justified heading into the election of 1860. James Buchanan opted not to seek a second term, leaving Stephen Douglas as the likely nominee of the party. Both expansionists and nonexpansionists knew where Douglas stood on the issue of manifest destiny.[10] In 1858 Douglas had delivered a speech to a large crowd in New Orleans denouncing the Republican Party and blaming it for sectionalizing politics. He called for the annexation of Cuba, telling his audience, "It will not do to say we have territory enough."[11] Douglas boasted that he had voted against the Treaty of Guadalupe Hidalgo and the Clayton-Bulwer Treaty, in both cases because they sought to confine the boundaries of the United States. Yet Douglas did not deliver proexpansion speeches only in southern climes. He repeated the same principles in a speech in New York.[12] Douglas stated, "I do not say that we ought, at one blow, to acquire a vast amount of new territory. On the contrary, let us proceed slowly, gradually, steadily—Americanizing first, and annexing afterwards." Heading into the election of 1860, Douglas set himself apart as the candidate of manifest destiny.[13]

Things did not work out as northern Democrats such as Douglas hoped. In April 1860 Democrats met in Charleston, South Carolina, to nominate a candidate for president. Squabbling broke out immediately over the platform. Southerners wanted a plank that guaranteed the protection of slavery in the territories; northerners, such as Douglas, continued to hold that territories should be able to decide for themselves whether to accept slavery or not.[14] When Douglas's supporters were able to pass their platform on a narrow vote, a group of delegates led by William Lowndes Yancey of Alabama stormed out of the convention.[15] Even without delegates from the Deep South, Douglas was unable to secure the Democratic nomination.[16] The delegates who remained in Charleston voted fifty-seven times, and each time Douglas emerged as the clear leader in votes.[17] Yet Douglas remained unable to secure two-thirds of the votes and, in stark contrast to previous conventions, the dissenting delegates refused to budge. The meeting in Charleston ended in a deadlock, without a nominee.

Democrats reconvened in Baltimore in June, but a contingent of southerners again walked out. Shortly thereafter, Douglas secured the nomination. A rump southern group held its own convention and nominated John C. Breckinridge.[18] In spite of the differences between the two Democratic factions, they did agree on one substantial issue: Cuba. The northern Democrats had the following plank in their platform: "That the Democratic party are in favor of the acquisition of Cuba on such terms as shall be honorable to ourselves and just to Spain."[19] The southern Democrats' platform read, "That the Democratic party are in favor of the acquisition of the Island of Cuba, on such terms as shall be honorable to ourselves and just to Spain, at the earliest practicable moment."[20] Differences over whether slavery should be allowed in the territories split the Democratic Party in 1860, but it still remained the party of expansion.

Republicans had far less difficulty finding a candidate. Convening in Chicago, the Republican delegates took a mere three ballots to select their candidate.[21] William Henry Seward emerged as the early favorite and took the first ballot, but his lack of popularity outside of New York helped to damage his chances.[22] Abraham Lincoln of Illinois gained momentum on the second ballot and captured the nomination on the third.[23] Lincoln lacked national political experience, as he had merely served a single term in the House of Representatives in the 1840s.[24] But he had run a strong campaign for the senate seat in Illinois against Stephen Douglas.[25] In terms of his views on expansion, Lincoln remained one of the more outspoken critics of manifest destiny.[26] He had denounced the U.S.-Mexican War, criticized filibustering, and mocked Stephen Douglas for believing in manifest destiny.[27]

Not all Republicans shared Lincoln's reservations about manifest destiny. William Henry Seward was disappointed about not securing the Republican nomination in Chicago, but he fully expected to play a significant role in Lincoln's administration.[28] After the Chicago convention, Seward delivered several speeches that stressed the beneficial effects of expansionism. In September 1860 Seward delivered a robust expansionist speech in St. Paul, Minnesota. Pandering slightly to his midwestern audience, Seward informed his listeners that he had always pictured Mexico City as the future center of the rapidly expanding United States, but that he had recently changed his mind and now saw it in Minnesota.[29] Seward promised that expansion would continue in the near future. All attempts to improve Canada, he informed his listeners, were simply preparing the way for its eventual annexation to the United States. "I can look southwest and see," he then observed, "amid all the convulsions that are breaking the Spanish American republics, and in their rapid decay and dissolution, the preparatory stage for their reorganization in free, equal and self-governing members of the United States of America."[30]

Seward differed from Democratic expansionists in one important respect; he believed slavery had to be removed for manifest destiny to be fulfilled. In October 1860 Seward delivered another lengthy speech in favor of expansion in Seneca Falls, New York.[31] In this speech he maintained that expansion was just and natural but that wise individuals were waiting for the eradication of slavery to continue the process of manifest destiny. He counseled patience, as "Canada and all British America to the shores of Hudson Bay, and Russian America . . . and Spanish America to the Isthmus of Panama, and perhaps to Cape Horn, [were] all coming into this republic as they would come, voluntarily . . . if you would only admit them as equal states and carry to them the blessings of your free states, but not the curse of slave states."[32] If Republicans could triumph in 1860, Seward seemed to be arguing, then the United States could expect to grow as a nation and fulfill its continental destiny. Canada and Mexico were merely waiting until enslavers lost their political power.

The *New York Herald* noticed Seward's speeches. Reporting on his speech in St. Paul, the paper commented that he seemed to be gearing up for a run in 1864. "What is there to prevent Mr. Seward's election in 1864," it asked its readers, "and the practical beginning, under his own official direction in 1865, of his grand continental scheme of annexation for the quiet suffocation of Southern slavery?"[33] The *Herald* suspected that Republicans were planning on creating a mighty empire for abolition. The following day the paper ran an article entitled "Seward's New Phase of Manifest Destiny— Mexico in the Foreground." The opening paragraph stated, "While the Southern politicians are splitting straws and quarrelling among themselves . . . Seward and the abolitionists are trying to steal the old original democratic thunder of 'manifest destiny,' and to paint it with a Northern as well as a Southern aspect."[34] If Democrats could successfully use annexation as a wedge issue to win voters, why could Republicans not wield that same power? The *New York Herald* suspected that was what Seward was planning.

Most Republicans, however, did not come to embrace Seward's grandiose vision of continental expansion. Instead, Republicans denounced the Democratic Party's attempts to seize Cuba and Mexico and warned that Douglas would continue those policies. In an address in June 1860, Justin Morrill, a Republican from Vermont, recounted the slave power's lust for new territory and its successful annexation of Louisiana, Florida, and Texas. Morrill noted that in spite of party divisions, the Democrats agreed upon annexing Cuba and Mexico.[35] "But notwithstanding the vastness of our present territorial limits," Morrill concluded, "no serious disturbance would arise touching slavery, if it were not the manifest destiny of the Democratic party, should it be able to maintain itself in power, to nationalize slavery at home, and then to seek fresh acquisitions from foreign nations."[36] Many Republicans believed that any nominee for the Democratic Party would espouse expansionist principles because they were indebted, ultimately, to the agenda of the slave power. In light of this, Republicans throughout the campaign season lambasted Douglas as a doughface and called him a tool of the slave power.[37]

Many Republicans again focused their attention on the slave power and portrayed the election of 1860 as a contest between freedom and slavery. Carl Schurz, a German immigrant who would go on to become a leader of the Republican Party, delivered a blistering speech denouncing the slave power.[38] He told his audience, "In order to succeed . . . Slavery needs a controlling power in the General Government." Schurz averred that congressmen from slave states realized that they were losing power and so looked to new lands to offset the North's growing strength. Schurz observed, "The acquisition of foreign countries, such as Cuba and the Northern States of Mexico, is demanded, and, if they cannot be obtained by fair purchase and diplomatic transaction, war must be resorted to; and, if the majority of the people are not inclined to go to war, our international relations must be disturbed by fillibustering expeditions."[39] Republicans such as Schurz did not only focus their attention on slavery, but they also reminded voters that Democrats were anxious to add territory. As the *New York Tribune* put it, the election pitted Republicans against "the Slavery Extensionists."[40]

In addition to criticizing the slave power and the Democratic Party's penchant for poaching land, Republicans also reminded voters of Douglas's love for Cuba.[41] One paper advised voters, "Mr. Douglas *now* goes for Cuba annexation with her thousands of slaves, and denies all right to prohibit it in the territories."[42] Carl Schurz provided a similar reminder in a speech he delivered in New York called "Douglasism Exposed and Republicanism Vindicated." As the title portended, Schurz dug through Douglas's lengthy legislative record to help his audience understand why the man was unfit for office. This deep dive into "Douglasism" led Schurz to conclude that a President Douglas would use the White House "for the purpose of plunging the country into warlike enterprises, to result in the conquering of Cuba and a part of Mexico."[43] Douglas had always been a proponent of expansion, Schurz pointed out, and so there was no reason to doubt that he would use his office to push for the addition of slave states.

Opponents of manifest destiny such as Carl Schurz did not turn the election of 1860 into a referendum on expansion, but they certainly did not shy away from the topic. Cuba, Mexico, and the potential expansion of the United States were interwoven into discussions of domestic controversies. Foreign policy debates that had raged since the 1840s still played a role in political discussions. Certainly, the campaign of 1860 was different than the campaigns in 1848, 1852, and 1856, as four contenders ran campaigns that were only viable in specific regions of the country. The key contest, however, which pitted Abraham Lincoln against Stephen Douglas in the North, resulted in a resounding victory for Republicans.[44] Lincoln and the Republicans had shown that an electoral victory was possible without southern support.[45]

The triumph of Lincoln in 1860 signified that the United States would not actively pursue the annexation of Cuba and northern Mexico. The dreams of Stephen Douglas, James Buchanan, and John L. O'Sullivan had been dashed by the Republican Party. Yet the president-elect would have little time to cherish his victory. On December 20 South Carolina unanimously passed an "Ordinance of Secession."[46] Mississippi, Florida, Alabama, Georgia, Louisiana, and Texas followed suit, and a convention of southern delegates convened in February 1861 to set up a new government.[47] The delegates assembled in Montgomery, Alabama, drafted a constitution, and selected a provisional president and vice president.[48] On February 18, 1861, Jefferson Davis was inaugurated as provisional president of the Confederate States of America.

The creation of the Confederacy led some southerners to quickly envision a mushrooming empire for slavery.[49] At a reception for Jefferson Davis held in March 1861, Alexander Stephens delivered a proexpansion speech. According to one correspondent, "[Stephens] alluded to the probable expansion of the Confederate States, hinting that our territory might extend far down to the tropical country of Central America, taking in the whole, all united, and all based on the fundamental idea that the negro was inferior to the white race."[50] Stephens had expressed similar views in a speech that he delivered in Georgia in 1859, when he told those gathered, "We are looking out toward Chihuahua, Sonora, and other parts of Mexico—to Cuba, and even to Central America. Where are to be our ultimate limits, time alone can determine."[51] The difference in 1861 was that Stephens was the provisional vice president of the Confederacy.[52] Confederates such as Stephens believed that the time was ripe for annexation, as they could acquire Cuba, Mexico, and Central America without worrying about northern obstruction.

Stephens's proexpansion speech triggered dreams of empire within the Confederacy. The correspondent of the *Daily Sun*, a newspaper from Stephens's home state of Georgia, waxed eloquent on the future boundaries of the Confederate nation. "The new government must grow strong in order to work out its great destiny," the correspondent observed. "Expansion South into the rich mines and valleys of Mexico, Arizona, &c., and into the teeming plains of Central America, will, and must, give that strength." Like Stephens, the correspondent believed that the Confederacy could establish a massive empire for slavery, with the first step being the occupation of Mexico: "The South must have territory still to the South. She must occupy Mexico, to prevent the Abolitionists getting on the Southern border. . . . It is essential that slave-holders, with slaves, should go and work the rich soil of Mexico. Manifest destiny and inexorable necessity so decree it."[53] The establishment of the Confederacy did not kill off the dream of manifest destiny but instead channeled it in new directions.

Many southerners hoped that the Confederacy would soon fulfill the long-cherished dream of acquiring northern Mexico and Cuba.[54] An Alabama paper ran a lengthy article on manifest destiny that began, "The doctrine of manifest destiny has been taught in some form or other, in every age and country, in which the human intellect was sufficiently cultivated to commit its reflections to paper."[55] After briefly looking at the examples of ancient Israel, Greece, and Rome, the author turned to the landing of the "Anglo-Saxon race" at Plymouth Rock. This led the author to observe that the United States was "now being divided by political dissensions, into Southern and Northern Confederacies." Rather than bemoaning the breakup of the United States, this author foresaw the creation of two powerful empires. The North would soon annex Canada; the Confederacy would look southward. "For the annexation of Cuba and Mexico to the South," the author concluded, "is as much manifest destiny, as that of the Canadas to the North."[56] Optimistic observers looked at the Confederacy and saw a rapidly expanding empire.

Not all Confederates, however, shared this view of manifest destiny.[57] In December 1861 the *Richmond Dispatch* ran an article appropriately entitled "Demise of Manifest Destiny."[58] This article included a brief history of the idea of manifest destiny, arguing that it had once unified the American people. "There have been few ideas," it asserted, "which have so filled the imagination and exalted the pride of its people as this grand one of the 'manifest destiny' of the American Union." According to the *Dispatch*, manifest destiny had led the United States to expand over a vast territory. "Carried out in the spirit of the American Constitution, it would have been a grand and holy 'destiny,'" the author sadly observed. But it was not to be. For "no sooner did the . . . desolating breath of Puritanism blow upon it, than it blasted and withered beyond hope of recovery." Had puritanical Republicans not seized the government, the nation could have continued on to its manifest destiny, but the South could not submit to be "governed by such mountebanks and imposters as Seward, Sumner, Greeley, and those two offsprings of polluted beds, Lincoln and Fremont." Recognizing that manifest destiny meant a unified continent of North America, the *Dispatch* rejoiced at its demise. The death of manifest destiny meant that Confederates would not have to live under the rule of a "Puritan democracy."[59]

As did southerners, northerners entertained a variety of opinions regarding the future fulfillment of manifest destiny. Some northerners blamed the ideology for breaking up the United States. George Duffield Jr., a prominent Presbyterian minister, reminded his congregation that the United States had wronged Mexico and was paying the price for its seizure of Mexican territory.[60] William Hayes Lord told his congregation, "[One] cause of our present troubles is territorial extension."[61] Religiously inclined northerners hoped that southern secession would lead the United States to humble itself and reject manifest destiny.[62] "Our country lies under the frown of God," one minister argued, "and we must repent, and bring forth fruits meet for repentance, before that frown can be turned away."[63] With the outbreak of war, some northern ministers argued that the United States needed to repent, turn from the idea of manifest destiny, and abase itself before the Almighty.[64] Such ministers did not doubt that the United States could turn back to the paths of righteousness.

Others credited the formation of the Confederacy with causing the collapse of manifest destiny. "A few years ago it was a very common saying among our American people of all grades and classes, North and South," a paper in California observed, "that it was our 'manifest destiny' to obtain possession of all Mexico and all of the country lying between the Atlantic and Pacific oceans, including, of course, that gem of islands, Cuba."[65] This author then went back over the U.S. history of expansion, crediting manifest destiny with the acquisition of Louisiana, Florida, and California, and with attempts to purchase Cuba and invade Nicaragua. "The idea was current and popular that the United States of North America were destined to go on conquering and to conquer until every human being and every inch of land between the Atlantic and Pacific Oceans would be brought under the principles of our government," the paper explained. Nonetheless, the formation of the Confederacy had shattered these dreams. "This is the end of our manifest destiny," the author suggested, "as preached by the leaders of the Democratic party for years, and acquiesced in by the masses of that party for the last twenty years." Instead of bemoaning the downfall of manifest destiny, this writer rejoiced: "'Manifest destiny' is played out and thank God for it."

Yet not all northerners believed that manifest destiny was played out. As previously noted, William Henry Seward had openly embraced the theory in 1860, and southern secession did little to dampen his enthusiasm. Shortly after Lincoln appointed him secretary of state, Seward drafted a memorandum. Seward was bothered not only by the ongoing situation at Fort Sumter, where supplies were running low, but also by France, Spain, and Great Britain threatening to invade Mexico. Seward suggested that Lincoln take a bold new approach in foreign policy. "I would demand explanations from Spain and France, categorically, at once," Seward wrote. He then continued in a bellicose manner: "I would seek explanations from Great Britain and Russia, and send agents into Canada, Mexico, and Central America, to rouse a vigorous continental spirit of independence on this continent against European intervention." "And if satisfactory explanations are not received from Spain and France," he continued, "[I] would convene Congress and declare war against them."[66] Lincoln's cooler head prevailed and he did not contemplate declaring war on Spain and France. But Seward's memorandum shows that some expansionists saw the crisis as an opportunity to carry out manifest destiny.[67]

The *New York Herald* concurred with Seward's vision of expansion. The *Herald* had earlier embraced the idea that the North could allow the South to peacefully secede, as both could pursue their separate destinies.[68] After the outbreak of hostilities, however, the *Herald* soon became a militant defender of the United States and outstripped Seward in its support for expansion.[69] At the end of 1861, the *Herald* predicted that the rebellion would "probably be crushed by next summer." It suggested that Lincoln should then deploy his army of one million men to subdue the continent: "Cuba and Canada must be annexed at one blow. . . . All the West India islands must be conquered." The editorial concluded with a stridently warlike paragraph: "Under other auspices, therefore, will it be necessary to send forth our armies, conquering and to conquer, till this vast continent is ours. Such is the manifest destiny of the Anglo-Saxon and Celtic races."[70] The outbreak of the Civil War did not cause the *Herald* to abandon its dream of manifest destiny. Instead, it saw it as a "glorious epoch" in which the United States would subdue not only a rebellion but an entire continent.

During 1861 expansionists within both regions continued to keep their eyes upon Mexico, believing that one day it would fall into the orbit of their respective empires. Little did either side realize that another power was about to enter the fray. In December 1861 a joint coalition of Great Britain, Spain, and France landed in Mexico, ostensibly to collect debts owed by the Mexican government. Great Britain and Spain soon left, but France launched a full-scale invasion. Emperor Napoléon III saw the breakup of the United States as an opportunity to establish his own empire in Mexico.[71] Napoléon III believed that an unchecked United States would continue to expand until it dominated the continent of North America and the Caribbean. The French takeover of Mexico would be one means of preventing the fulfillment of manifest destiny.[72]

Not surprisingly, northern expansionists condemned the invasion of Mexico.[73] Although they had often spoken of dismantling Mexico and annexing it to the United States, they bristled at the thought of a European monarch conquering the region. "This nation is by no means dead," a writer for *Frank Leslie's Illustrated Newspaper* reminded the French, "nor is it impotent, as the proceedings of France in Mexico would seem to imply."[74] The author went on to label the attack "a defiance of the avowed and intelligible policy of the United States, and, consequently, an act of hostility." Expansionists were not overly concerned about the damage France would do to Mexico, but rather worried that the French would become an obstacle to manifest destiny. They pointed out that the war against the Confederacy would not last forever and that the United States would have a massive army, more than capable of subduing the French.[75] "And when all our domestic troubles are settled," the *New York Herald* threatened, "and there is no further need of the immense armies of the North and South, there can be little doubt that new employment will be cut out for them. United under one government, they will go forth conquering and to conquer. Their first attentions will be paid to England and to France."[76] Expansionists recognized that putting down the rebellion remained the priority, but it would be followed by driving European powers out of North America.

Confederates reacted quite differently to the French occupation of Mexico. The *Daily Picayune* of New Orleans believed that the invasion benefited the Confederacy. "There was an American Union once," the paper explained, "in which the Southern people had faith as the beneficent guardian of liberty and happiness. . . . Its unlimited expansion over this continent was its manifest destiny, and every approach of foreign influence over the affairs of the neighboring States, was jealously watched as a movement against the genius of American freedom."[77] Northerners had broken the trust of southerners, however, and destroyed both the dream of manifest destiny and the Monroe Doctrine. Because of this, the Confederacy had nothing to fear from the French. "We shall, therefore, accept whatever may be done for Mexico," the paper concluded, "as something, which so far as it checks and humbles our enemy is a comparative good." By 1862 the *Picayune*, which had routinely supported expansion during the 1850s, was willing to accept a European invasion of its southern neighbor, so long as it harmed the Yankees. The survival of the Confederacy was more important than manifest destiny.

Indeed, the French occupation of Mexico triggered a new line of attack on manifest destiny. Many Confederates portrayed manifest destiny as a doctrine of northern aggression. The *Charleston Mercury* mocked the impotence of northerners, who were unable to prevent the French from occupying Mexico. "The Yankees," it scoffed, "who look upon the whole Continent of North America as theirs, 'by manifest destiny,' are very much exercised . . . with this impeachment of their pretensions. Every wooden nutmeg maker in the North boils with wrath, as he sees Mexico passing away from the domain of his rapacity."[78] In a manner similar to how some northerners had portrayed manifest destiny as a cover for rapacious enslavers, southerners now argued that manifest destiny had been concocted by religious fanatics living in New England. The *Charleston Mercury* went so far as to goad northerners into attacking Mexico. To some Confederates, it clearly seemed amusing and ironic that the French had blocked manifest destiny.

The *Richmond Dispatch* crowed that the French occupation of Mexico had shattered forever the Yankee dream of manifest destiny. "It treats with such profound contempt," one author wrote, speaking of the French occupation, "the Monroe doctrine, and all other cardinal doctrines of Manifest Destiny, and it opposes such an effectual barrier to the ambitious plans, purposes, and territorial and political progress of Yankee Doodle, that it may well stir up the bile of that interesting nation to the profoundest depths."[79] The *Dispatch* cast manifest destiny as a northern ideology and boasted that southerners would infinitely "prefer to be a colony of France than a province of Yankeedom." Although the author still hoped that the Confederacy would succeed in securing its independence, he admitted that he found amusement in "the desperate dilemma to which Napoleon's bold move in Mexico [had] reduced the Manifest Destiny Yankees."

In fact, however, as the war progressed, northerners continued to view manifest destiny in a variety of ways. Many northerners still blamed the South for manifest destiny and for the United States' aggressive foreign policies of the 1840s and 1850s. The *North American and United States Gazette* faulted the South for breaking up the United States and slaveholders for attempting to conquer Cuba and

Mexico.[80] This paper argued that the South had been solely responsible for the conquest of Mexico and for filibustering attempts into Cuba and Central America.[81] Postmaster General Montgomery Blair made a similar argument in an 1863 speech during which he portrayed the slave power as an insatiable cormorant that refused to be appeased by northern concessions.[82] "Their filibustering operations having failed in their attempt to steal Cuba and Central America," he noted, "they prepared to take these countries openly by the power of the government." Using pronouns such as "they" placed the blame for expansionism squarely on the shoulders of the South. Many northerners interpreted the Civil War as a contest between the virtuous and long-suffering United States and a slave power hell-bent on overrunning its neighbors and creating a massive slave empire.[83]

At the same moment, many northern Democrats believed that manifest destiny could be revived once the South was brought back into the Union. The *New York World* boasted in 1863 that the Democratic Party had been responsible for the acquisition of Louisiana, Texas, and California. All of these measures had been opposed by Whigs and Republicans, yet Republicans were unwilling to give California back to Mexico. "By fighting to retain what they opposed the Democracy in acquiring," the paper casually explained, "they make a tacit admission that the Democrats have always been in the right and their opponents always in the wrong."[84] Democratic organs such as the *New York World* continued to boast that it was the Democratic Party that supported manifest destiny and expansion. Clement Vallandigham, a Democrat from Ohio who served in the House of Representatives, delivered a passionate plea for reconciliation in Congress in 1863.[85] "Union is empire," Vallandigham declaimed. "Hence, hitherto we have continually extended our territory, and the Union with it, South and West. The Louisiana purchase, Florida, and Texas all attest it."[86] Vallandigham did not see expansion as playing a role in the breakup of the United States and instead portrayed it as a reason for reunification, believing that after reunifying, the United States could continue on the path of manifest destiny.

Northern opponents of manifest destiny tended to disagree with Vallandigham's reading of history. In an 1863 article, Horace Greeley lamented that, prior to the Civil War, the United States had pursued an aggressive foreign policy that targeted weaker neighbors.[87] The Rev. Ezra H. Gillett labeled manifest destiny one of the greatest sins of the United States. "We had all the self-exaltation and self-glorification of the King of Babylon," he declared in a sermon in 1862. "We talked of *manifest destiny*. . . . We forgot that we had enough to do to train and educate and christianize our own masses."[88] True greatness, Gillett noted, consisted of taking care of those in need. Northern critics of manifest destiny hoped that the turmoil, death, and destruction of the Civil War would lead a reunified United States to be humble and contrite.[89] Instead of seeing the Civil War as a means through which manifest destiny would be fulfilled, many northerners hoped it would cause Americans to rethink how the United States acted on the international stage.

As the war progressed, southerners hoped northerners would abandon the idea of manifest destiny. Although many had begun the war with dreams of southern expansion, as Union victories piled up, the southern press increasingly denounced manifest destiny as epitomizing Yankee insolence.[90] Once again, the *Richmond Dispatch* led the charge. One article mocked the United States for coveting Mexico: "We wonder if the French Emperor never reads the editorials of the Yankee-newspapers, or the speeches in the Yankee Congress, or has never heard of the 'Manifest Destiny' of the amiable and interesting Yankee people!"[91] Another article taunted the Yankees for being unable to fulfill manifest destiny because a French puppet sat upon the throne of Mexico.[92] Time and again, the *Richmond Dispatch* assailed manifest destiny as a Yankee doctrine.[93] In the pages of the *Richmond Dispatch*, manifest destiny was transformed into a prototypical Yankee notion, one that southerners were boldly resisting by establishing an independent nation.[94]

Throughout 1864 northerners focused most of their attention on the conflict with the Confederacy and not on what would happen once the Confederacy was subdued. Nowhere was this more evident than in the election of 1864, which pitted Abraham Lincoln against George B. McClellan. The Republican Party only mentioned its foreign policy at the conclusion of its platform, where it stated that it could "never regard with indifference the attempt of any European Power to overthrow by force or to supplant by fraud the institutions of any Republican Government on the Western Continent."[95] Without mentioning Mexico or France by name, this plank made it clear that Republicans were opposed to the French occupation of Mexico. The Democratic platform of 1864 made no mention of foreign policy at all, as it instead called for a reunification of the United States and chastised Republicans for abandoning the Constitution.[96] The party that had nominated expansionists since 1844, that had openly boasted of securing Louisiana, Florida, Texas, and California, and that had recently promised to annex Cuba opted to ignore territorial expansion in the midst of the Civil War.

If discussions of manifest destiny largely disappeared in the North throughout 1864, the defeat of the Confederacy in 1865 triggered renewed attention to the continental destiny of the United States. Although Lincoln himself did not embrace the idea, many northerners saw the conclusion of the Civil War as an opportunity for the United States to fulfill its manifest destiny. The Chicago *Republican* boasted that the Civil War had "settled beyond all question the permanency of the American Republic."[97] As the nation would continue united, there would be nothing to prevent the United States from carrying out its manifest destiny. "Douglas, twenty years ago uttered the truth that will one day be verified to the letter," the paper observed, "when he said that the continent was too small for more than one government, as long as that government was a Republic." The Civil War had proved to be a necessary purgative for the United States. The paper concluded, "The war through which we have passed has been . . . at least a healthful preparation for that destiny which will only be realized in the glory of an American Continental Empire." With debates over slavery silenced and the question of secession firmly settled, there could be nothing to prevent the continued growth of the United States.

Not surprisingly, the *New York Herald* returned to manifest destiny. Shortly after Lincoln's assassination, the paper predicted that Andrew Johnson would be an effective president who would promote manifest destiny.[98] The *Herald* explained, "It was as a war democrat that he was nominated for the Vice Presidency . . . and as a vigorous and perhaps rough-handed war democrat of the mixed Crom-wellian, Jacksonian, 'manifest destiny' and 'Monroe doctrine' types, Andrew Johnson . . . will carve out for himself a splendid name in the world's history."[99] The *Herald* sensed that disbanded soldiers would soon travel to Mexico to drive out the French usurpers and that Canada would petition to join the Union, as it was "well known that the Canadas would long ago have striven to secure admittance into the Union but for the bugaboo of slavery." With a burgeoning antislavery empire, the United States would be able to add Cuba to the constellation of states: "The now dominant anti-slavery senti-ment of the United States cannot, for any great length of time, tol-erate the existence and rivalry near our shores of the slave-holding and slave-importing colonial government of Cuba."[100]

Visions of empire also danced before the eyes of former Confed-erates. In November 1865 a group of prominent southerners gathered in Nashville "in honor of the commercial nuptials of Memphis and Nashville." On this festive occasion, several individuals gave speeches, including Sam Tate, a Tennessean most noted for his role in financing the development of southern railroads.[101] Tate admitted in his speech that he had served the Confederacy, but he claimed to have been a reluctant supporter of secession. Tate urged his fellow Confederates to gracefully accept their defeat, as a unified United States would be vir-tually impossible to oppose. "I believe in the manifest destiny doctrine that was advocated by a distinguished statesman at St. Paul in eighteen hundred and sixty," Tate stated, speaking of William Henry Seward. He then continued with a full-throated defense of manifest destiny, proclaiming that Canada and Mexico were in the process of "puri-fying" themselves to "become one of this family of great free States, the home of the free man and the white man." Like the *Herald*, Tate believed that the Civil War had paved the way for the fulfillment of manifest destiny. He told his audience, comprising many former Con-federates, "Manifest destiny has declared it that these stars and stripes should wave over every foot of soil on the continent of America, and the laws of the United States should reign supreme all over this con-tinent." Southerners like Tate were quick to abandon the dream of a Confederacy in favor of a continent-spanning United States.[102]

There was a decided uptick in expansionist sentiment after the fall of the Confederacy. The *New Orleans Times* refocused its attention on Mexico, portraying it as ripe for annexation. "Texas was lost in 1836, California and New Mexico in 1848, and a considerable portion of its northern territory in 1854," it explained. "Thus it will be, till manifest destiny is entirely accomplished."[103] Papers such as the *Picayune* picked up where they had left off in the 1850s, calling for the annexation of Mexico as a solution to the "Mexican problem."[104] A South Carolina paper casually informed its readers, "Never before did the old and popular doctrine of 'Manifest Destiny' seem so likely of fulfillment as it does now, with this universal extension of Americans and their ideas all over this continent."[105] As they had in the 1850s, expansion-minded individuals turned their attention to Mexico.

In the years from 1860 to 1865, opponents of manifest destiny did not have to create new arguments against the ideology. Abraham Lincoln's victories in 1860 and 1864 ensured that the North would not embrace manifest destiny, at least in the short term. Although William Henry Seward continually threatened war with Britain and France, the Lincoln administration showed no desire to annex Canada, Cuba, or Mexico. The Civil War did not destroy manifest destiny, however. As countless newspapers attested, and as the speeches of men such as Sam Tate and William Henry Seward demonstrated, manifest destiny proved to be far more durable than the Confederacy. No sooner had the Confederacy surrendered than papers such as the *Daily Picayune* renewed their calls for the annexation of Mexico. The *New York Herald* still anticipated the acquisition of Cuba, Mexico, and Canada. Within the halls of Congress, representatives again proclaimed that it was the manifest destiny of the United States to expand over the continent.[106] For expansionists, the Civil War had brushed away one of the largest impediments to the fulfillment of manifest destiny: the issue of slavery. No longer did the questions of free soil, slavery, and popular sovereignty loom before Congress with each possible acquisition. Proponents of manifest destiny, therefore, found themselves reinvigorated by the war and saw a path cleared to fulfill their dreams.

6

Worthless Real Estate

The Environmental Critique of Manifest Destiny, 1866–1868

In June 1867 William H. Seward basked in an unusually fine mood. Seward had recently negotiated with Russia for the purchase of Alaska and had decided to give a celebratory address in Boston. Seward offered a raucous audience what could only be classified as a manifest destiny speech. "I know that nature designs that this whole continent," he proclaimed to the cheering multitude, "not merely these thirty-six States, but this whole continent—shall be, sooner or later, within the magic circle of the American Union."[1] As the crowd burst into cheers, Seward continued, "Give me then fifty, forty, or thirty more years of life, and I will engage to give you the possession of the American Continent and the control of the entire world."[2] Seward believed that the purchase of Alaska was merely a stepping stone, a first acquisition that prepared the way for the fulfillment of manifest destiny. The Civil War had ended, the smoke had cleared, and all impediments had seemingly been swept away. For fervent disciples of manifest destiny, it appeared as if the realization of their dreams was at hand.

Seward's words illustrated how manifest destiny remained a vibrant ideology in the aftermath of the Civil War.[3] Because many of the old standbys no longer sufficed, opponents of manifest destiny had to mold their arguments to the changing circumstances of the postbellum world. Critics of manifest destiny could no longer claim that expansion only stood to benefit enslavers, as slavery had been abolished by the Thirteenth Amendment. Nor could they dredge up the ideas of filibustering and robbery, as expansionists showed no inclination toward aggressive expansionism. Because of these changes, opponents increasingly relied upon an environmental critique of manifest destiny. They posited that the United States already controlled the best land and that the regions being sought now were worthless. They portrayed Alaska as a frozen tundra filled with icebergs and polar bears, and they presented the Danish West Indies as a pestilent region riven by earthquakes and volcanoes. This environmental critique of manifest destiny failed to prevent the purchase of Alaska, but it did help scuttle Seward's Danish treaty. Seward promised to gain "this whole continent," but could not even deliver the Danish West Indies. Like so many others, Seward left office having failed to bring about the fulfillment of manifest destiny.[4]

During the Civil War, Seward had not had an opportunity to expand the United States. Preventing European intervention and dealing with the French occupation of Mexico kept him busy.[5] Almost as soon as the conflict ended, however, Russia approached Seward with an offer. In December 1866 Tsar Alexander II sent out orders to his ambassador, Edouard de Stoeckl, to sell what would be known as Alaska to the United States.[6] Seward jumped at the opportunity and he and Stoeckl wrapped up negotiations in five days.[7] Seward submitted the final treaty to the Senate on March 30, 1867, the day Congress was set to adjourn.[8] An executive session was called, senators debated the merits, and on April 9, 1867, the Senate voted 37–2 to ratify the treaty. The entire process of negotiating and ratifying had taken under thirty days.[9]

The rapidity with which the treaty was written and ratified meant that there was little opportunity to challenge it. The Senate held its debate in a closed session, and a motion to publish the record was rejected. According to historian Thomas A. Bailey, proponents of the Alaskan treaty relied upon three key arguments. First, they maintained that the territory would be an economic asset to the United States, as it abounded in natural resources.[10] Second, Russia had been a loyal ally during the Civil War and ratification would cement friendly relations.[11] Unlike Britain and France, Russia had not contemplated recognizing the Confederacy.[12] Northerners such as Seward appreciated that support and warned that rejection of the treaty would be an insult to Russia. Third, proponents hoped that the treaty would prepare the way for the eventual annexation of Canada.[13] This purchase would supposedly enable the United States to "surround" Canada, causing Britain to relinquish it.[14]

Proponents of expansion saw the Alaskan purchase as the next step toward fulfilling manifest destiny. Many Republicans who had long opposed adding territory suddenly swung into the annexationist camp.[15] Charles Sumner, a prominent senator from Massachusetts who had railed against the slave power in the 1850s, played a pivotal role in securing the ratification of the treaty. In 1867 Sumner delivered a lengthy address in which he declared, "Our territorial acquisitions are among the landmarks of our history."[16] Sumner boasted of the additions of Louisiana, Florida, Texas, and New Mexico, ignoring the fact that Federalists and later, Whigs, had opposed most of those purchases. Sumner overlooked the sectional hostility that expansion had engendered, instead telling his fellow senators, "With an increased size on the map there is an increased consciousness of strength, and the citizen throbs anew as he traces the extending line."[17] Alaska was merely the next step in the destiny of the United States "to spread over the northern part of the American quarter of the globe."[18] With Alaska, it seemed that Republicans were poised to steal the Democratic idea of manifest destiny.[19]

Republican support for Alaska did not deter some familiar voices from favoring the purchase. The *New York Herald* continued to trumpet the idea of manifest destiny in its pages, seeing the purchase as evidence that the forces of expansion could not be stopped. "Manifest destiny . . . marks out the North American continent as the future map of the United States," the *Herald* proclaimed shortly after the ratification of the treaty.[20] In the not-so-distant future, the *Herald* believed, Congress would seat representatives from places ranging from Quebec to Mexico to Sitka. "If within the last six years we have put down a rebellion of over half a million of armed men," it concluded, "liberated four millions of slaves, reconquered eight hundred thousand square miles of territory, and purchased four hundred and fifty thousand square miles more, how long will it take us to absorb all North America?"[21] The purchase of Alaska confirmed to the *New York Herald* that the fulfillment of manifest destiny was at hand.

Other papers joined the *Herald* in discussing the fulfillment of manifest destiny in the near future.[22] One editor declared, "Our people have faith in the manifest destiny of the nation. They look to the eventual absorption of the whole North American continent."[23] According to the *Brooklyn Eagle*, Alaska prepared the way for the fulfillment of manifest destiny because Canada could not long remain in the hands of a European power.[24] The *Alexandria Gazette* predicted, "'Manifest Destiny' will probably urge on the 'expansion' until the 'whole boundless continent is ours.'"[25] So often was the phrase "manifest destiny" bandied about that a paper in South Carolina concluded, "[The] cession is regarded with great favor by nearly all the journals of the country, and causes many of them to predict that all of North America will ultimately be absorbed by the United States."[26] Alaska helped to breathe new life into the idea of manifest destiny.

Opponents of manifest destiny, however, were unwilling to buckle under this expansionist onslaught. Almost as soon as the treaty was announced, critics complained about the territory itself. Horace Greeley's *New York Tribune* quickly published a short article on the treaty that treated the purchase in a contemptuous manner. Greeley highlighted the fact that the "Arctic territory" had not been given an official name.[27] He then joked, "We venture to suggest, at once in recognition of the most valued inhabitants of this western Greenland, and as a compliment to the great nation which does us the honor to pocket our money, that Gov. Seward's hard bargain be known as Walrussia." Although other names would be suggested, it was Walrussia that stuck.[28]

Over the course of 1867 and into the ensuing year, editors routinely referred to the area as Walrussia.[29] Articles that appeared in 1867 bore titles such as "Natives of Walrussia" and "Gold in Walrussia."[30] The *New York Tribune* continued to derisively use the term, often deploying it in articles that mocked the climate and the produce of the region.[31] The term appeared so often that a newspaper in Wyoming commented, "[The] title of Walrussia sticks to our new possessions like pitch, or Russian salve."[32] Most often newspapers used the name in passing reference to the poor climate, such as when a paper in Kentucky observed, "If this purgatorial weather endures much longer we shall all have to 'pilgrimate' to Walrussia."[33] Even though the name Alaska would eventually supplant Walrussia, the humorous moniker proved to be quite popular.

The name Walrussia was part of a broader critique of Alaska's climate. Critics alleged that the United States had acquired the land of icebergs, walruses, and polar bears. One paper in Kansas commented, "If ever any people were profoundly astonished, certainly the people of these United States were on learning that the Senate had been induced to confirm the treaty with Russia, by which this country acquired the ice-bergs, the polar bears, and the Esquimaux who constitute what is known as Russian America."[34] Opponents of the purchase continually trotted forth the argument that Alaska was not a fit habitation for humans and that it added nothing of value to the United States.[35] Even a paper from Wisconsin, a place well acquainted with snow and ice, lamented that the United States had purchased "a frozen desert, a land of storms and fogs."[36]

Other critics ridiculed the man responsible for the treaty. A paper in Iowa called Seward a "poor old man" and denounced him for being a poor statesman.[37] It satirically noted that Seward had used a "magical wand" to transform the barren region into a "lovely country," filled with sunshine and fragrant flowers.[38] The *New York Herald* joined in the merriment at the secretary of state's expense. On April 12, 1867, the paper ran a series of fictional advertisements on its sixth page that poked fun at Seward. One of these advertisements read, "William H. Seward, having gone into the real estate business, is prepared to buy property, improved or unimproved, either North or South. Land that grows oranges or icebergs preferred. Apply to Washington, D.C."[39] Another "advertisement" carried a similar theme: "Owners of real estate who are in need of ready money may hear of something to their advantage by applying at the old brick building adjoining the Treasury Department, Washington, D.C. No questions asked as to title."[40] Given that the *Herald* supported the purchase of Alaska, this seems to have been an attempt to poke fun at William Henry Seward as an individual. Whatever the exact reason for the

THE TWO PETER FUNKS.

RUSSIAN STRANGER—" *I say, little boy, do you want to trade ? I've got a fine lot of bears, seals, icebergs and Esquimaux—They're no use to me, I'll swap 'em all for those boats you've got.*"
[Billy, like other foolish boys, jumps at the idea.]

10. Opponents of the Alaska purchase not only focused on the snow, ice, and climate, but they also mocked Seward for his willingness to purchase such real estate. "The Two Peter Funks," *Frank Leslie's Illustrated Newspaper*, May 25, 1867. From House Divided: The Civil War Research Engine at Dickinson College, http://hd.housedivided.dickinson.edu/node/46558.

mock advertisements, the *Herald* aptly demonstrated that Seward could be a target for ridicule.[41]

Poets, writers, and humorists also joked about the purchase.[42] John Stanton was a humorist who created the character of Corry O'Lanus to amuse readers of the *Brooklyn Eagle*.[43] In contrast to Seba Smith, whose stories centered on politics, Stanton favored domestic scenes, and his short epistle each week revolved around the hazards of married life. O'Lanus's wife's nagging, his children's unruliness, and his struggle to fit into his middle-class surroundings became the basis for the humor. In 1867, however, O'Lanus turned his attention to Alaska. In the midst of his ninth epistle, in which he explains religious weeklies and how much they cost, O'Lanus suddenly changes the subject. "I begin to think this is an ungrateful country," he observes, "and that genius is not appreciated here . . . I have some thoughts of leaving Brooklyn and going where talent is recognized."[44] That comment leads O'Lanus to turn his attention to Walrussia as a possible place to immigrate. "There are none of the sudden changes of temperature you experience here," he quips. "It freezes the year round." He then continues to unleash a torrent of squibs. "They have a short summer about the first of August," he jokes, "which lasts about twenty minutes." Like many of those who came before him, Stanton found it humorous that anyone would wish to migrate to Walrussia.

Throughout the article Stanton referred to the territory as Walrussia, but he also turned his attention specifically to the name. "The new territory has not been named yet," O'Lanus observes, "and Secretary Seward is open for proposals on the subject."[45] O'Lanus, of course, is willing to provide some suggestions. After noting that all Russian places must conclude with an "off" or a "ski" he comes down firmly on the side of the "offs." "'Damlongwayoff' is Russian, peculiar and expressive," he deadpans. "'Eversofaroff' is not so emphatic," he comments, before suggesting "Jumpingoff" as a final possibility. Each of these names, of course, was a not-so-subtle comment on the distance of Alaska from the rest of the United States. Between the jokes about the weather and the distance from the contiguous states, Stanton was making it clear that moving to Alaska was not a real option for Corry O'Lanus. Moving to Alaska was a joke.

David Ross Locke worked several of these themes into his satire of the Alaska purchase. Locke was an Ohio newspaperman who created the character Petroleum V. Nasby.[46] Nasby was a revolting figure, an overweight, hard-drinking, red-nosed Democrat who railed against African Americans. As Seba Smith had done with Major Jack Downing, Locke wrote fictional letters in the guise of Nasby and used his extreme views to satirize the Democratic Party. Locke continued to pen the "Nasby Papers" through the Johnson administration and Locke himself became something of a national celebrity.[47] His letters were widely read and reprinted.

Shortly after the Alaska purchase, Nasby penned a letter that mocked the entire purchase. In this letter Nasby brags that he concocted the entire scheme to purchase Alaska. "The idea originatid in these massive intelleck," Nasby boasts in his comically misspelled style.[48] Nasby, by this time an advisor of President Johnson, and William Henry Seward had thought of ways to get rid of the Blair family, who were always asking for political appointments for family members. Nasby convinced Seward that they could dump the Blair clan in Alaska, along with hordes of office-seekers. This argument persuaded Seward to buy Russian Alaska. The joke revolved around the fact that Nasby and Seward had to then convince President Johnson that the territory of Alaska was worth purchasing. Johnson considered it cold and worthless territory and so Seward explained to Johnson that Alaska was filled with "whales, and walruses, and seals, and white bears, and pine-apples, and wheat, and sea-lions, and fields uv ice the year round, in a climit ez mild and equable ez the meridian uv Washington." Johnson remained skeptical until Seward and Nasby patiently explained that Alaska would become a new home for the Blairs. Thinking he could dispatch the Blair family, Johnson sent the treaty to Congress.

Locke, through Nasby, satirized Seward and the corruption of those who supported the Alaskan purchase. As Nasby relates, Seward solicited letters of recommendation from a learned professor and from a naval officer to help convince Johnson that Alaska was valuable. Both men provided glowing reviews of the territory under consideration. The distinguished professor wrote, "The Gulf Stream sweeps up the coast, causing a decided twist in the isothermal line, wich hez the effeck uv making it ruther sultry than otherwise. Anywheres for six hundred miles back uv the coast strawberries grow in the open air."[49] The learned professor followed up this analysis with a request that he would be appointed to lead any scientific expeditions to the newly acquired territory. Likewise, the naval officer demanded a naval command if Congress approved the treaty. These "experts" had a vested interest in seeing the purchase approved by Congress and

"THE BIG THING."

Old Mother Seward. "I'll rub some of this on his sore spot: it may soothe him a little."

II. Republicans frequently alleged that President Johnson and Seward had ulterior motivations for purchasing Alaska. In the background is a map of Alaska with a polar bear chasing an American. "The Big Thing," *Harper's Weekly Magazine*, April 20, 1867. From House Divided: The Civil War Research Engine at Dickinson College, http://hd.housedivided.dickinson.edu/node/46472.

so they willingly lied about Alaska's fecundity and climate. Locke aimed his satire at the Johnson administration, but also pointed out that promoters had vastly oversold Alaska. It was the land of icebergs, cold, and polar bears. Those who sought the territory had ulterior motives and so they spun tales of a fertile, temperate land filled with fresh strawberries.

Asserting that Alaska had little value often led to the larger argument that expansion was unnecessary because the United States already possessed ample territory. The *Milwaukee Daily Sentinel* maintained that the United States already possessed all the land that was necessary for its prosperity. "We occupy the best part of the continent," it argued, "South of us tropical heats will ever enervate and enfeeble. North of us the rigors of an Arctic winter will ever resist the march of civilization."[50] Why bother to purchase a vast, underpopulated, and frozen territory when the United States already had more land than it knew what to do with in climates that were far more agreeable? The writer concluded, "With our unequaled commercial advantages of river, lake and ocean . . . in the name of reason ought we not to rest content?"[51] The purchase of Russian Alaska provided the opponents of manifest destiny with an opportunity to offer pragmatic objections, which had been a harder case to make with Cuba or northern Mexico.

Whether humorous or serious, criticism of the Alaska purchase had little effect on public policy. After all, most of these arguments were crafted in the wake of Senate ratification of the treaty. Additionally, most papers begrudgingly accepted the purchase.[52] *Frank Leslie's Illustrated Newspaper* published cartoons mocking Seward, called the territory Walrussia, and joked about the icebergs, polar bears, and cold weather. Yet it advised Congress to go ahead and pay for the purchase.[53] The critique of Alaska was politically impotent, but it nevertheless mustered arguments that would soon be applied to other territories.[54] Joking about the poor climate proved useful to those who opposed expansion and to those who thought that the United States already had ample territory.

Opponents of manifest destiny would soon have the opportunity to deploy the environmental argument again. As early as 1865, Seward had explored the possibility of purchasing several islands in the Caribbean to serve as naval coaling stations, and in 1866 he toured Santo Domingo and St. Thomas.[55] Seward paid the most attention to the Danish West Indies, a group of islands—most notably St. Thomas, St. Croix, and St. John—that would later become known as the U.S. Virgin Islands.[56] Seward engaged in negotiations with Denmark throughout 1867, as both sides squabbled over the price, which islands would be included in the sale, and how the territory would be transferred.[57] After months of diplomatic wrangling, a treaty between the United States and Denmark was finally signed in Copenhagen on October 24, 1867. It appeared that Seward had added another territory to the United States.

Ratification of the treaty, however, required certain stipulations. Besides the U.S. Senate and the Danish Parliament ratifying the treaty, a plebiscite had to be held and the people of the Danish West Indies had to vote to annex themselves to the United States. The U.S. Congress had recessed and would not reconvene until December, but in the meantime Seward dispatched the Rev. Charles Hawley as a commissioner to oversee the plebiscite, which was scheduled for December.[58] Hawley arrived at Christiansted on St. Croix and planned to meet with a Danish commissioner.[59] But nature intervened. On November 18, 1867, a massive earthquake struck the West Indies and devastated the islands.[60] Fierce hurricanes had already ripped through the region in September.[61] In spite of the damage, the commissioners eventually met and a plebiscite was scheduled for January 1868.

Seward's treaty appeared at a less than auspicious moment. Just as the negotiations had been completed, reports of the massive earthquake were trickling into the United States.[62] Not surprisingly, opponents of the treaty drew upon the same rhetoric that they had used to challenge the purchase of Alaska. The *Milwaukee Daily Sentinel* sarcastically remarked, "We need not be surprised, perhaps, that Mr. Seward, having secured a sufficient supply of icebergs and aurora borealis, should be anxious to make an investment in hurricanes and earthquakes."[63] As with Alaska, the landscape was described as bleak and forbidding: "At frequent intervals the most terrible cyclones visit them and destroy all the shipping and houses, besides causing often great loss of life." If Alaska was a barren and cold wasteland filled with icebergs, the Danish West Indies was a hot and humid land, forever rocked by earthquakes and hurricanes. It appeared that Seward had been swindled yet again.

As usual, the *New York Tribune* crafted the most biting critique. On December 14, 1867, an article entitled "Porter's Pastoral" mocked a letter that Vice Adm. David D. Porter had written in favor of the acquisition. To persuade the Senate about the usefulness of the Danish West Indies, Seward had submitted several letters in support of the treaty.[64] In one letter Admiral Porter had waxed eloquent on the islands' wonders, calling St. Thomas a "Gibraltar" that would be nearly impossible for other nations to conquer. Touting more than military advantages, Porter extolled the beautiful climate. "There is no place where a stranger enjoys himself more than at St. Thomas," he claimed, "and if the island was the property of the United States it would become a popular resort."[65] Porter's missive made it appear that the island was a lush, tropical paradise that would also allow the United States to control the Caribbean.

The *Tribune* did not agree with Porter's assessment.[66] "Since Mr. Seward . . . described the rosy Polar Arcadia," the *Tribune* scoffed, "where the slopes of the icebergs were clad in perpetual verdure and the walrus disported in the flowery meads . . . no more beautiful pastoral poem has been given to the world than the lovely piece which Admiral Porter has just written."[67] A biting piece of satire, the article worked through each of Porter's claims and critiqued them: "Mr. Seward found beauty in the polar bear; Mr. Sumner drew inspiration from train oil, pine trees, and cannibals; and now, amid the rumble of earthquakes, the bellowing of volcanoes, the shriek of the whirlwind, the crash of timbers, and the roar of the angry waters, our sentimental sailor pipes his pastoral notes . . . and makes us a most elegant little song out of the uproar."[68] Doubting that St. Thomas could ever be a resort, the editor asked who would want to live among the earthquakes, volcanoes, and hurricanes? Much like Alaska, it was a place hardly fit for habitation.

Disclaiming any belief in superstition, *Frank Leslie's Illustrated Newspaper* noted that it was odd how disasters had hit territories recently purchased by the United States.[69] Immediately after the United States acquired "Wall-Russia," there came "a storm, the like of which was almost unknown in those high latitudes." When the United States entered into a treaty for the Danish West Indies, "a cyclone swept through it." The point of this article was not to claim that providence had intervened, but rather to provide a hint that perhaps the United States was not purchasing prime real estate. "Plain folks like ourselves," the author pithily noted, "without attaching any supernatural meanings to such a cataclysm, argue from it that St. Thomas is a very good place to be avoided." If Alaska was a bad purchase because of the cold, then why bother to acquire earthquake-prone islands?

Earthquakes, hurricanes, and volcanoes were bad enough, but they could be written off as sporadic events. Yellow fever was a different story. "The surviving inhabitants of St. Thomas who are averse to the sale of the Island to the United States," one paper proclaimed, "and inclined to superstitious feelings, must believe that a judgment has come upon them. . . . For some time they have languished under an unusually fatal plague of yellow fever."[70] These and other reports made it appear that the climate was deadly to Americans who traveled to the region.[71] These accounts appeared even more credible in November 1867 when Rear Adm. James S. Palmer, commander of the North Atlantic Squadron, died of yellow fever at St. Thomas.[72] His death, along with general fears about the climate, allowed opponents of expansion to describe the islands as inhospitable for immigration. As *Frank Leslie's Illustrated Newspaper* put it in 1868, the United States could never establish a colony in a region that was "riven by earthquakes, swept by hurricanes, and pestilent with the yellow fever."[73]

Opponents of expansion soon began to call Seward a real estate broker and the Seward Real Estate Agency became a running joke.[74] Seward had negotiated four treaties in 1867, a Kansas newspaper remarked, and two of them involved acquiring territory.[75] "Nor is there any probability that we have reached the end of this purchasing business," the paper complained, "unless Mr. Seward is made to see that he has not been given carte blanche to buy all creation." This author called upon Congress to see that Seward did not make

WILLIAM THE GLUTTON.

"Why, then, the world's mine oyster.'

BILLY SEWARD—"'Pon my word, my dear gal, this is a monstrous fine oyster—just the thing to give me an appetite."

12. Seward's propensity to gobble up unwanted parcels of real estate is again turned to humorous effect. Having secured the ice of Alaska, he is seen purchasing the windswept Danish West Indies. "William the Glutton," *Frank Leslie's Illustrated Newspaper*, September 28, 1867. From House Divided: The Civil War Research Engine at Dickinson College, http://hd.housedivided.dickinson.edu/node/47474.

more bad bargains. Unless Congress stepped in, Seward would continue to buy up all the unwanted territory that European potentates were willing to pawn.

Commenting on Seward's real estate agency readily segued into jokes about the climate of the Danish West Indies and Alaska. Newspaper articles ridiculed the secretary of state for attempting to buy a windswept land that seemed to be at the mercy of Mother Nature.[76]

"Mr. Seward would do well to examine a little more into his St. Thomas purchase," the *Bangor Daily Whig and Courier* observed. "We cannot afford to buy hurricanes and volcanoes to add to our other internal convulsions."[77] If Seward was a real estate agent, he was a bad one, or so his critics alleged. And nothing pleased them more than to jest about other possible territories to purchase. "Does he propose to give us another sensation by still larger operations in the real estate line?" one paper asked. "Is the dreadful measure of his ambition for the acquisition of National Ice-Houses, Earthquakes and Tornadoes, not yet complete?"[78] This editor recommended that Seward look into buying the land near Mount Vesuvius, as it was only partially buried under ash. As such witticisms erupted, they drove home a simple point; Seward was not an adept expansionist. His only accomplishment had been buying up tracts of land that nobody coveted.

Critics even questioned Seward's mental state. A Kansas editor ran a lengthy article that implied that the hardships that Seward had endured over the course of his life had led him to seek out the advice of spiritualists and astrologers.[79] Although this article was written in a humorous style, it managed to both poke fun at Seward and proffer an explanation for his "land mania." In the story a spirit visited Seward and told him of a buried treasure in Alaska, and so Seward purchased the entire territory. "Next," the story continued, "an astrologer informed him that the fabulous treasures of the pirate Kidd were buried on the island of St. Thomas, and that the stars revealed to him that the year 1868 would witness their recovery. . . . Immediately the purchase of St. Thomas was negotiated . . . under the idea that the prevalent earthquakes and hurricanes were to unearth the treasure." Finally, a necromancer approached Seward and encouraged him to purchase Cuba because it held Henry Morgan's pirate treasures. The editor did not expect readers to believe this story, but it aptly captured the creative ways that individuals mocked Seward for his attempts to purchase territory.[80] Buying earthquakes, hurricanes, and ice was something that only an irrational person would do.

More serious critics also demanded that Seward's schemes be thwarted. In the past most treaties had been negotiated at the behest of the president. The treaties for Alaska and the Danish West Indies were different in that Andrew Johnson had little interest in expanding the nation and spent much of his presidency battling Congress over Reconstruction policy. It would therefore be Congress's job to rein in Seward and end his land deals. "The wholesale real estate business lately entered into by Mr. Seward," one paper noted, "has naturally awakened some inquiring on the point whether there is any way in which to put any check upon his extraordinary proceedings."[81] *Frank Leslie's Illustrated Newspaper* agreed that Seward was abusing his authority as secretary of state and that action was necessary to prevent such overreach in the future.[82] No action was taken against Seward, but many feared that he was setting a dangerous precedent in seizing extraordinary powers for the secretary of state.

Seward's opponents also complained that he was recklessly spending the public's money. It was one thing to buy land that was desirable and fertile, but it was another to dole out large sums for regions that Americans had never coveted. One paper sarcastically observed that Seward desired "more icebergs, used-up whaling grounds, extinct volcanoes and speculative guano beds" so that he could "associate with the polar bear and sport with crocodiles, speculate in ice and pay the national debt in sand and gravel."[83] Given that the United States had emerged from the Civil War with a sizable national debt, many critics questioned whether it was wise for Seward to be spending large sums on his foolish "real estate speculations."[84] "The Secretary wanted to balance his polar investment by a tropical purchase," another paper sardonically explained, "and if he looks around he may yet succeed in his laudable endeavors to get rid of some of the cash which the government is now so overburthened with."[85] Seward was not a great diplomat, these critics alleged, as his only accomplishment was spending inordinate sums of money for territory that would produce nothing valuable in return.[86] It was perhaps wiser to begin paying down the national debt.

As they had with Seward's purchase of Alaska, writers and humorists soon began adding references to the Danish West Indies to their poems, short stories, and letters. One of the most notable letters appeared from "Our Special Correspondent" in the *New York Tribune*. This letter was in fact written by Mark Twain and revolves around the tribulations of his fictional uncle, a man looking for a peaceful spot to settle down and farm. "Could you give me any information respecting such islands, if any, as the Government is going to purchase?" Twain asked. "It is an uncle of mine that wants to know. He is an industrious man, and well-disposed, and wants to make a living in an honest, humble way." Setting up his story in this straightforward way, Twain then delved into his kinsman's recent difficulties. His uncle had landed in St. Thomas, thinking that it might be a nice place to settle down. However, as soon as he arrived his briefcase was stolen.[87] His uncle then came down with the cholera. "He is not a kind of man that enjoys fevers," Twain deadpanned, "though he is well-meaning . . . and so he was a good deal annoyed when it appeared that he was going to die."[88]

The second half of Twain's story relates the troubles that ensued. But the humor derives from two freakish meteorological events. His uncle first settled upon a mountain, which appeared to be a prime piece of real estate. Then a massive earthquake struck. Frustrated but undaunted, he moved to the low ground. Soon a great volcano erupted and tossed his property "2,000 feet in the air." Twain's phlegmatic uncle considered asking the United States government for assistance "but all he wants is quiet, and so he is not going to apply for the subsidy he was thinking about." In the end, Twain's uncle hoped that the United States government would one day purchase real estate with some tangible value.[89]

Twain creatively captured the major arguments against the Danish treaty. Within this short piece he managed to work in disease, earthquakes, and volcanoes. Twain even included a jibe about Alaska. He noted in his concluding paragraph that his uncle "tried Walrussia; but the bears kept after him so much, and kept him so on the jump . . . that he had to leave the country. He could not be quiet there, with those bears prancing after him all the time."[90] Twain deployed his satirical talents to hammer home the point that the United States was spending money on worthless pieces of real estate. Who in their right mind would want to settle down in Walrussia or the island of St. Thomas? What American would want to start up a farm in the frozen fields of Alaska or among the volcanoes of the West Indies?

Much like Corey O'Lanus, Twain's uncle demonstrated that expansion was not necessary.

Mark Twain did not mention Seward, but by 1868 humorists directly targeted the hapless secretary of state.[91] In April 1868 Bret Harte wrote an entire poem that mocked Seward for his purchase of a windswept and desolate island.[92] David Ross Locke, who remained the most famous humorist during the era, also did not mind taking shots at Seward. On March 5, 1869, Locke penned a Nasby letter in which Andrew Johnson said goodbye to his cabinet.[93] As Johnson bade farewell, each cabinet member reacted differently, which allowed Locke to make specific jokes about each one. When it came to Seward, Locke described the situation in the following manner: "Sekretary Seward wuz vizably effected. That afternoon he hed heerd uv a Island for sale, the principal volcano on wich hed mostly stopped gushin, and he wept to think he hedn't time to complete negociashens for it. It wuz offered for $20,000,000, and he considered the price a mere bagatelle." Of all the jokes that could be made about Seward, who had a long and controversial political career, Locke decided to send him off with a dig about his proclivity for purchasing worthless real estate.

Jokes about Seward and his real estate agency soon made it into the halls of Congress. In February 1868 the House of Representatives was discussing "appropriations for the consular and diplomatic expenses of the Government" when John A. Logan, a Republican from Illinois, offered an amendment designed to mock Seward: "That the Secretary of State shall be empowered to appoint some suitable person to become the agent of the United States . . . to at once enter negotiations for the purchase of empires, kingdoms, rebellions, wars, volcanoes, icebergs, snow and rainstorms, earthquakes, or submerged and undiscovered islands."[94] This amendment further required that the agent would be paid in "Russian bears," provided that the agent was able to catch them. More jokes about walruses and icebergs followed before Logan turned to St. Thomas: "Earthquakes at ten dollars each, with a stipulation that they shall not shake our confidence in the State Department."[95]

Although Logan's amendment was not taken seriously, other congressmen peppered their speeches with references to Walrussia, polar

WORTHLESS REAL ESTATE

bears, and the hurricanes and earthquakes of St. Thomas. Republican Benjamin F. Butler of Massachusetts deemed Seward "insane" and called him the only person willing "to buy the earthquakes in St. Thomas and ice-fields in Greenland."[96] Thomas Williams, a Republican from Pennsylvania, objected to an appropriation for the Alaska treaty. "But if the rocks, and icebergs, and volcanoes, and earthquakes of Alaska," he sarcastically argued, "are worth ten millions of our money . . . how much more valuable are the glaciers of Greenland, and the geysers of Iceland in the Atlantic sea."[97] Williams, like many others, believed that the United States was better served by saving its money and improving what it had.[98]

These arguments against the purchase of the Danish West Indies were effective. Even Seward's defenders admitted that the personal attacks had swayed popular opinion. In January 1868 the *Boston Daily Advertiser* defended the secretary of state against his critics, but admitted that his defenders were outnumbered. "Mr. Seward is one of those men who, fortunately or unfortunately," the paper observed, "is believed by the public in general to have a leading part in all that goes on about him, and to have some deep motive for whatever he does."[99] Noting that this was unfair and prejudicial, the paper asked Americans to consider the treaties on their merits. The editor admitted, however, that most people would not do so. "We say that this superstition about the Secretary of State is perhaps unfortunate," the paper continued, "because it happens as a natural result that to pronounce a project 'one of Mr. Seward's schemes' is enough to set half the world on the alert against it." Although exaggerating slightly, the paper captured a crucial point; by 1868 many Americans no longer considered the merits of the treaty so much as they focused on the man who was responsible for it. If William Henry Seward negotiated it, then it had to be a poor bargain.[100]

Unlike the Alaska treaty, which was rammed through within a month, the Danish treaty languished in the Senate. In January 1868 a plebiscite was held and the Danish West Indies voted for annexation, but the Senate refused to act.[101] The treaty was ratified by the Danish parliament and signed by King Christian IX, yet Charles Sumner, chair of the Senate Foreign Relations Committee, held the treaty in committee and refused to allow it to come up for a vote.[102] It seems most likely that Sumner recognized his inability to secure ratification.[103] The Senate never ratified the treaty and so Denmark retained sovereignty of the islands until 1917, when they were sold to the United States for $25 million.

Supporters of the Danish treaty recognized that the environmental argument played a key role in their defeat. Frederick W. Seward, the son of William Henry Seward, admitted as much in a memoir.[104] The younger Seward concluded that the hurricane and earthquake had helped bring down the treaty, writing, "At any other time, perhaps, this natural convulsion would only have excited that interest and commiseration which are roused by the news of a disastrous flood or fire. But in the inflamed state of the public mind it was eagerly seized upon for political effect. Its details, magnified and spread abroad, were used as arguments against the purchase of the islands."[105] If all that Americans knew about the Danish West Indies was that they were likely to be hit by earthquakes and hurricanes, then why purchase them? Like Mark Twain's fictional uncle, they queried whether there was perhaps better territory available for purchase.

Opponents of manifest destiny were thus successful in thwarting Seward's ambitions. They achieved this by focusing on two central arguments. The first was deeply personal. They attacked Seward directly and portrayed him as an insatiable expansionist whose appetite for territory was unmatched. Opponents of manifest destiny had used this technique in the past and had mocked and labeled as dangerous men such as Lewis Cass, James Buchanan, and, of course, Stephen Douglas. Seward was slightly different, however, in that he was an opponent of slavery and a Republican. Old arguments, such as calling a man a doughface or arguing that he wanted to extend the institution of slavery, no longer sufficed. In spite of these difficulties, opponents of manifest destiny managed to craft a caricature of Seward that challenged his ability to carry out his expansionist dreams. Mocking his physique, calling him a failed real estate agent, and joking about Walrussia, polar bears, and earthquakes all created a popular image of a secretary of state who craved expansion, but who was only able to purchase scraps offered by European powers.

Manifest destiny seemed somehow less grandiose when it included Alaska and St. Thomas.

The second argument against expansion would be more enduring, however. In the U.S.-Mexican War, critics had warned that California and New Mexico were deserts unfit for habitation. But the environmental critique had faded from popular use as the United States contemplated the purchase of Cuba, Nicaragua, and northern Mexico. As the areas to be acquired shifted, and as expansionists turned their eyes to colder and then more tropical climes, the environmental critique gained force. After the Civil War opponents of manifest destiny frequently criticized the territory that expansionists sought, and they continued to do so after Seward had left office. To cite one example of this, in 1871 a magazine joked, "The most earnest annexationists had recently had their enthusiasm frozen by the icebergs of Alaska." It then quipped that "during the discussion of the proposition to annex St. Thomas the ardor of the most liberal extensionists had cooled as suddenly as the lava of its volcanoes, and their faith had been shaken as violently as was the island by its earthquakes."[106] Picturing regions as unfit for habitation became a standard argument for opponents of manifest destiny.

Part of the reason for the environmental critique's success was that it built upon the idea, stressed by Whigs in the 1840s, that the United States already controlled the most valuable land in North America. Henry Clay and Daniel Webster had both argued during the U.S.-Mexican War that expansion was unnecessary because the United States had all the natural resources that it would ever need. By the 1860s opponents of manifest destiny returned to the idea that the United States controlled the most habitable land in North America. Territories to the north, such as Alaska and Canada, were too cold, and additions from the south, such as St. Thomas, were too warm and liable to be hit with extreme weather. This critique forced proponents of expansion to explain why the territories they wished to acquire were valuable. Certainly, the environmental argument was not always effective, but it did help stifle expansion in the immediate aftermath of the Civil War.[107] Ultimately, it forced William Henry Seward to abandon his dream of establishing a continental empire.

7

Destiny's Demise

The Racial Critique of Manifest Destiny, 1868–1872

In April 1869 Charles W. Willard, a Vermont Republican, warned his colleagues in the House of Representatives that manifest destiny had not yet been defeated. "The lust for territory seems yet to possess others than Mr. Seward," Willard proclaimed, "and real estate operations and projects for annexation, if they abandoned the State Department, did not leave all branches of the Government with the late Secretary." Although the United States had elected a new president in 1868, Willard still worried that the Ulysses S. Grant administration would seek to expand the country's borders. "The 'manifest destiny' men still live," Willard announced, "and although our flag does not yet fully protect or give free government to all upon our own soil, they would run our boundaries beyond the limits of the unsettled and fighting populations of the West Indies and the turbulent factions of Mexico, and would make American citizens alike of the Esquimaux toward the north pole and the naked natives of the tropics." If Republicans were not careful, Willard admonished, they would find themselves embroiled in a host of international difficulties. It was wiser to fix the problems at home instead of turning their eyes abroad.[1]

Willard recognized that the retirement of William Henry Seward did not mark the end of manifest destiny. Indeed, his words proved to be somewhat prophetic, as Ulysses S. Grant turned his attention to expansion and lobbied for the annexation of the Dominican Republic. To challenge this rising expansionist sentiment, opponents of manifest destiny turned to a racial critique of expansion.

As Willard warned of the "turbulent factions of Mexico" and the "naked natives of the tropics," other opponents of manifest destiny cautioned against extending rights to "unruly" Dominicans. Opponents of annexing the Dominican Republic considered Dominicans lazy, unsophisticated, and unworthy of citizenship. In speech after speech opponents focused on race and compared the people of the Dominican Republic unfavorably with Cubans. Grant entered office believing that he could potentially bring about the fulfillment of manifest destiny, but he was unable to get Congress to accept the Dominican Republic. His failure to maneuver a treaty through the Senate effectively ended the dream of manifest destiny.

By 1868 critics of expansion were well-versed in using racial appeals. During the U.S.-Mexican War opponents of manifest destiny had railed against the "mixed-race" people of Mexico, whom they deemed unfit for citizenship.[2] More recently, opponents of manifest destiny had raised the specter of race over the Alaskan purchase. Critics of the Russian treaty often jested about the polar bears and ice, but they had also derided Alaska Natives.[3] In 1867 William Mungen, a Democratic congressman from Ohio, confidently told his fellow congressmen, "The Fins and Laps and Esquimaux are all dark skinned men, the latter nearly black."[4] If the United States continued to expand, he warned, then it would directly lead to "a hybrid race—a set of mongrels, mulattoes, crosses between Chinese, Esquimaux, whites, mulattoes, Indians, half-breeds, and nondescripts."[5] It was far better, Mungen asserted, to arrest the growth of the United States and develop the nation by internal improvements.

Throughout the debates on Alaskan annexation, opponents regularly compared the Indigenous peoples of the region to barbarians and savages. "In the Russian American question," one paper quipped, "the shabbiest item is the native people."[6] It then observed, "This race of train-oil eaters seems to have followed the Arctic circle around the globe." The drinking of train oil and the eating of tallow candles, another stereotype that became a punchline, seemed to be proof that these were an inferior people unworthy of annexation to the United States.[7] The *Daily Courier*, a Kentucky paper, sarcastically noted, "Before this splendid purchase our population was not of suffi-

WHAT WE MAY LOOK FOR SOON.

"The Hon. Tookooloto Jabinkoker, Delegate from the Kodiak District of the former Russian Possessions, arrived yesterday from New Archangel. He dined at Delmonico's, and ordered the repast in the *haute cuisine* of Kodiak: train oil for two; tallow candles for one; whale blubber for one (but substituted raw pork, as the other was not to be had); asked for a seal's fin, but took India-rubber, *faute de mieux*, with a glass of spirits of turpentine; wanted a rat in an advanced state of decomposition, but had to put up with a bad egg."

13. Those opposed to expansion often mocked nonwhites for their alleged dietary preferences. In this instance, a delegate from Alaska shocks the patrons at Delmonico's with his order. "What We May Look for Soon," *Harper's Weekly Magazine*, May 4, 1867. From House Divided: The Civil War Research Engine at Dickinson College, http://hd.housedivided.dickinson.edu/node/46514.

cient variety, consisting only of white men, Indians, negroes and Chinese; now we have the addition of a Slavonic-Esquimau population, extraordinarily proficient in the consumption of train oil."[8] Mocking the eating and drinking habits of the Indigenous population made the larger point that Alaska Natives would not be good citizens.[9]

Often this critique led to sarcastic warnings about the specter of

OUR NEW SENATORS.

SECRETARY SEWARD—"*My dear Mr. Kamskatca, you really must dine with me. I have some of the very finest tallow candles and the loveliest train oil you ever tasted, and my whale's blubber is exquisite— and pray bring your friend Mr. Seal along with you. The President will be one of the party.*"

14. Opponents of expansion frequently objected to a Senate that included nonwhites. Here, the new senators from Alaska are introduced to Seward and Johnson. "Our New Senators," *Frank Leslie's Illustrated Newspaper*, April 27, 1867. From House Divided: The Civil War Research Engine at Dickinson College, http://hd.housedivided.dickinson.edu/node/46381.

darker-hued representatives being sent to Congress. The *Daily Courier*, for instance, followed up its remarks about train oil with facetious commentary on Indigenous representation in Congress.[10] "We do not know," the writer concluded, "whether our new domain is to go through a territorial pupilage. . . . Nor are we advised whether Congress contemplates the admission of grizzlies to the right of suffrage." It then deadpanned, "Esquimaux nor grizzlies being in any manner connected with the rebellion . . . it is probable they will be allowed at once to send Senators and Representatives to Washing-

DESTINY'S DEMISE

ton."[11] Another newspaper mockingly looked forward to the day when "Mr. Ewee-ta-oke-toke, of Tschutskoi" and "Mr. Kei-seukke-poke, of Oonalaski" sat in Congress.[12] If African Americans were granted the vote, then why not the Indigenous population within Alaska? Opponents of manifest destiny believed that racial fears could help block expansionist schemes.

Humorists also jested about the Indigenous population. In his letter dealing with the Alaska purchase, comedian John Stanton cast aspersions on Alaska Natives. "The population is of mixed descent," he jibed, "like that of the Eastern States. The principal races are Esquimaux, Seals, Russians, Bears and Walruses."[13] After assuring his readers that Russians loved to eat "fried candles," Stanton argued that the annexation would boost the economy. "The annexation to the States," he promised, "of so large a candle consuming population would create a revival in the trade."[14] Stanton not only derived humor from the dietary preferences of the Indigenous population but he also quipped about voting rights. Foreseeing a day when the franchise would be granted to the "seals and walruses," he mused, "Barnum's learned seal might be one of the first Senators sent to Washington."[15] Stanton's jokes were hardly original, but they demonstrate the manner in which certain lines of argument seeped into popular culture.

These jokes about Native Alaskans appeared simultaneously with a presidential election. In July 1868, the same month that the House voted to approve funds for the Alaska purchase, Democrats nominated Horatio Seymour of New York as their candidate for the presidency.[16] The Democratic platform said nothing about foreign policy and instead lambasted "the Radical party for its disregard of right."[17] Democrats focused on Reconstruction and hoped to win the election by portraying Republicans as tyrants who were trampling upon the Constitution. Republicans unanimously selected the war hero Ulysses S. Grant on the first ballot at their convention in Chicago. Republicans did have a plank that expressed "sympathy with all the oppressed people . . . struggling for their rights," but they largely ignored foreign policy.[18] Like the Democrats, Republicans focused their attention on domestic issues.

Neither Republicans nor Democrats officially embraced expansion in 1868, but proponents of manifest destiny still cast their eyes abroad. Many expansionists continued to covet Mexico, believing that the French intervention had prepared the way for a U.S. take-over.[19] "There are other kinds of fillibustering than those accompanied by drums and muskets," a paper in Wyoming observed, "and the manifest destiny of Mexico is to be peaceably absorbed by the United States."[20] Even the *Richmond Dispatch*, which had mocked manifest destiny throughout the Civil War as a Yankee innovation, anticipated the annexation of Mexico and admitted that it was "the manifest destiny of [the] Republic to have '*provinces*.'"[21] Editors continued to write about the eventual spread of the United States over the continent of North America.[22] "Whether it be called manifest destiny or inordinate ambition," one journal stated, "this much seems to be certain, that if the sense of the people were taken at any time in regard to the acquisition of any new territory—whether it were Alaska or St. Thomas or Cuba or Porto Rico or Canada or Greenland—the chances would be in favor of an affirmative vote."[23] Expansionists continued to believe in manifest destiny, in spite of the seeming ambivalence of the two major parties.

Grant's victory intensified such dreams of empire. In April 1869 the Democratic *New York World* proclaimed, "President Grant has a definite policy for the future—a policy bold, ambitious, and which may involve war."[24] As a military leader, Grant had favored bold action during the Civil War and would likely continue to do so. "The hints of his executive advisers, the statements of persons known to be in his confidence," the paper continued, "and the actual facts of his administration which are publicly or partially known, indicate that the new President has resolved to signalize his career by the acquisition—if this be possible—of all North America to the dominion of one American government!" The *New York World* did not support Grant, and would turn into one of his sharpest critics, but it suspected he was an expansionist at heart.[25]

The *New York Herald* hoped that the *World's* prediction would prove accurate and claimed, "[The] opportunity offered to General Grant for the extension of the boundaries of the nation . . . is without a precedent in American history, and without a comparison in the records of the human race."[26] Always given to hyperbole, the *Herald* detected opportunity where others saw problems. It predicted that Cuba would soon fall into U.S. hands; intervention in Mexico to restore "law and order" was likely inevitable. Soon, Canada would willingly link up with the United States. "We rely, however, upon the progressive ideas, sagacity and moral courage of General Grant," the article concluded, "sustained by the general drift of public opinion, in our expectations of a foreign policy which offers not only the Continent for our occupation, but its boundless resources from which to meet our national debt." In the eyes of the *Herald*, Grant was the ideal man to usher in this new phase of manifest destiny.

Such territorial acquisitions would presumably be popular.[27] "It is idle to conceal the fact that the great body of the American people are in favor of an increased extension of territory," a paper in South Carolina announced, before concluding that Canada and Cuba were ready to join the United States.[28] According to a correspondent for the *Cleveland Herald*, Grant had his eyes on Canada and Americans expected him to complete the "ocean-bound republic." "Every addition to our territory has proved popular with the people," the correspondent observed, "and disastrous to the party or politicians who were short sighted enough to oppose it."[29] Enthusiastic editors revisited the history of U.S. expansion, leaving out the struggles that had occurred over Louisiana, Texas, Mexico, and Cuba. Based on this retelling of history, expansionists portrayed annexation as a reliable way for a president to ensure both his popularity and his place in history.

Many individuals, however, did not forget how divisive expansion had been in the past and warned that adding territory would endanger the United States. A Philadelphia newspaper commented that expansion was unnecessary because the United States already covered "the choicest section of the continent."[30] After briefly mocking William Henry Seward for having "been bitten with the annexation mania," the author looked at Mexico, Cuba, and the West Indies and pointed out that white men could not survive in those environments. More importantly, if the United States annexed these territories, it would acquire unruly citizens: "They are already inhabited by turbulent races that have never been able to govern themselves or to develop their resources, and to keep these in subjection, at least until our political ascendency was secured by a large increase of the Anglo-Saxon race in their midst, would be a difficulty of the first magnitude." To opponents of manifest destiny, there was nothing to be gained but problems by annexing Cuba, Mexico, or the Danish West Indies.

As the merits of manifest destiny were being debated, Grant set in motion his plans for acquiring the Dominican Republic, then called Santo Domingo.[31] Seward had attempted to acquire Samaná Bay, the central port of Santo Domingo, while he was trying to buy the Danish West Indies.[32] Political instability, coupled with the willingness of Denmark to part with its portion of the West Indies, caused Seward to abandon the plans for Santo Domingo. Upon taking office, Grant scrapped the Danish treaty and instead fixated on Santo Domingo.[33] Grant dispatched his personal secretary, Orville Babcock, as a special agent to investigate the nation. The timing was propitious, as Buenaventura Báez had recently returned to power as president.[34] Báez was a noted proponent of annexation and more than willing to negotiate with the United States.[35]

Negotiations took up half a year, but in November 1869 the two sides reached an agreement.[36] Shortly thereafter, President Grant sent the treaty to the Senate.[37] The debate on the Santo Domingo treaty dragged into 1871, engaging both the Senate and the broader public. The struggle over Santo Domingo revived older questions about expansionism and helped fracture the Republican Party.[38] With the possible exception of the earlier debate over Texas, Santo Domingo was the most fiercely contested annexation scheme of the mid-nineteenth century. Both sides hauled out their most powerful rhetorical guns and the outcome was far from certain.

Proponents of the treaty listed several reasons why annexing Santo Domingo was beneficial. In December 1869 Grant wrote a memorandum that explained his reasons for pursuing annexation. Grant described the place as "an island of unequaled fertility," capable of producing timber, coffee, sugar, and fruit. It had a strategic location in the Caribbean. Furthermore, if the United States refused to annex the island, then a European power was more than likely

DESTINY'S DEMISE

to seize the prize. Location, the fecundity of the soil, and the fear of European encroachment were all traditional reasons that expansionists had used in the past. In his final paragraph, however, Grant turned to a broader argument: "Its acquisition is carrying out Manifest destiny. It is a step towards claring [*sic*] . . . all European flags from this Continent. Can any one favor rejecting so valuable a gift who voted $7.200.000 for the icebergs of Alasca?"[39] In this hastily scribbled memorandum, replete with misspellings and repetitions, Grant never explained what he meant by "carrying out Manifest destiny." But it seems clear that he saw Santo Domingo as part of a larger project of expansion.

The *Herald* unsurprisingly became one of the strongest supporters of the treaty. In January 1870 a lengthy article downplayed the dangers of annexation and recounted its glorious history. Events were aligning to fulfill the dream of manifest destiny, as the "revolution in Cuba," uprisings in Canada, and turmoil in Mexico were preparing the way for the United States to acquire the continent.[40] After explaining how the wheels of history were already in motion, the paper boldly proclaimed: "Manifest destiny is not a mere sentiment, but a fact." Throughout the rest of the year, it continued to praise Grant's Santo Domingo treaty.[41] In June 1870 the paper explained how the annexation of Santo Domingo would enable the United States to acquire Cuba and would then allow for the acquisition of "the awaiting States of Mexico and Central America."[42] The *Herald* saw Santo Domingo as a fine appetizer to the main course of manifest destiny.

Opponents of manifest destiny, however, dismissed any notion that the United States would benefit from annexing Santo Domingo. As soon as the treaty was introduced, denunciations of both the land and its inhabitants appeared. "The people don't want to buy any more real estate at present," a writer for the *Milwaukee Daily Sentinel* concluded, "and as for the half-civilized, bigoted and turbulent Dominicans, we have enough fellow's [*sic*] of that description to take care of already."[43] The *Brooklyn Eagle* estimated that the vast majority of newspapers opposed Grant's foreign policy.[44] And for good reason, as the Santo Domingo treaty was "a proposition of something for nothing—of millions of the people's money for a territory of which the inhabitants [were] barbarians by nature, and thieves and cutthroats by practice." The *Eagle's* assessment of the Dominican people was widespread. Many papers hurled racial slurs and derided Dominicans as an unruly people.[45] "To all intents and purposes they are barbarians," a paper in Kansas concluded, "having learned the vices of the whites and none of their virtues. The Dominicans are as ignorant of the science of self-government as the Hottentots, and . . . are not disposed to recognize any constituted authority which goes counter to their whims and caprices."[46] Opponents of the treaty sought to stir up racial fears.

Congressmen soon chimed in on this racist critique. In February 1870 Fernando Wood, a former mayor of New York and notorious copperhead during the war, pointedly asked, "What will posterity say of the proceedings of these times? What will be the verdict of impartial history. . . . It will record of us how a great people sought to degrade themselves; how a nation possessing all the attributes of superiority over other nations, not content with this supremacy, willingly adulterated its own blood, demoralized its own elevation, and by negro amalgamation contaminated its own purity of race."[47] Wood applied racist stereotypes of African Americans to the people of Santo Domingo. His words spat contempt: "I can conceive of no people so depressed in the scale of humanity as those of San Domingo. They are the product of the lower order of Spaniard with the negro in a semi-barbarous condition, a cross between the African savage and the more debased descendant of the blood-thirsty West Indian creole." If the United States annexed Santo Domingo, Wood feared, posterity would remember it as being the moment when the nation began its precipitous decline.

Some senators picked up these same arguments. Perhaps the most noted opponent of the treaty, apart from Charles Sumner, was Carl Schurz. Although debates on the treaty occurred in closed session, newspapers did report on the substance of the speeches. The *New York Tribune* told readers that Schurz "held that the proposed annexation would only bring another element of trouble into [the U.S.] political and social system. . . . These people, like the people of Mexico and the other Spanish colonies, had thoroughly demonstrated their incapacity for self-government. Their whole history was a history of revolutions."[48] Schurz further alleged that Dominicans "were immoral, vicious, and lazy."[49] Schurz brought up a variety of reasons to oppose annexation and did not merely rely upon the racial critique. But he stated emphatically that he would not vote to ratify the treaty.[50]

Many Republicans agreed with Schurz. Grant had entered office believing that he could avoid Seward's errors and successfully handle the Senate. He was mistaken. The bill to annex Santo Domingo came up for a vote on June 30, 1870 and was rejected 28–28.[51] All nine Democrats who were present voted against the treaty, but Republican defections destroyed the measure. Twenty-eight Republicans voted in favor of annexing Santo Domingo, but nineteen Republicans voted in opposition. Previous annexation measures, including Texas, had been partisan affairs; never before had a party split to such an extent over adding territory. In its postmortem analysis of the vote, the *Herald* remarked, "It is a little curious that the democrats, who have always been annexationists, should have voted against the treaty. Probably they do not like the negro element in St. Domingo, and they may have opposed the treaty because it was an administration measure and on party grounds."[52] The *Herald* frankly admitted that it had expected more Republicans to vote yes. It hoped that Grant would try to annex Santo Domingo through a joint resolution.

Many newspapers rejoiced over the treaty's failure. "The Senate yesterday earned the thanks of the whole people by rejecting the San Domingo treaty," the *Chicago Tribune* gloated.[53] It then described Dominicans as "ignorant, idle, shiftless, [and] revengeful" and blamed them for being in a constant state of revolution. Some papers scoffed at Grant for being unable to get his pet measure through a Republican Senate.[54] Others compared his failure to Seward's recent treaty defeat.[55] Many Republican papers were not exactly saddened by the Senate's action. The *Milwaukee Daily Sentinel* credited Grant for his honest intentions but feared "the adoption of a general policy of territorial extension, and the attempt to assimilate unhomogenous populations."[56] The *New York Tribune* did not regret the treaty's failure: "We accept the vote as a declaration by the Senate of its hostility, not to the Administration . . . but to the premature and dangerous tendency of the country to swallow up adjacent lands and foreign peoples."[57]

In spite of a stinging defeat, Grant refused to let the issue go. Over the next year, Grant continued to press Republicans to annex Santo Domingo.[58] Wielding his considerable power within the Republican Party, Grant managed to get Charles Sumner, the man he blamed for blocking the treaty, removed from his position on the Senate Foreign Relations Committee.[59] Grant recalled John Lothrop Motley, his minister to the United Kingdom, who had been appointed at Sumner's request.[60] He also had Congress dispatch a special commission to investigate the worth of Santo Domingo. The committee included Frederick Douglass, a noted proponent of annexation, as an assistant secretary to the three commissioners.[61] Not surprisingly, when the special commission released its report, it was highly favorable to annexation. And so the debate continued over the value of Santo Domingo and the desirability of adding it to the United States.

Expansionists remained sanguine that Grant would eventually prevail. A Pennsylvania newspaper predicted that the commissioners' report would spur the annexation of Santo Domingo, which would then trigger the acquisition of Haiti, Jamaica, and Cuba. "Once in possession of these," the editor enthused, "will not 'manifest destiny' urge us on to the acquisition of all the other West India islands, and finally to the acquisition and incorporation into the Union of Mexico and all the States of South and Central America."[62] The rejection of the San Domingo treaty was a temporary setback, which Grant would soon overcome. A Kansas newspaper depicted the president as a strong proponent of manifest destiny: "General Grant was a Democrat when 'Manifest Destiny' was its popular outcry. He has not forgotten that early impulse, and is now changing Republicans to Democrats, Democrats to Republicans in the pursuit of this cherished purpose."[63] Annexation might be a dubious undertaking, but Grant would ram the annexation of Santo Domingo through the Senate, thanks to his personal popularity. Even after the events of 1870, expansionists remained hopeful that Grant would successfully annex Santo Domingo and then move on to other projects.[64]

Opponents of manifest destiny, however, kept up the fight. In April

1871 William Lloyd Garrison, the famous abolitionist, challenged Grant's judgment on Santo Domingo.[65] After laying out the reasons why annexing Santo Domingo would not economically benefit the United States, Garrison ripped into manifest destiny. "If there be a phrase which excites my special abhorrence," he wrote in his inimitable prose, "it is that of 'manifest destiny.' In the past it has been the slogan of filibusters, Southern slave speculators, and landgrabbing adventurers generally. . . . Good men should not soil their lips or their paper by using it approvingly." Garrison was disheartened to see the phrase emerge as a justification for the Santo Domingo purchase. Garrison saw Grant's project as part of a larger scheme, warning, "'Manifest destiny' means, as the first step, the acquisition of San Domingo; next Hayti; next Cuba; next the West India Islands . . . next Mexico; next the South American republics." If leaders did not rise to block the acquisition of Santo Domingo, Grant would be allowed to demand annexation after annexation until manifest destiny was fulfilled.

Garrison did not base his critique of manifest destiny upon race, but many opponents of the Santo Domingo treaty did. Noted journalist Donn Piatt denounced the annexation scheme in no uncertain terms.[66] "We have had the negro crowded down our throats sugar-coated," he bemoaned. "But we are not exactly prepared to go crazy upon the subject of this proposition to admit, by resolution, a State made up of barbarians black as the ace of spades and ignorant as horses, to say nothing of the cruelty and beastly practices peculiar to the race in that condition."[67] Why Grant insisted on annexing Dominicans baffled Piatt. A Georgia editor agreed that Dominicans were incapable of civilization.[68] Adding such voters to the United States was unthinkable to this paper, which also protested against allowing African Americans voting rights. If African Americans should not be allowed to vote, then why would the United States annex a territory and provide those citizens with the franchise?

It was not merely disgruntled southerners who used race as a reason to reject Santo Domingo. *Frank Leslie's Illustrated Newspaper*, a popular New York newspaper, became one of the strongest voices opposing the treaty. When the treaty was first announced in early

1870, the paper ran a somewhat favorable article on Santo Domingo, dwelling on the pleasant climate and the cheerful, if lazy, Dominicans. "The inhabitants, although, like those of all tropical countries, indolent and inefficient," it observed, "are a docile, tractable people, remarkably free from crime and vice."[69] By the ensuing year, however, *Frank Leslie's Illustrated Newspaper* had changed its opinion. Writing in January 1871, it described those same "docile" and "tractable" Dominicans as "a mongrel population," who spoke "a different language," and who had "a different religion, different civil and social organizations."[70] It argued that the incorporation of such people would endanger the safety and stability of the United States. As the country struggled with what to do with recently freed African Americans in the South, *Frank Leslie's* opposed adding a "mongrel" population.[71]

Frank Leslie's based much its opposition to the treaty on racial fears. In March 1871 it repeated the assertion that Dominicans were unworthy of citizenship, calling them "as ignorant, careless or reckless as African savages." It alleged, "Their natural political condition is that of anarchy, more or less pronounced." After labeling the people of Santo Domingo barbarians and savages, the article's author argued that the annexation of Santo Domingo would lead to the annexation of Haiti—the other half of the island of Hispaniola—and that would be even worse: "Its population of about 800,000 is wholly negro, and is turbulent, lawless, ignorant and debased to the last degree."[72] Annexing Santo Domingo with its 200,000 citizens and Haiti with its 800,000 would lead the United States into acquiring one million "savages" who would greatly weaken the United States. Such was the logic of the popular *Frank Leslie's*. Its racial animus was hardly hidden.

Congressmen amplified these arguments. James Robinson McCormick, a Missouri Democrat, considered it impractical to develop tropical countries without slavery. "As soon as it became a free country," he observed of Santo Domingo, "the inhabitants, of their own volition, retrograded to a state of semi-barbarism."[73] McCormick opposed annexing Santo Domingo because it would be impossible to civilize Dominicans and get them to work. Fernando Wood of New York delivered another lengthy speech explaining that although Democrats had traditionally supported annexation, they had never contemplated annexing a people who were of a "degraded and utterly abandoned character."[74] Wood's colleague from New York, Samuel S. Cox, also defended the Democratic Party from the charge of opposing the treaty on partisan grounds. Cox, who had a well-deserved reputation as an expansionist, argued that he opposed annexation "because it [was] a corrupt, specious, prearranged device and jobbery." Yet in the same speech, Cox also called Dominicans "idle, turbulent, unproductive, and worthless."[75] Even when Democrats tried to distance themselves from racist arguments, it remained evident that they feared granting citizenship to nonwhites.

The objections of McCormick, Cox, and Wood were unimportant, insofar as the Democratic Party did not have the votes to block annexation. What mattered was that many Republicans continued to disparage Santo Domingo and Dominicans. In January John Franklin Farnsworth, an Illinois Republican, claimed to have "no objection to expansion in the direction of the people who speak a common language and whose laws are derived from a common source."[76] Dominicans did not fit these criteria because they were "a motley mixture of French, Spanish, and other Europeans, with Indians, savages, and negroes from every part of western Africa."[77] In the Senate Carl Schurz again denounced manifest destiny and warned his colleagues that it would be dangerous for the United States to acquire southern regions. Schurz agreed with Charles Sumner: "The tropics should belong to the colored race . . . let them cultivate that soil in freedom; let them be happy there."[78] As the United States was large enough, there was no need to annex Santo Domingo.

In the Senate Schurz became the foremost critic of manifest destiny and explained in detail why he believed that its fulfillment would lead to the "doom" of the United States. "Imagine 'manifest destiny' to have swallowed up Mexico also," Schurz explained, "and you will not be able to stop when you are once on the inclined plane." Schurz then continued, "And then fancy ten or twelve tropical States added to the southern States we already possess; fancy the Senators and Representatives of ten or twelve millions of tropical people, people of the Latin race mixed with Indian and African blood; people who . . . have neither language, nor traditions, nor habits, nor political institutions, nor morals in common with us."[79] Schurz pondered whether his colleagues in the Senate would be comfortable with nonwhite colleagues who spoke a different language. If not, then they should leave Santo Domingo alone.

Many of Schurz's Republican colleagues advanced similar arguments. In April 1871 Justin Morrill opposed annexation, arguing, "The people of Dominica are confessedly in the lowest state of poverty, and must remain so forever, because they will not work."[80] In his speech Morrill unleashed a torrent of insults against Dominicans, calling them lazy, priest-ridden, and uneducated. Morrill wanted nothing to do with a people whom he saw as "reeking in filth and laziness . . . who never invented anything nor comprehended the use of the inventions of others."[81] Morrill advanced several reasons for opposing annexation, but racial animosity stood out. Like so many other Republicans, he refused to support Grant's project.

Periodicals reinforced these arguments in both text and illustrations. The widely read magazine *Harper's Weekly* denounced Dominicans for their "ignorance and barbarism" and opposed annexation.[82] As the debate over annexation raged, the magazine, not coincidentally, ran a series of four "Character Sketches in San Domingo and Hayti," depicting scenes from the island of Hispaniola. These racist caricatures include a bombastically dressed general, a bedraggled soldier standing at attention, and one entitled "Visiting in High Life" that mocks a poor family for its social pretensions. The characters all lack adequate clothing or go barefoot and are drawn in such a way as to amuse white readers.[83] These "humorous" depictions aligned with the editorial stance of the magazine and supported *Harper's Weekly*'s argument that Dominicans were unworthy of annexation. This popular magazine found it amusing that Grant would even consider turning Dominicans into citizens of the United States.[84]

Other humorists also ridiculed Grant for attempting to make Santo Domingo part of the United States. *Frank Leslie's Budget of Fun* devoted an issue to Grant and Santo Domingo. The cover page depicts Grant holding hands with a dark-skinned, barefoot woman named

Miss Domingo.[85] A Black Cupid is shown in the upper-right corner, who has shot Grant with an arrow to make him fall in love with Miss Domingo. The caption underneath the image reads, "My dear Miss Domingo, I have always had a sneaking liking for you, but now cupid has quite done the business! Never mind what granny Sumner says, 'We may be happy yet!'" Equating Grant's desire to annex Santo Domingo with amorous affection toward a dark-skinned woman demonstrated the pervasiveness of the racial argument against manifest destiny.

In the same issue, *Frank Leslie's Budget of Fun* ran several additional cartoons that relied heavily upon the racial critique of expansion. Perhaps the most notable was a cartoon that contrasted Santo Domingo with Cuba. In this image there is a building labeled "United States" that has a window. A woman, who represents Cuba, stands outside of the door and knocks alongside a sign that reads "Manifest Destiny." A pair of hands extend out the window and grab a Dominican man, who is remonstrating against forcible annexation. There could be no mistaking the point. Cuba, depicted as a white woman, is anxious to join the United States. Cuba is a part of the manifest destiny of the United States. In contrast, the darker-skinned Dominican, who does not want annexation, is being pulled into the United States. Cartoons such as this contrasted the valuable island of Cuba with the worthless island of Hispaniola. The key difference between the two islands was the people.[86]

Although the commission sent to Santo Domingo returned a favorable report, Grant was unable to revive a movement to pass the treaty. The dream of annexation, which had burned so brightly at the beginning of Grant's term, faded. Renominated by the Republican Party, Grant easily won reelection.[87] But Grant's dream of obtaining Santo Domingo had been buried. The Republican platform in 1872 made no mention of Santo Domingo, offering instead a largely meaningless plank stating: "[The United States] should seek to maintain honorable peace with all nations, protecting its citizens everywhere, and sympathizing with all people who strive for greater liberty."[88] Republicans were unwilling to become the party of manifest destiny. So were Democrats, who offered a single plank on foreign policy, stating that it was "the duty of the Government, in its intercourse with foreign nations, to cultivate the friendships of peace by treating with all on fair and equal terms."[89] In 1872 neither party was willing to take up the burden of manifest destiny.

Most expansionists recognized that the election of 1872 had driven the final nail in the coffin of manifest destiny. In contrast to other presidential elections, which had triggered renewed calls for territory, astute observers understood that Grant would no longer press the issue. Shortly after Grant's reelection, the *New York Herald* published a lengthy examination of U.S. expansion, beginning with the Louisiana Purchase and moving through the acquisition of Alaska. The author averred that most of these annexation projects had been popular, but that Seward's blunders had turned the nation against manifest destiny. "Then from this arctic and this tropical adventure there was a reaction," the author explained, "and it was made manifest in the significant opposition to General Grant's fascinating St. Domingo scheme. The people began to inquire, 'If we annex all these outside barbarians, what can we do with them?'" The *Herald* believed that the failures of Seward and Grant, and especially the racial questions revolving around the Santo Domingo purchase, had soured white Americans on the idea of expansion and signified "that the fever of annexation has died out."[90]

Not only did the *New York Herald* believe that Americans were tired of territorial expansion, but it explicitly denounced manifest destiny. Ignoring how it had lavished praise upon Seward for his manifest destiny views a mere two years before, the paper bashed him for his purchases and hoped that they taught Americans a valuable lesson.[91] "Our white bear of Alaska has proved a white elephant," it observed, "but he will pay for his keeping if we profit from his instructions and go no further after this will-o'-the-wisp of 'manifest destiny.'" Calling manifest destiny a will-o'-the-wisp was only the beginning. "Let us suppose that we have annexed the Canadas and British Columbia and Cuba and St. Domingo and Mexico and Central America," the *Herald* continued, "for this is the manifest destiny of Mr. Seward— and let us suppose that all these countries and peoples, to the number of thirty or forty new States and Territories, are represented in Congress, what would follow?"[92] The paper then answered its own question, suggesting that the resulting confusion would be akin to the tower of Babel and that "such a congress of lunatics could not hold together." The paper that had seriously proposed that Lincoln unleash his armies to conquer Canada and Mexico now argued that manifest destiny was evil. "We want no more annexations," the *Herald* concluded, "our country is large enough."[93] In the space of a single year, the *New York Herald* had switched camps to become one of the leading opponents of manifest destiny.[94]

The defection of the *New York Herald* represented a broader trend, as few believers remained. The *Democratic Review* had folded in 1859, still anxiously anticipating the day when the United States would swarm over the continent. Stephen Douglas had died suddenly in 1861 at the age of forty-eight, upon which the Democratic Party abandoned territorial expansion and dropped Cuban annexation from its platform. Republican proponents of manifest destiny hardly fared better than their Democratic counterparts. Seward and Grant proved remarkably unsuccessful at convincing their own party and struggled to maneuver treaties through the Senate. Seward's death in 1872, coupled with the editorial about-face of the *New York Herald*, deprived manifest destiny of its foremost champions.

Not everyone abandoned the dream of manifest destiny. Indeed, individuals continued to anticipate the fulfillment of manifest destiny for the next fifty years. One Louisiana paper observed in 1875, "It seems to be a prevalent opinion, a fixed idea, with a numerous class of American citizens that the Republic of the United States is of necessity bound, forced, and obligated and compelled to expand her boundary lines until they shall be made to embrace all of North and South America and the neighboring islands."[95] This paper went on to discuss the possible annexation of Canada, Cuba, and Mexico. In 1883 the *Washington Post* declared itself firmly in favor of manifest destiny, noting, "The belief is general that it is the destiny of this Republic to extend its area until it embraces the entire continent."[96] As they had in the past, expansionists read international events as evidence of manifest destiny's rapidly approaching fulfillment. "With a rebellion impending in Canada and an insurrection in Cuba," a paper in Minnesota claimed in 1887, "it only needs a revolution in Mexico to complete this country's opportunity to annex to it all the territory that Destiny has decreed to be embraced within the limits of the American republic. It is coming, Destiny is manifesting itself."[97] Although the *New York Herald* no longer stumped on behalf of manifest destiny, other organs picked up the traditional refrain.

These expansionists did not believe that manifest destiny had been "fulfilled" or "realized" in the nineteenth century. As they had since the 1840s, expansionists defined manifest destiny as the belief that the United States would be one with the continent of North America. "The manifest destiny of the people of the United States is to acquire, have and hold every square mile of territory on the North American continent," an Ohio paper announced.[98] Speakers who stood up and proclaimed their belief in the doctrine of manifest destiny spoke of acquiring the entire continent.[99] "We believe in the doctrine of Monroe, and in our manifest destiny," another paper declared. "One day this whole continent will be ours."[100] Even after the United States had gone to war with Spain over Cuba in 1898, papers still concluded, "'Manifest destiny' marks the West Indies, Mexico and Canada for our own."[101] Up through the early twentieth century, some anticipated the fulfillment of manifest destiny.[102]

In spite of the expansionists' lingering optimism, Grant's attempt to annex Santo Domingo torpedoed whatever limited chance the United States had of fulfilling its manifest destiny. As a war hero who was replacing an unpopular president, Grant had an opportunity to add to the national domain. With sizable Republican majorities in the House and Senate, Grant seemingly had fewer obstacles to overcome than previous expansion-minded presidents. Yet his decision to target Santo Domingo, instead of Cuba, and his inability to overcome his own party's racial prejudices sank his annexationist efforts. White Americans seemed uninterested in expanding the borders of the nation when that expansion entailed giving citizenship rights to nonwhites.[103] Thus the racial critique of expansion provided the final nail in the coffin of manifest destiny. In 1869 Grant had confidently predicted that the annexation of Santo Domingo would be "carrying out Manifest destiny."[104] He left office having failed to achieve that goal. With his departure from the White House, the dream of manifest destiny had effectively been ended.

Epilogue

Overturning the Myth

In November 1988 the *Baltimore Sun* ran a short quiz designed to test readers on their knowledge of U.S. history. It included fifteen questions classified as "basic" and an additional fifteen that were defined as "tougher." Under the basic label, the first question asked "Who is the main author of the Declaration of Independence?" Subsequent basic questions included "What famous black leader led his movement with non-violent, civil disobedience?" and "Who was president during the Civil War?" The readers of the *Sun* were expected to know the answers. The fourth question in the basic category asked, "What was the theory that supported our country's expansion from sea to shining sea?" The answer to that question, as the *Sun* presumed its readers would know, was "Manifest Destiny." In the opinion of the *Baltimore Sun*, the fulfillment of manifest destiny was as established a fact as Thomas Jefferson being the primary author of the Declaration of Independence, or Ulysses S. Grant being buried in Grant's tomb. It was a fact that every American was expected to know.[1]

Perhaps the author of this quiz should have searched the files of the *Baltimore Sun* a little more closely. If the author had done so, he or she might have noticed something strange. Articles in the *Baltimore Sun* in the nineteenth century that discussed manifest destiny did not revolve around western expansion, nor did they bring up the acquisition of the Pacific Coast.[2] Instead, articles that mentioned the phrase analyzed whether or not the United States would "extend itself over the American continent."[3] In 1870, for example, the *Sun* ran an article suggesting that if the United States fulfilled its manifest destiny and annexed Canada, Cuba, Mexico, and Central America, then it would make sense to move the capital of the United States to Central America.[4] Five years later, the paper was still discussing the possibility of annexing the entire continent. "As to absorbing the whole of North America," one writer suggested, "that may be our 'manifest destiny,' but whether such enlargement will tend to the national unity, and consequently to the magnificent population which is anticipated, is another question."[5] Each time that the *Baltimore Sun* discussed manifest destiny, it explored whether or not it was wise to acquire the continent.[6]

Furthermore, in the nineteenth century the *Baltimore Sun* never spoke of manifest destiny in the past tense, as something that had been fulfilled or completed.[7] Articles that brought up the subject of manifest destiny analyzed the potential annexation of Canada, Hawaii, Puerto Rico, the Philippines, Cuba, and Mexico.[8] As late as 1898, opponents of manifest destiny still opposed adding territory; proponents still spoke of the necessity of acquiring the continent.[9] Even after the turn of the century, the *Sun* continued to discuss the possible fulfillment of manifest destiny. It examined whether the "whisperings of 'manifest destiny'" were leading the United States to absorb Mexico; it questioned the wisdom of annexing Cuba; and it pondered whether Canada was on the verge of annexing itself to the United States.[10] Manifest destiny remained something yet to be accomplished.[11]

This brief glance through the *Baltimore Sun* illustrates the drastic redefinition that occurred in the twentieth century. Well into the 1920s, papers such as the *Baltimore Sun* defined manifest destiny as the theory that the United States would annex Canada, Mexico, Cuba, and, as time passed, other places such as the Hawaiian Islands, the Dominican Republic, and Haiti. Although expansionists often favored one of these nations over another, they would not have defined manifest destiny as "the theory that supported our country's expansion from sea to shining sea."[12] Indeed, as late as 1927, when famed Baltimore journalist H. L. Mencken wrote about manifest destiny he discussed the acquisition of the continent.[13] "Such small and feeble countries as Haiti and Nicaragua," Mencken concluded, "can no more resist the suction of the United States than the tides can resist the suction of the moon. They are doomed to succumb, just as Mexico is doomed to succumb, and maybe Canada after it . . . let us not forget that Rhode Island also resisted, and Utah a century later." Mencken's article was typical for the 1920s, but it was a view of manifest destiny that would soon be forgotten.

Within a decade academic historians reimagined manifest destiny and crafted a narrative that gained broad acceptance. In the early twentieth century, manifest destiny became almost exclusively identified with western expansion, as discussions of Canada, Mexico, and Cuba faded from popular memory. Historians increasingly portrayed the ideology as the dominant belief of the 1840s, an ideology that spread like a fever and drove white Americans westward with the zeal of religious enthusiasts. Spurred on by manifest destiny, white Americans annexed Texas, claimed New Mexico, and conquered California. History had proven the *Democratic Review* and John L. O'Sullivan correct.

Nowhere is this drastic redefinition better captured than in an image that has become almost exclusively identified with manifest destiny. In 1873 George Crofutt printed an image called *American Progress* in his magazine *Crofutt's Western World*.[14] The image was a copy of a painting by John Gast, which Crofutt then reprinted and sent to all those who subscribed to *Crofutt's Western World*. As described by Crofutt himself, the image depicted the march of American Progress. "In the foreground," Crofutt explained, "the central and principal figure, a beautiful and charming female, is floating westward through the air, bearing on her forehead the 'Star of Empire.' She has left the cities of the east far behind, crossed the Alleghanies and the 'Father of Waters,' and still her march is westward." Crofutt was immensely proud of this image and worked to distribute it as widely as possible.

It took over a century before the image reached a truly national audience. In 1982 an art historian named Rena N. Coen analyzed the influence of French painter Jacques-Louis David on the U.S. West. Coen sought to trace how David's depictions of women influenced U.S. artwork, and so she investigated a handful of paintings, including *American Progress*.[15] Coen did not call the painting *American*

15. Although frequently used to illustrate manifest destiny, John Gast's image is better seen as a key element of the myth that has grown up around the ideology. Proponents of manifest destiny desired the continent of North America and were hardly satisfied with the Pacific Coast. John Gast, *American Progress* (George A. Crofutt, 1873). From Library of Congress Prints and Photographs Online Catalog, https://www.loc.gov/pictures/item/97507547/.

Progress, but instead labeled it *Westward Ho! (Manifest Destiny)*, a title that Gast and Crofutt had never used. In addition, Coen argued, "This voluptuous female, who floats so decorously westward, is not only a symbol of civilization but the moral justification for westward expansion or Manifest Destiny."[16] Defining manifest destiny as synonymous with western expansion, Coen believed Gast's image was a perfect visual representation of the ideology. Others soon interpreted the image in a similar way. J. Gray Sweeney argued, "Gast's painting symbolizes in one concise image the self-serving ideology of westward expansion, its allegorical figure floating across the sky making explicit the conflation of sacred and secular in the visual rhetoric of Manifest Destiny."[17] By the middle of the 1990s, academic presses frequently selected Gast's image as the cover image for works on manifest destiny.[18]

Gast's image is an apt representation of the myth of western expansion as a benevolent process, but there is no evidence that Crofutt intended the image to illustrate manifest destiny. This can clearly be seen in Crofutt's own description of his image. In an article accompanying the image, he wrote, "This beautiful picture . . . is purely national in design, and represents the United States' portion of the American Continent in its beauty and variety, from the Atlantic to the Pacific Ocean, illustrating at a glance the grand drama of Progress in the civilization, settlement and history of this country."[19] Crofutt's use of the phrase "the United States' portion of the American Continent" is informative. Believers in manifest destiny averred that the entire continent of North America belonged to the United States. No proponent of manifest destiny would have spoken of the "United States' portion of the American Continent." If Crofutt had desired to depict manifest destiny, even as an allegory, the angel of progress would have aimed toward Canada, Cuba, or Mexico, not toward the Pacific Coast.

Crofutt's contemporaries, including John Gast, would not have associated manifest destiny with western expansion. For example, Isaac H. Sturgeon, a resident of St. Louis, penned an open letter to the Missouri *Tribune* in 1873 that pushed for manifest destiny. "Our government can not be weakened by natural and healthy expansion," Sturgeon wrote. "Its manifest destiny is to absorb all of North America under one government, and we should bravely and manfully fulfill that mission allotted to us."[20] Proponents of manifest destiny such as Sturgeon still believed that the United States would acquire the continent of North America. Manifest destiny did not pertain to the past, as Americans continued to debate the potential acquisition of Canada, the Danish West Indies, Cuba, and Mexico.[21] To cite another example, in 1872 the *Chicago Tribune* wrote, "If our 'manifest destiny' is ever fulfilled, we must welcome a Cuban, a Canadian, and a Mexican, and can claim that we have a Government such as the world hath ne'er seen,— and will ne'er see again."[22] Whether they were in favor of annexation or against it, Americans understood what manifest destiny meant. Only after historians redefined manifest destiny would Gast's image be seen as a fitting allegory of the ideology.

The use of *American Progress* to symbolize manifest destiny is an example of how the myth of manifest destiny grew over the decades.[23] With the passage of time, other elements were added. For instance, historians in the 1920s and 1930s increasingly capitalized manifest destiny to signify its importance.[24] So prevalent did the capitalization become that some took it for granted that nineteenth-century Americans had capitalized it. Most notably, in 2001 Bruce A. Harvey stated that manifest destiny was "one of the few ideologies, in the history of nations, that in its own time became so reified as to garner initial capitals in its name."[25] Yet, in spite of Harvey's assertion, most nineteenth-century Americans did not capitalize the phrase. The *Democratic Review*, certainly the leading authority on the topic, never capitalized manifest destiny and typically surrounded it with quotation marks.[26] When John L. O'Sullivan wrote his public letter to William Henry Seward in 1860, he did not capitalize manifest destiny.[27] The *New York Herald* did not capitalize it, even though the paper churned out hundreds of articles that discussed manifest destiny.[28] A quick search through articles shows that most papers did not capitalize the phrase.[29] Like so many other things, capitalizing manifest destiny turned out to largely be an invention of later historians.[30]

The assertion that Americans have always capitalized manifest destiny and the use of Gast's image to represent the ideology are poignant reminders of the enduring power of the myth of manifest destiny. Over the last hundred years, so many elements have been added to the myth that the ideology itself has lost its original meaning. Recovering that original meaning, understanding that manifest destiny had a precise definition, that it was not a synonym for western expansion, that it was mocked, maligned, and challenged, and that it was certainly not fulfilled, will not be a simple process. The myth of manifest destiny has obtained a remarkably stable hold in the historical profession and within the broader public, as the *Baltimore Sun* exemplified. Yet it is a myth that is well worth overturning, as it will lead to a richer, and certainly more nuanced, narrative of U.S. empire.

Dispensing with the myth of manifest destiny will lead to a greater understanding of the failures of U.S. empire. Throughout the nineteenth century, policymakers were not successful at implementing their grandiose dreams of empire. Polk did acquire a large chunk of Mexico, but the Treaty of Guadalupe Hidalgo failed to satisfy the dreams of the proponents of manifest destiny, who wanted all of Mexico. Polk himself was unhappy with the treaty and hoped to acquire more Mexican territory, but he submitted it believing a treaty that included more territory would be voted down in the Senate.[31] Polk's effort to buy Cuba floundered.[32] Polk's term, in short, did not fulfill his own plans of empire, much less the vision of uncompromising expansionists like O'Sullivan and Douglas. Subsequent presidents had even less success. Pierce rode into the White House on a wave of expansionist sentiment, but his plan for acquiring Cuba exploded at Ostend. Pierce's own party refused to renominate him, a humiliating defeat for a man who entered office boasting of his expansive plans. Buchanan was less successful than his predecessor, who managed, at least, to procure the Gadsden Treaty. Republicans stymied Buchanan in all his attempts to purchase Cuba and northern Mexico. In short, expansionist presidents from 1845 to 1860 hardly realized their dreams of empire. Most of their plans went down to ignominious defeat.

A similar pattern emerged after the Civil War. With the threat of the slave power eradicated, some Republicans attempted to revive manifest destiny. William Henry Seward managed to get a treaty through a contentious Senate, procuring Alaska. But Seward's treaty, like Polk's, failed to satisfy its leading proponent's expansive plans. Seward dreamed of a continental United States and thought the purchase of Alaska would lead to bigger things. This never came to pass. Seward's attempt to purchase the Danish West Indies backfired, as Americans relentlessly mocked him for trying to buy volcanoes, earthquakes, and hurricanes. He left office with his dream of empire in shambles. Ulysses S. Grant took over with thoughts of pushing the United States toward its manifest destiny. His own party quashed his treaty to acquire Santo Domingo, making it clear that most white Americans were unwilling to add territory that contained a significant nonwhite population. The failures of Seward and Grant, and the refusal of the Republican Party to officially embrace expansionism, rendered manifest destiny impotent.

Manifest destiny's failure, not its fulfillment, triggered policymakers to pursue commercial empire in the latter half of the nineteenth century. Historians have often explained the shift to commercial empire in terms of political preferences; Democrats favored territorial expansion, whereas Whigs and later Republicans sought a commercial empire.[33] The rise of the Republican Party, particularly William Henry Seward, triggered the abandonment of territorial expansion in favor of securing ports and markets and opening trade with other nations.[34] Having accomplished manifest destiny, policymakers turned their attention outside North America.[35] A better interpretation, one that takes into account the failures of Seward and Grant, is that policymakers shifted to commercial expansion because of the difficulty of territorial expansion. Battles over Alaska, the Danish West Indies, and Santo Domingo taught Republicans the futility of trying to annex outside regions.

It was not merely internal opposition, however, that led to the abandonment of manifest destiny. Mexico, Great Britain, and Spain played an equally significant role in thwarting the United States' presumed destiny. After 1854 Mexico refused to sell any more of its territory, and expansion-minded Democrats proved inept at procuring their desired territorial concessions without armed force. The prediction that Mexico would prove unable to govern itself and that the United States would be forced to annex it, made countless times by proponents of manifest destiny, never came to pass. Mexico retained its sovereignty and refused to relinquish its territory. In a similar manner, Spain remained uninterested in selling Cuba to the United States, regardless of price. Unwilling to embrace filibustering as an official policy, expansionists were unable to find a way to pry Cuba loose from Spain's grasp. Spain successfully put down López's filibuster invasions and refused to be intimidated into selling the island.[36] Finally, Britain stood as a bulwark against manifest destiny. In Central America, Britain retained its hold on Belize and its alliance with the Miskito Kingdom, which enabled it to negotiate the Clayton-Bulwer Treaty. This treaty forced the United States to abandon colonization in Central America. The belief that Canada would one day annex itself to the United States, and that acquiring Alaska would hasten that process, proved to be an illusion.[37]

Internal resistance to manifest destiny was equally potent. Historians have vastly overestimated the popularity of manifest destiny in the United States. Although a small group of expansionists continually prated of the inevitability of continental domination, many, if not most, Americans remained skeptical that the United States would benefit from expanding over too vast of a territory. Prior to the Civil War, these skeptics warned that the United States was abandoning its founding principles by pursuing an aggressive war with Mexico. They pointed out, quite correctly, that adding territory would stoke sectional tension. As time passed, many northerners turned to a sectional critique, questioning why the government always sought to expand in a southerly direction. In the aftermath of the Civil War, opponents of manifest destiny pointed out that the United States had plenty of land and did not need to purchase volcanoes, earthquakes, and ice. They warned that annexing Mexico, Santo Domingo, or Haiti would add "turbulent" peoples to the United States. A substantial majority of white Americans, north and south, feared enfranchising African Americans and had no interest in annexing a substantial nonwhite population. In the nineteenth century Americans did not fall under the sway of manifest destiny. For a variety of reasons, many worked to make sure that the dream of Stephen Douglas, John L. O'Sullivan, and William Henry Seward never came to pass.

Far more prosaic motivations undergirded the expansion that occurred during the middle of the nineteenth century. White Americans did not swarm into Texas, Oregon, New Mexico, and California infused with the romantic belief that Providence had provided them with a title to the territory stretching from sea to shining sea. Some lusted after new markets and desired to expand the U.S. economy, while others sought to open up more territory for the institution of slavery. Some of those fleeing to what became the Southwest hoped to escape from the authority of the United States altogether. There was hardly a unified belief, even among white Americans, that the United States would take the shape that it eventually did. John Tyler maneuvered Texas annexation through a divided Congress.[38] Shortly thereafter, James K. Polk, elected by a slim margin over Henry Clay, provoked a war with Mexico and sent a treaty to the Senate that he did not fully endorse.[39] After the war expansionists tried and failed to acquire Canada, Cuba, Nicaragua, Mexico, and Santo Domingo. Proponents of manifest destiny envisioned a republic that covered the entirety of North America. Assailed from within and without, this dream of manifest destiny unraveled over the nineteenth century, demonstrating the limits of the United States and the inability of many of its policymakers to enact their visions of empire. Manifest destiny was left unfulfilled, except in the pages of most history books.

NOTES

Introduction

1. "Manifest Destiny,'" *Courier-Journal* (Louisville KY), March 21, 1870.

2. "Manifest Destiny,'" *Courier-Journal* (Louisville KY), March 21, 1870.

3. Chaffin, *Met His Every Goal?*, 122.

4. Heidler and Heidler, *Manifest Destiny*, 132.

5. Reynolds, *America, Empire of Liberty*, 125; see also Woodworth, *Manifest Destinies*, 103; Weeks, *Building the Continental Empire*, 61.

6. Pratt, "The Origin of 'Manifest Destiny,'" 795–98.

7. Hudson, *Mistress of Manifest Destiny*, 46; Sampson, *John L. O'Sullivan and His Times*, 244–45.

8. "Annexation," *United States Magazine, and Democratic Review* 17, no. 85 (July/August 1845): 6. It should be noted that the magazine changed editors and its own name several times from 1845 to 1859 without altering its philosophy. It became the *United States Review* in 1853; the *United States Democratic Review* in 1856; and the *United States' Democratic Review* in 1859, its final year. It remained stridently Democratic and unabashedly supported manifest destiny.

9. "Our Mission—Diplomacy and Navy," *Democratic Review* 31, no. 1 (July 1852): 38.

10. "The Monroe Doctrine versus the Clayton and Bulwer Treaty: An Expose," *United States Review* 1, no. 3 (March 1853): 199; see also "The Message: Political Considerations Suggested by the President's Message of December, 1852," *United States Review* 1, no. 2 (February 1853): 103; "Cuba! Philosophy of the Ostende Correspondence," *United States Review*, June 1855, 449–50.

11. "Chronicle of the Month: Foreign," *United States Review*, June 1856, 512.

12. "The Fate of Mexico," *United States Democratic Review*, May 1858, 345.

13. "Continental Policy of the United States—the Acquisition of Cuba," *United States' Democratic Review*, April 1859, 2.

14. "The Diplomacy of the Sword," *United States' Democratic Review*, October 1859, 360.

15. "The Science of Manifest Destiny," *New York Times*, September 9, 1852.

16. "The Prevailing Sentiment," *New York Times*, October 4, 1852.

17. "Manifest Destiny," *New York Times*, July 7, 1853.

18. "Manifest Destiny," *New York Times*, July 7, 1853.

19. "Anglo-American Progress," *New York Times*, December 22, 1854.

20. "Anglo-American Progress."

21. *New York Tribune*, July 8, 1858.

22. "The Tribune on Manifest Destiny," *New York Times*, July 10, 1858.

23. "The Tribune on Manifest Destiny."

24. "Central America and the Monroe Doctrine," *New York Times*, December 18, 1858; Edward E. Dunbar, "Arizona and Sonora—No. X," *New York Times*, February 21, 1859; F. A. M., "The Evil and the Remedy: Suggestions as to the Nature of the Political Crisis, and the Means of Meeting It." *New York Times*, January 13, 1861.

25. "Mexico and America," *New York Times*, October 9, 1868.

26. "Mexico," *New York Times*, March 7, 1870.

27. "A New Era for Mexico," *New York Times*, November 20, 1872.

28. For other examples of this, see J. B. Austin, "Manifest Destiny," *Lippincott's Magazine of Literature, Science and Education* (August 1869): 183; "Manifest Destiny," *Round Table: A Saturday Review of Politics, Finance, Literature, Society and Art* (June 1869): 387; "Manifest Destiny," *Appletons' Journal of Literature, Science, and Art* (March 26, 1870): 353.

29. "Canada and Annexation," *New York Times*, May 5, 1879.

30. "Hapless Mexico," *Galveston Daily News*, July 8, 1877.

31. "Mexico and the Annexationists," *Daily Evening Bulletin*, October 5, 1875.

32. Blaine, *Twenty Years of Congress*, 99.

33. "Canada and Annexation."

34. "Slavery and Conquest," *St. Louis Globe-Democrat*, April 29, 1881; Robert E. Thompson, "Imperialism and Slavery," *Irish World and American Industrial Liberator*, October 7, 1899.

35. Roosevelt, *Life of Thomas Hart Benton*, 40.

36. Roosevelt, *Life of Thomas Hart Benton*, 41.

37. See Boucher, "In Re That Aggressive Slaveocracy," 13–79.

38. Turner, "The Problem of the West," 289–97.

39. Turner, "The Problem of the West," 293.

40. Turner, "The Problem of the West," 293.

41. See also Turner, *The United States, 1830–1850*, 567, 572.

42. Adams, *The Power of Ideals in American History*, 65–66.

43. Adams, *The Power of Ideals in American History*, 66.

44. Adams, *The Power of Ideals in American History*, 88.

45. Adams, *The Power of Ideals in American History*, 93.

46. Adams, *The Power of Ideals in American History*, 94.

47. Adams, *The Power of Ideals in American History*, 85.

48. Adams, *The Power of Ideals in American History*, 91.

49. Adams, *The Power of Ideals in American History*, 93.

50. See especially Dodd, *Expansion and Conflict*. Dodd's work, published in 1915, covered the same time period and focused on U.S. expansion. Dodd never mentioned manifest destiny in his volume.

51. Fish, *The Rise of the Common Man*, 291–312.

52. Fish, *The Rise of the Common Man*, 302. Recent historians have repeated this claim. See Greenberg, *Lady First*, 140; and Leonard, *James K. Polk*, 73.

53. Fish, *The Rise of the Common Man*, 303.

54. Fish, *The Rise of the Common Man*, 329.

55. Pratt, "The Origin of 'Manifest Destiny,'" 795–98.

56. Pratt, "John L. O'Sullivan and Manifest Destiny," 213–34.

57. Pratt, "John L. O'Sullivan and Manifest Destiny," 220.

58. Pratt, "John L. O'Sullivan and Manifest Destiny," 221.

59. Weinberg, *Manifest Destiny*, 2.

60. Weinberg, *Manifest Destiny*, 8.

61. Weinberg, *Manifest Destiny*, 100, 125.

62. Burns, *The American Idea of Mission*, 5.

63. Tuveson, *Redeemer Nation*, 91.

64. Tuveson, *Redeemer Nation*, 97.

65. Bercovitch, *The Puritan Origins of the American Self*, 108; Bercovitch, *The American Jeremiad*, 92; Bercovitch, *Rites of Assent*, 35; Stephanson, *Manifest Destiny*, xiii; McDougall, *Promised Land, Crusader State*, 77–80.

66. Pinheiro, *Missionaries of Republicanism*, 14.

67. Weeks, *Building the Continental Empire*, 61.

68. Nugent, *Habits of Empire*, 22–23. See also Buck, *Religious Myths and Visions of America*, 28–31; Gomez, "Deus Vult," 236–62; Wilsey, *American Exceptionalism and Civil Religion*, 16–17.

69. Horsman, *Race and Manifest Destiny*.

70. Horsman, *Race and Manifest Destiny*, 208.

71. Slotkin, *Regeneration through Violence*; Slotkin, *The Fatal Environment*, 15; Drinnon, *Facing West*, xxvii–xxviii; Miller, *Native America, Discovered and Conquered*, 2; Pierce, *Making the White Man's West*, 20.

72. Kaplan, "Manifest Domesticity," 582.

73. Magnuson, "In the Service of Columbia," 17–21.

74. See most recently, Shire, *The Threshold of Manifest Destiny*, 197–98.

75. Caughfield, *True Women and Westward Expansion*, 8.

76. Greenberg, *Manifest Manhood*, 17.

77. Caughfield, *True Women and Westward Expansion*, 136.

78. Schlesinger, *The Age of Jackson*, 369–90.

79. Schlesinger, *The Age of Jackson*, 427, 372.

80. Widmer, *Young America*, 12.

81. Kerrigan, "'Young America!,'" 282–93; Widmer, *Young America*, 15–16; Eyal, *The Young America Movement*, 130–32; Allen, *A Republic in Time*, 17–36.

82. See especially, Sampson, *John L. O'Sullivan and His Times*, 138, 240.

83. Sundquist, *Empire and Slavery in American Literature*, 13–18; Harvey, *American Geographics*, 7; Rowe, *Literary Culture and U.S. Imperialism*, 6–12; Fresonke, *West of Emerson*, 15.

84. Clark, "Manifest Destiny and the Pacific," 1–17.

85. Greenberg, *Manifest Manhood*, 17.

86. Johannsen, "The Meaning of Manifest Destiny," 15.

87. Hahn, *A Nation without Borders*, 123.

88. Greenberg, *Manifest Destiny and American Territorial Expansion*, 20.

89. Adams, *The Power of Ideals in American History*, 93.

90. Graebner, *Empire on the Pacific*, v.

91. Graebner, *Empire on the Pacific*, 217.

92. Graebner, *Empire on the Pacific*, 227.

93. Merk and Merk, *Manifest Destiny and Mission in American History*.

94. Merk and Merk, *Manifest Destiny and Mission in American History*, 256.

95. Merk and Merk, *Manifest Destiny and Mission in American History*, 216.

96. Hietala, *Manifest Design*.

97. Hietala, *Manifest Design*, 2.

98. Hietala, *Manifest Design*, xi.

99. Streeby, *American Sensations*, 57.

100. Streeby, *American Sensations*, 66.

101. LeMenager, *Manifest and Other Destinies*.

102. LeMenager, *Manifest and Other Destinies*, 4.

103. Baker, *Heartless Immensity*, 1.

104. Reséndez, *Changing National Identities at the Frontier*, 5.

105. Reséndez, *Changing National Identities at the Frontier*, 116–23, 170–74, 264.

106. Reséndez, *Changing National Identities at the Frontier*, 267.

107. Reséndez, *Changing National Identities at the Frontier*, 5–6.

108. See McDonough, "Manifestly Uncertain Destiny," 2; Kastor, *William Clark's World*, 8.

109. Rodríguez, "'Children of the Great Mexican Family,'" 19.

110. Rodríguez, "'Children of the Great Mexican Family,'" 5.

111. Rodríguez, "'The Greatest Nation on Earth,'" 50–83.

112. St. John, "The Unpredictable America of William Gwin," 58.

113. St. John, "Contingent Continent," 39–40.

114. St. John, "The Unpredictable America of William Gwin," 59.

115. Isenberg and Richards, "Alternative Wests," 9.

116. Isenberg and Richards, "Alternative Wests," 16.

117. Isenberg and Richards, "Alternative Wests," 16–17.

118. Richards, *Breakaway Americas*.

119. Richards, *Breakaway Americas*, 42.

120. Richards, *Breakaway Americas*, 13.

121. Bryan, "'Everybody Needs Some Elbow Room,'" 1–14.

122. Merk and Merk, *Manifest Destiny and Mission*, 228–60.

123. For the argument that manifest destiny endured past the 1840s, see especially Greenberg, *Manifest Manhood*, 16–17.

124. DeVoto, *The Year of Decision*, 9; Nevins, *Ordeal of the Union*; Wilentz, *The Rise of American Democracy*, 577–78; Woodworth, *Manifest Destinies*, xiv.

1. Delaying Destiny

1. Appendix to Cong. Globe, 29th Cong., 1st Sess. 99 (1846).

2. Appendix to Cong. Globe, 29th Cong., 1st Sess. 99; Pratt, "The Origin of 'Manifest Destiny,'" 795–98.

3. Appendix to Cong. Globe, 29th Cong., 1st Sess. 99.

4. Appendix to Cong. Globe, 29th Cong., 1st Sess. 99.

5. "Modern Demagoguism," *Nassau Literary Magazine* 8, no. 1 (September 1848): 26.

6. Silbey, *Storm over Texas*; Haynes, *Unfinished Revolution*; Torget, *Seeds of Empire*.

7. Guardino, *The Dead March*, 34–35.

8. McCaffrey, *Army of Manifest Destiny*, 207–8.

9. Graebner, *Empire on the Pacific*, 119; Kiser, *Coast-to-Coast Empire*, 5–6.

10. Guardino, *The Dead March*, 326.

11. "The Mexican War—Its Origin and Conduct," *United States Magazine, and Democratic Review* 20, no. 106 (April 1847): 291.

12. "New Territory versus No Territory," *United States Magazine, and Democratic Review* 21, no. 112 (October 1847): 291.

13. "Occupation of Mexico," *United States Magazine, and Democratic Review* 21, no. 113 (November 1847): 381.

14. "The Mexican War—Its Origin, Its Justice and Its Consequences: The Boundary of Texas Discussed," *United States Magazine, and Democratic Review* 22, no. 116 (February 1848): 119–20.

15. Crouthamel, *Bennett's New York Herald*, 4.

16. Crouthamel, *Bennett's New York Herald*, 60–63.

17. "Mexico—Its Castes," *New York Herald*, June 5, 1846.

18. "Telegraphic Summary," *New York Herald*, January 25, 1848.

19. "Highly Important—Settlement of the Mexican Question," *New York Herald*, January 14, 1848; Crouthamel, *Bennett's New York Herald*, 56.

20. For detailed analyses see Fuller, *The Movement for the Acquisition of All Mexico*; Pletcher, *The Diplomacy of Annexation*, 302.

21. For insight into the formation of the Whig Party and the issues it advocated, see Howe, *The Political Culture of the American Whigs*, 33–35; Holt, *The Rise and Fall of the American Whig Party*, xiii–xiv; Pearson, *The Whigs' America*, 2.

22. Wilson, *Space, Time, and Freedom*, 108.

23. Klotter, *Henry Clay*, 294–316.

24. Historians who have discussed the opponents of manifest destiny have generally focused on intellectuals, abolitionists, and ministers who resided in the northeast. See Schroeder, *Mr. Polk's War*, 34; Horsman, *Race and Manifest Destiny*, 257;

Johannsen, *To the Halls of the Montezumas,* 275–80; and Stephanson, *Manifest Destiny,* 49.

25. See Cong. Globe, 30th Cong., 1st Sess. 321 (1848).

26. See Cong. Globe, 30th Cong., 1st Sess. 347.

27. D. D. B., "The Whigs and the War," *American Review: A Whig Journal of Politics, Literature, Art and Science* 6, no. 4 (October 1847): 338.

28. "From the Richmond Republican," quoted in "Public Sentiment," *National Intelligencer,* November 4, 1847.

29. Appendix to Cong. Globe, 30th Cong., 1st Sess. 308 (1848).

30. Ritchie, *Press Gallery,* 13–34.

31. "Political Clap-Trap," *National Intelligencer,* January 14, 1848.

32. Many Americans at the time believed that God actively intervened in human history and punished nations for their transgressions. See Guyatt, *Providence and the Invention of the United States,* 3–4, 173–74.

33. "The 'Manifest Destiny,'" *Richmond Whig,* July 30, 1847.

34. "Mr. Editor—We Are Engaged in a War with a Sister Nation," *Raleigh Register, and North-Carolina Gazette,* December 4, 1847.

35. "Mr. Editor."

36. "T. F. Marshall's Speech—Gen. Taylor," *Richmond Whig,* June 25, 1847.

37. "Manifest Destiny," *National Intelligencer,* August 6, 1847.

38. Sanford, "The True Elements of National Greatness and Prosperity," 295–307.

39. Sanford, "The True Elements of National Greatness and Prosperity," 301.

40. Sanford, "The True Elements of National Greatness and Prosperity," 306.

41. Sanford, "The True Elements of National Greatness and Prosperity," 306.

42. Braman, *The Mexican War,* 5.

43. Braman, *The Mexican War,* 10.

44. Braman, *The Mexican War,* 11.

45. See also "New York Correspondence," *Vermont Chronicle,* May 17, 1848.

46. For an examination of how this religious critique of expansion developed before the U.S.-Mexican War, and continued long after, see Burge, "Stealing Naboth's Vineyard," 40–55.

47. "The Foreign Policy of the United States," *National Intelligencer,* January 31, 1845. For a detailed analysis of the legacy of Washington's Farewell Address, see Malanson, *Addressing America.*

48. "The True Whig Sentiment of New-Hampshire," *New-Hampshire Statesman and State Journal,* November 20, 1846; "Text from Washington," *Watchmen & Journal* (Montpelier vt), November 29, 1846.

49. "Progressive Democracy," *Fayetteville Observer* (nc), March 31, 1846.

50. "Opinion of Honest Men at Home," *National Intelligencer,* February 12, 1848.

51. Congleton, "George D. Prentice," 94.

52. *Louisville Journal,* December 11, 1847; *Louisville Journal,* December 14, 1847.

53. *Louisville Journal,* December 24, 1847.

54. "The Wisdom of Washington and the Folly of Polk," *Louisville Journal*, March 1, 1848.

55. "Seizure of Santa Anna's Property," *Louisville Journal*, March 8, 1848.

56. Appendix to Cong. Globe, 29th Cong., 1st Sess. 110 (1846); "Manifest Destiny," *National Intelligencer*, August 6, 1847.

57. D. D. B., "The Whigs and the War," 340.

58. D. D. B., "The Whigs and the War," 341.

59. "The 'Manifest Destiny,'" *Richmond Whig*, July 30, 1847.

60. Horsman, *Race and Manifest Destiny*, 229–30; McCaffrey, *Army of Manifest Destiny*, 69; Pinheiro, *Missionaries of Republicanism*, 109.

61. "Reception of the Volunteers at New Orleans," *Niles' National Register* (Baltimore MD), July 10, 1847.

62. Cong. Globe, 30th Cong., 1st Sess. 328.

63. "Prospects of Peace," *Richmond Whig*, April 30, 1847.

64. Cong. Globe, 30th Cong., 1st Sess. 394.

65. "Civilizing Mexico," *Cincinnati Atlas*, quoted in *National Intelligencer*, August 24, 1847.

66. "Political Clap-Trap."

67. See Morrison, *Democratic Politics and Sectionalism*; Earle, *Jacksonian Antislavery and the Politics of Free Soil*, 123–24; Brooks, *Liberty Power*, 123.

68. Childers, *The Failure of Popular Sovereignty*, 103–23.

69. "Let It Not Be Forgotten!," *Richmond Whig*, October 1, 1847.

70. Cong. Globe, 29th Cong., 2nd Sess. 326 (1847).

71. Appendix to Cong. Globe, 29th Cong., 2nd Sess. 330 (1847).

72. "The Meeting of Congress—the Importance of the Session," *Louisville Journal*, December 6, 1847; Phocion, "Correspondence of the Gazette," *Arkansas Gazette*, January 6, 1848; "Manifest Destiny," *Weekly Courier and Journal* (Natchez MS), January 5, 1848; *Vicksburg Daily Whig*, February 17, 1848.

73. See Klotter, *Henry Clay*.

74. For a detailed analysis of Clay's foreign policy views, see Jones, "Henry Clay and Continental Expansion," 241–62.

75. Clay, *Henry Clay's Advice to His Countrymen*.

76. Clay, *Henry Clay's Advice to His Countrymen*, 44–45, 46, 56.

77. Cong. Globe, 29th Cong., 2nd Sess. 555.

78. Cong. Globe, 29th Cong., 2nd Sess. 555.

79. Cong. Globe, 29th Cong., 2nd Sess. 217.

80. Cong. Globe, 29th Cong., 2nd Sess. 218.

81. Clay, *Henry Clay's Advice to His Countrymen*, 37.

82. Clay, *Henry Clay's Advice to His Countrymen*, 37.

83. Cong. Globe, 29th Cong., 2nd Sess. 556.

84. Appendix to Cong. Globe, 30th Cong., 1st Sess. 386.

85. Appendix to Cong. Globe, 30th Cong., 1st Sess. 388.

86. Appendix to Cong. Globe, 30th Cong., 1st Sess. 392.

87. Expansionists believed that the land was valuable. See Kiser, *Coast-to-Coast Empire*, 7–9, 30–33.

88. Appendix to Cong. Globe, 30th Cong., 1st Sess. 393.

89. Appendix to Cong. Globe, 30th Cong., 1st Sess. 420; Cong. Globe, 30th Cong., 1st Sess. 534.

90. Appendix to Cong. Globe, 30th Cong., 1st Sess. 517.

91. Appendix to Cong. Globe, 30th Cong., 1st Sess. 517.

92. Appendix to Cong. Globe, 30th Cong., 1st Sess. 393.

93. Appendix to Cong. Globe, 30th Cong., 1st Sess. 499.

94. Cong. Globe, 29th Cong., 2nd Sess. 577.

95. Cong. Globe, 29th Cong., 2nd Sess. 330.

96. Appendix to Cong. Globe, 30th Cong., 1st Sess. 158.

97. Lander, *Reluctant Imperialists*.

98. Cong. Globe, 30th Cong., 1st Sess. 429.

99. Appendix to Cong. Globe, 30th Cong., 1st Sess. 283.

100. Cong. Globe, 30th Cong., 1st Sess. 429.

101. A Volunteer, "Affairs in New Mexico," *Missouri Republican*, quoted in *National Intelligencer*, May 13, 1847.

102. A Volunteer, "Affairs in New Mexico."

103. "Republic of Sierra Madre," *National Intelligencer*, July 21, 1848.

104. For two excellent studies that trace the contested history of expansion in what became the U.S. West, see Blackhawk, *Violence over the Land*; and DeLay, *War of a Thousand Deserts*.

105. "Mr. Editor."

106. Wyman, *Two American Pioneers*, 10–13.

107. Wyman, *Two American Pioneers*, 30–31.

108. Smith, *My Thirty Years out of the Senate*.

109. "Editors' Correspondence," *National Intelligencer*, July 2, 1847.

110. Schroeder, "Major Jack Downing and American Expansionism," 214–33; and Winter, "The Laughing Dove," 137–44.

111. Smith, *My Thirty Years out of the Senate*, 273.

112. Smith, *My Thirty Years out of the Senate*, 285, 290.

113. Smith, *My Thirty Years out of the Senate*, 273.

114. Smith, *My Thirty Years out of the Senate*, 275.

115. Smith, *My Thirty Years out of the Senate*, 276.

116. Smith, *My Thirty Years out of the Senate*, 281.

117. Smith, *My Thirty Years out of the Senate*, 281.

118. Smith, *My Thirty Years out of the Senate*, 282.

119. For the terms of the treaty, see Griswold del Castillo, *The Treaty of Guadalupe Hidalgo*.

120. Schroeder, *Mr. Polk's War*, 158.

121. Greenberg, *A Wicked War*, 261–63.

122. Senate Executive Journal, 30th Cong., 1st Sess. 340 (1848).

123. "Annexation," *United States Magazine, and Democratic Review* 17, no. 85 (July/August 1845): 6.

124. "Mr. Clay's Speech—Again," *Independent Monitor* (Tuscaloosa AL), December 9, 1847.

125. "Discordant Opinions among the Annexationists," *Louisville Journal*, February 16, 1848.

126. See, for example, the *North Carolinian*, January 22, 1848, which described Daniel Dickinson of New York as a "manifest destiny man."

127. "T. F. Marshall's Speech."

128. "Rev. Mr. Maffit's Lecture," *Alexandria Gazette*, September 3, 1847.

129. Johannsen, *Stephen A. Douglas*, 217–18.

130. "The Fate of Mexico," *United States Democratic Review*, May 1858, 344.

2. Promises of Peace

1. "Several of the Candidates," *Adrian Expositor* (MI), quoted in *Lancaster Gazette* (OH), June 23, 1848; "Several of the Candidates," *Richmond Palladium* (IN), June 28, 1848.

2. Smith, *The Presidencies of Zachary Taylor and Millard Fillmore*, 36–37.

3. Greenberg, *A Wicked War*, 179–83; Johannsen, *To the Halls of the Montezumas*, 114–18.

4. Congleton, "Contenders for the Whig Nomination in 1848," 119–33.

5. Bauer, *Zachary Taylor*, 217.

6. Hamilton, *Zachary Taylor*, 48–52.

7. Taylor wrote a series of letters to friends and acquaintances that baffled his potential supporters. See Bauer, *Zachary Taylor*, 222–24. For one such letter, see Zachary Taylor to R. C. Wood, July 20, 1847, Helen Marie Taylor Collection, Virginia Museum of History & Culture.

8. Owen, *The Taylor Anecdote Book*, 149. It is not clear if Taylor actually wrote the letter. See Rayback, "Who Wrote the Allison Letters," 51–72. It is clear, however, that the original letter expressed Taylor's views on foreign policy. See, for example, Zachary Taylor to Orlando Brown, March 15, 1848, Zachary Taylor Papers, Kentucky Historical Society; Zachary Taylor to John Clayton, September 4, 1848, Clayton Papers, Library of Congress.

9. Owen, *The Taylor Anecdote Book*, 149.

10. Owen, *The Taylor Anecdote Book*, 149.

11. Cong. Globe, 30th Cong., 1st Sess. 1011; "The Taylor Platform," *New Hampshire Statesmen*, July 21, 1848; "The Burner's Platform Contrasted with the Taylor Platform," *Cleveland Herald*, August 22, 1848.

12. "How Gen. Taylor Is Supported," *Cleveland Herald*, July 8, 1848.

13. "Andrew Stewart's Resolves—the Debate on Yucatan, in the Senate," *Boston Daily Atlas*, May 10, 1848; "Gen. Taylor's 'Platform,'" *Daily Sentinel and Gazette* (Milwaukee WI), May 22, 1848.

14. Childers, *The Failure of Popular Sovereignty*, 137–45.

15. Cong. Globe, 30th Cong., 1st Sess. 184.

16. Cong. Globe, 30th Cong., 1st Sess. 184.

17. Klunder, *Lewis Cass and the Politics of Moderation*, 171, 172, 188.

18. "Of Conquest," *Semi-Weekly Raleigh Register*, October 28, 1848.

19. "In Favor of Conquest and Dismemberment," *Semi-Weekly Raleigh Register*, October 28, 1848.

20. "The Sentiments of Two Men," *Evansville Weekly Journal* (IN), June 29, 1848.

21. "The Sentiments of Two Men," *Memphis Daily Eagle*, June 28, 1848; "The Sentiments of Two Men," *Sheboygan Mercury* (WI), July 1, 1848; "The Sentiments of Two Men," *Middlebury Register* (VT), July 4, 1848.

22. "Precept and Example," *Cleveland Herald*, July 18, 1848; "Taylor and Washington," *Star and Banner* (Gettysburg PA), October 27, 1848.

23. *A Brief Review of the Career, Character and Campaigns of Zachary Taylor*, 14–15.

24. Poore insisted on spelling his first name with the colon after Ben, writing it as Ben: Perley Poore.

25. Poore, *Life of Gen. Zachary Taylor*, 15.

26. *A Sketch of the Life and Public Services of General Zachary Taylor*, 28–30.

27. *A Sketch of the Life and Public Services of General Zachary Taylor*, 23.

28. "Gen. Taylor—the Peace Candidate," *Raleigh Register, and North-Carolina Gazette*, October 14, 1848.

29. "Gen. Taylor—the Peace Candidate."

30. "Hon. Truman Smith," *Cleveland Herald*, July 1, 1848.

31. An Old Fashioned Whig, "The People's Candidate," *Boston Daily Atlas*, July 7, 1848; see also "Cass vs. Taylor," *Daily Sentinel and Gazette* (Milwaukee WI), August 8, 1848.

32. "Letter from Hon. C. B. Smith," *North American and United States Gazette* (Philadelphia PA), July 19, 1848.

33. "Taylor, Van Buren, and Cass," *Boston Atlas* quoted in *Daily Banner* (Milwaukee WI), August 25, 1848.

34. "To the Editors of the Daily Banner," *Daily Banner* (Milwaukee WI), June 30, 1848.

35. Daniel Webster to Edward Everett, May 29, 1848, in *The Papers of Daniel Webster: Correspondence*, 6:290.

36. Taylor was not pleased when he read one of Webster's speeches, but he nonetheless remained grateful for Webster's begrudging support. See Zachary Taylor to George Lunt, September 27, 1848, Rauner Special Collections Library, Dartmouth College.

37. Webster, *Mr. Webster's Speech at Marshfield*, 13.

38. Daniel Webster, "Speech of Hon. Daniel Webster, At Abington, October 9, 1848," Webster Papers, Rauner Special Collections Library, Dartmouth College.

39. Mott, *American Journalism*, 272–76.

40. Lundberg, *Horace Greeley*, 71–72.

41. "The Choice," *New York Tribune*, September 29, 1848.

42. "The Choice."

43. D. D. B. "The Whigs and Their Candidate," *American Review: Devoted to Politics and Literature* 2, no. 3 (September 1848): 224.

44. D. D. B. "The Whigs and Their Candidate," 224.

45. X, "War or Peace," *National Intelligencer*, October 28, 1848.

46. X, "War or Peace."

47. Smith, *My Thirty Years out of the Senate*, 305.

48. Smith, *My Thirty Years out of the Senate*, 306.

49. See also Rose, *The Poetry of Locofocoism*.

50. Dow, Jr. [Elbridge Gerry Paige], *Dow's Patent Sermons*.

51. Dow, Jr. [Elbridge Gerry Paige], *Dow's Patent Sermons*, 219.

52. For the election of 1848, see Rayback, *Free Soil*, who viewed the election as hinging upon the idea of Free Soil and debates over the Wilmot Proviso (however muted). Frederick J. Blue argued, "For both northern and southern voters the only issue of major significance was that of slavery in the territories." See Blue, *The Free Soilers*, 130. More recently, Silbey revisited the election of 1848 and argued that both Whigs and Democrats relied upon their traditional issues (tariffs, foreign relations, executive power) and that discussion of the Wilmot Proviso and slavery were not that disruptive. See Silbey, *Party over Section*, 60–62.

53. Rayback, *Free Soil*, viii.

54. Cooper, *The South and the Politics of Slavery*, 246–67.

55. Silbey, *Party over Section*, 140.

56. "Lewis Cass," *Charlotte Journal*, November 10, 1848. See also X, "War or Peace"; "The People's Ticket," *Raleigh Register, and North-Carolina Gazette*, October 28, 1848.

57. "The Result," *National Intelligencer*, November 11, 1848.

58. *New York Courier and Enquirer*, quoted in "America," *Morning Post* (London), December 5, 1848.

59. *New York Express*, quoted in *Alexandria Gazette*, February 24, 1849.

60. "General Taylor's Views and Policies," *New York Herald*, January 20, 1849; and "Important Disclosures of the Views and Principles of General Taylor," *New York Herald*, January 27, 1849.

61. Zachary Taylor, "Inaugural Address," in Richardson, *A Compilation of the Messages and Papers of the Presidents, 1789–1907*, 5:5.

62. Taylor, "Inaugural Address," 5:5.

63. Historians have been critical of Taylor's inaugural. See Bauer, *Zachary Taylor*, 257; Holt, *The Rise and Fall of the American Whig Party*, 415.

64. "The New Administration and Its Prospects," *New York Herald*, March 10, 1849.

65. "Gen. Taylor's Inaugural," *Daily National Whig* (Washington DC), March 14, 1849.

66. "The Inaugural," *Lancaster Examiner* (PA), March 7, 1849.

67. *Cincinnati Chronicle*, quoted in "The Inauguration," *Lancaster Gazette* (OH), March 16, 1849. The *Lancaster Gazette* provided excerpts from a wide range of papers that approved of Taylor's inaugural.

68. "President Taylor's Inaugural Address," *Vermont Union Whig* (Rutland), March 14, 1849; "Gen. Taylor's Inaugural," *Weekly Memphis Eagle*, March 15, 1849.

69. "Prospectus of the National Intelligencer," *National Intelligencer*, June 9, 1849.

70. Williams, *Anglo-American Isthmian Diplomacy*, 57.

71. Travis, *The History of the Clayton-Bulwer Treaty*, 58–59.

72. Curry, "British Honduras," 33; Grunewald, "The Anglo-Guatemalan Dispute over British Honduras," 29–30.

73. Travis, *The History of the Clayton-Bulwer Treaty*, 40, 43.

74. Hamilton, *Zachary Taylor*, 202.

75. Wire, "John M. Clayton and the Search for Order," 208.

76. Williams, *Anglo-American Isthmian Diplomacy*, 89.

77. Wire, "John M. Clayton and the Search for Order," 308–11; John M. Clayton to Mr. Bulwer, February 18, 1850, Papers of John M. Clayton, Library of Congress; Van Alstyne, "British Diplomacy and the Clayton-Bulwer Treaty," 154.

78. "The Clayton-Bulwer Treaty," in Miller, *Treaties and Other International Acts of the United States of America*, 5:671–802.

79. "Clayton-Bulwer Treaty," 671–72.

80. "Clayton-Bulwer Treaty," 672.

81. Zachary Taylor, "To the Senate of the United States," in Richardson, *A Compilation of the Messages and Papers of the Presidents*, 5:42.

82. Taylor, "To the Senate of the United States," 42–43.

83. Senate Executive Journal, 31st Cong., 1st Sess. 185 (1850).

84. "The Nicaragua Treaty, and the Nicaragua Negotiations," *New York Herald*, April 24, 1850.

85. "The Nicaragua Treaty," *Daily National Intelligencer*, April 27, 1850; "Correspondence of the Louisville Courier," *Louisville Courier*, May 1, 1850.

86. Senate Executive Journal, 31st Cong., 1st Sess. 186.

87. Appendix to Cong. Globe, 30th Cong., 1st Sess. 86–89 (Dickinson); Appendix to Cong. Globe, 30th Cong., 1st Sess. 195 (Davis); Appendix to Cong. Globe, 30th Cong., 1st Sess. 270 (Turney); Appendix to Cong. Globe, 30th Cong., 1st Sess. 305 (Yulee).

88. "The Nicaragua Treaty," the *Pennsylvanian*, quoted in the *Union* (Washington DC), May 16, 1850; The *Union* prefaced the article by noting, "We invite the attention of our readers to the following able and powerful article upon the Nicaragua treaty." *Union* (Washington DC), May 16, 1850; the *Richmond Enquirer* also reprinted the article. See *Richmond Enquirer*, June 5, 1850.

89. "The Nicaragua Treaty," *Union* (Washington DC), May 18, 1850.

90. Buchanan to McClernand, April 2, 1850, in "Letters of Bancroft and Buchanan on the Clayton-Bulwer Treaty," 100–101.

91. Mr. King to James Buchanan, May 8, 1850, in Buchanan, *The Works of James Buchanan*, 8:381–82. Buchanan's first letter is not included in Buchanan's papers, but the contents can be deduced from King's response; James Buchanan to Mr. King, May 13, 1850, in Buchanan, *The Works of James Buchanan*, 8:383.

92. See also James Buchanan to Mr. Foote, May 31, 1850, in Buchanan, *The Works of James Buchanan*, 8:385–86.

93. Mr. King to James Buchanan, May 8, 1850, in Buchanan, *The Works of James Buchanan*, 8:381.

94. "To-day Here—To-morrow Where?," *Natchez Courier*, June 4, 1850.

95. "Ratification of the Nicaragua Treaty," *New York Courier and Enquirer*, quoted in *Milwaukee Daily Sentinel*, May 31, 1850.

96. "We Are Sold to the British!," *Natchez Courier*, June 7, 1850.

97. "Clayton-Bulwer Treaty," 681.

98. Bauer, *Zachary Taylor*, 314.

99. See, for example, Independent [pseud.], "From Washington," *North American and United States Gazette*, December 27, 1852: "Gen. Cass supported the resolution, and enlarged upon his favorite doctrine of 'manifest destiny.'"

100. E. L. Seaman to Horace Mann, November 18, 1848, Horace Mann Papers, Massachusetts Historical Society.

101. Horace Mann to S. Downer, June 28, 1850, Horace Mann Papers, Massachusetts Historical Society.

102. Bauer, *Zachary Taylor*, 286.

103. May, *Slavery, Race, and Conquest in the Tropics*, 89.

104. Appendix to Cong. Globe, 32nd Cong., 2nd Sess. 270 (1853); Cong. Globe, 34th Cong., 1st and 2nd Sess. 1071, 1072 (1856); "Speech of the Hon. Stephen A. Douglas, at the Meeting in the Odd Fellows' Hall, New Orleans, on Monday Evening, the 6th December," *New Orleans Delta*, quoted in *Missouri Republican*, December 18, 1858; "Senator Douglas in New York," *Boston Daily Advertiser*, January 3, 1859.

105. See, for example, "The Monroe Doctrine versus the Clayton and Bulwer Treaty: An Expose," *United States Review* 1, no. 3 (March 1853): 199; "British Aggression in Central America," *United States Magazine, and Democratic Review* 28, no. 151 (January 1851): 11; and "Who Owns British North America?," *Democratic Review* 31, no. 170 (August 1852): 152.

3. Rejecting Robbery

1. William L. Marcy to L. B. Shepherd, Washington, April 15, 1855, William L. Marcy Papers, Library of Congress.

2. Rayback, *Millard Fillmore*, 173–91.

3. Maizlish, *A Strife of Tongues*, 15–16.

4. Potter, *The Impending Crisis*, 97–98.

5. Morrison, *Slavery and the American West*, 124–25.

6. For a detailed examination of the importance of the Texas and New Mexico boundary issue, see Stegmaier, *Texas, New Mexico, and the Compromise of 1850*.

7. For an overview of the political debates in 1850, see Hamilton, *Prologue to Conflict*.

8. For filibustering, see Scroogs, *Filibusters and Financiers*; Brown, *Agents of Manifest Destiny*; May, *John A. Quitman*; Chaffin, *Fatal Glory*; May, *Manifest Destiny's*

Underworld; Stout, *Schemers and Dreamers*; Greenberg, *Manifest Manhood*; Tucker, *Newest Born of Nations*.

9. "A New and Important Movement in the South—Revolutionary Expedition to Mexico," *Weekly Herald*, August 8, 1849.

10. Thomas Ewing to William Ballard Preston, August 9, 1849, Preston Family Papers, Virginia Museum of History & Culture.

11. For details on the expedition, see de la Cova, "The Taylor Administration versus Mississippi Sovereignty," 299–303.

12. Zachary Taylor, "Proclamations," in Richardson, *A Compilation of the Messages and Papers of the Presidents, 1789–1907*, 5:7–8.

13. Rauch, *American Interest in Cuba*, 121.

14. Vilá, *Narciso López y su época*, 27.

15. Vilá, *Narciso López y su época*, 143.

16. Lightfoot, "Manifesting Destiny on Cuban Shores," 396–98.

17. De la Cova, "The Kentucky Regiment That Invaded Cuba in 1850," 571–615.

18. Chaffin, *Fatal Glory*, 127.

19. Chaffin, *Fatal Glory*, 134–39.

20. "Great News from Cuba!," *Natchez Courier*, May 28, 1850.

21. See, for instance, "A Bold Prophecy," *Richmond Whig*, July 12, 1850, which mocked López and ridiculed the *New York Sun* for its continued trumpeting of manifest destiny; "How They Were Duped," *National Intelligencer* June 7, 1850; "Louisiana Democratic Views of the Cuban Expedition," *National Intelligencer*, June 15, 1850; "The Cuba Affair," *Boston Daily Atlas*, June 17, 1850.

22. "The Cuban Expedition," *Semi-Weekly Eagle* (Brattleboro VT), May 20, 1850.

23. "The Cuban Buccaneers," *Richmond Whig*, May 31, 1850; "Matanzas, Cardenas," *National Intelligencer*, June 12, 1850.

24. F., "Cuba," *North American and United States Gazette*, June 3, 1850.

25. *Hartford Daily Courant*, June 3, 1850.

26. "Narcisso Lopez and His Companions," *United States Magazine, and Democratic Review* 29, no. 160 (October 1851): 299.

27. "Pick Your Flint and Try It Again," *Mississippian* (Jackson), June 6, 1850.

28. Kimball, *Cuba, and the Cubans*.

29. Kimball, *Cuba, and the Cubans*, 190.

30. Kimball, *Cuba, and the Cubans*, 193. Expansionists frequently argued that acquisitions were necessary to limit British influence on the continent. See Hietala, *Manifest Design*, 93; Haynes, *Unfinished Revolution*, 240.

31. Kimball, *Cuba, and the Cubans*, 198.

32. Kimball, *Cuba, and the Cubans*, 188.

33. Kimball, *Cuba, and the Cubans*, 188.

34. Kimball, *Cuba, and the Cubans*, 199; "The Cuban Expedition," *Natchez Courier*, June 4, 1850.

35. Millard Fillmore, "Proclamations," in Richardson, *A Compilation of the Messages and Papers of the Presidents, 1789–1907*, 5:111.

36. "Rumors from Cuba," *Daily Scioto Gazette* (Chillicothe OH), August 5, 1851.

37. *New Orleans Picayune*, quoted in "Cuba," *Daily Morning News* (Savannah GA), August 8, 1851.

38. Chaffin, *Fatal Glory*, 203.

39. See Brown, *Agents of Manifest Destiny*, 87–88.

40. *Pittsburgh Commercial Journal*, quoted in "The Lopez Expedition," *National Intelligencer*, September 2, 1851.

41. "Give Us Light!," *National Intelligencer*, September 30, 1851.

42. "Cuba—the Havana Massacre—Collateral Questions," *Daily Ohio States-man* (Columbus), August 27, 1851.

43. *Detroit Free Press* quoted in "Views of Gen. Cass—the President's Procla-mation," *Mississippian State Gazette* (Jackson), September 26, 1851.

44. "Narcisso Lopez and His Companions," 299.

45. "Destiny of Cuba, and the Late Expedition of Lopez," *Daily Ohio Statesman* (Columbus), October 30, 1851.

46. "The Position of the United States on the Cuban Question," *Union* (Wash-ington DC), September 4, 1851.

47. "The Republic and the Treaty of 1795," *Union* (Washington DC), October 7, 1851.

48. "Cuba—the Havana Massacre—Collateral Questions."

49. "Cuba Meeting," *Savannah Morning News*, August 22, 1851; "Cuba Public Meeting," *Republic* (Washington DC), August 28, 1851; "Cuban Sympathy Meetings—Movement of Troops," *Daily Ohio Statesman* (Columbus), August 29, 1851; "The Cuba Meeting," *Alta California* (San Francisco), October 1, 1851.

50. "Late from Cuba—Condition and Prospects of the Island," *New York Her-ald*, March 8, 1852.

51. Holt, *The Rise and Fall of the American Whig Party*, 722–25.

52. For details of the Baltimore Convention see Smith, *The Presidencies of Zach-ary Taylor and Millard Fillmore*, 243–46.

53. Johannsen, *Stephen A. Douglas*, 114–25.

54. See Appendix to Cong. Globe, 32nd Cong., 2nd. Sess. 171–72.

55. Spencer, *Louis Kossuth*, 119–27.

56. Eyal, *The Young America Movement*, 99.

57. Widmer, *Young America*, 191–92.

58. "Eighteen-Fifty-Two and the Presidency," *Democratic Review* 30, no. 1 (Jan-uary 1852): 2.

59. "Eighteen-Fifty-Two and the Presidency," 12.

60. "Progress of Democracy, vs. Old Fogy Retrogrades," *Democratic Review* 30, no. 4 (April 1852): 289; "The Nomination—the 'Old Fogies' and Fogy Conspiracies," *Democratic Review* 30, no. 4 (April 1852): 366.

61. Riepma, "Young America," 204; "State of Parties—Old Fogydom and Young America—the Wants of the New Age," *New York Herald*, April 14, 1852; "The Acqui-sition of Cuba," *National Intelligencer*, April 14, 1852.

62. Spencer, *Louis Kossuth*, 119–20.

63. Nichols, *Franklin Pierce*, 203–4.

64. Holt, *Franklin Pierce*, 41–43.

65. Eyal, *The Young America Movement*, 216–18.

66. *Louisville Journal*, October 23, 1852.

67. "Modern Democracy," *New Orleans Bulletin*, quoted in *Flag of the Union* (Jackson MS), September 17, 1852.

68. "Possibilities of the Future," *Semi-Weekly Eagle* (Brattleboro VT), September 30, 1852.

69. "Possibilities of the Future."

70. *Savannah Republican* quoted in "'Signs' from Georgia," *National Intelligencer*, August 19, 1852.

71. "Freemen of Vermont!," *Vermont Journal*, October 29, 1852.

72. "Freemen of Vermont!"

73. "From Our New York Correspondent," *Milwaukee Daily Sentinel*, November 9, 1852.

74. "Mind Your Own Business," *North American and United States Gazette* (Philadelphia PA), February 1, 1853; "Fillibusterism's Hostility to the Continuance of Monarchy on the American Continent," *Louisville Journal*, December 3, 1852.

75. "The Herald—Onward!," *Democratic Review* 31, no. 173 (November–December 1852), 409–19.

76. "The Administration of General Pierce and Our Foreign Relations," *Weekly Herald*, December 4, 1852.

77. "Gen. Pierce's Administration—a New Epoch—the Annexation Question—the Monroe Doctrine," *New York Weekly Herald*, February 19, 1853.

78. Smith, *My Thirty Years out of the Senate*, 401.

79. Smith, *My Thirty Years out of the Senate*, 401.

80. Smith, *My Thirty Years out of the Senate*, 404.

81. Smith, *My Thirty Years out of the Senate*, 404.

82. "Fillibusterism," *Union* (Washington DC), December 29, 1852. Pierce would make the *Union* the official organ of his administration.

83. "Fillibusterism."

84. "Fillibusterism."

85. The *Union* continued to make this point through 1853. See "The Inaugural and the *National Intelligencer*," *Union* (Washington DC), March 18, 1853; "The Last Whig Complaint," *Union* (Washington DC), September 2, 1853.

86. Franklin Pierce, "Inaugural Address," in Richardson, *A Compilation of the Messages and Papers of the Presidents, 1789–1907*, 5:198.

87. Pierce, "Inaugural Address," 5:199. Historians have focused most of their attention on the fact that Pierce was in favor of annexation. See Nichols, *Franklin Pierce*, 235; and Holt, *Franklin Pierce*, 53.

88. Pierce, "Inaugural Address," 5:199.

89. This is not to say that Pierce refused to consider the possible benefits of filibustering. He allowed John Quitman, for example, to raise a filibustering force. It

was not until after the passage of Kansas-Nebraska that Pierce released his procla-mations against filibustering and distanced himself from Quitman. See May, *John A. Quitman*, 282–85.

90. "The New Administration," *National Intelligencer*, March 12, 1853.

91. "The Inaugural Address and the *National Intelligencer*," *Union* (Washington DC), March 15, 1853.

92. "The New Administration," *National Intelligencer*, March 17, 1853.

93. Nichols, *Franklin Pierce*, 224–29.

94. Johannsen, *Stephen A. Douglas*, 377. For Cushing's views on empire, see Belohlavek, *Broken Glass*, 252–67; for Jefferson Davis, see Cooper, *Jefferson Davis*, 284–85.

95. For a discussion of conflicting southern attitudes toward Cuba at the time, see Karp, *This Vast Southern Empire*, 191–97.

96. Spencer, *The Victor and the Spoils*, 228–29. For the reasons that Pierce made these seemingly odd choices, see Holt, *Franklin Pierce*, 2–3.

97. While serving in the Senate, Soulé delivered one of the only speeches in favor of filibustering. See Appendix to Cong. Globe, 32nd Cong., 2nd. Sess. 119.

98. Ettinger, *The Mission to Spain of Pierre Soulé*, 100–105.

99. Ettinger, *The Mission to Spain of Pierre Soulé*, 118.

100. "The Mission to Spain—Mr. Soule—Cuba—'Manifest Destiny,'" *New York Herald*, April 9, 1853.

101. See Ettinger, *The Mission to Spain of Pierre Soulé*, 228–33.

102. For Marcy's original instructions to Soulé, see William L. Marcy to Pierre Soulé, July 23, 1853, in Manning, *Diplomatic Correspondence of the United States*, 11:162–63.

103. William L. Marcy to Pierre Soulé, March 17, 1854, in Manning, *Diplomatic Correspondence of the United States*, 11:175–76. See also William Marcy to John Y. Mason, May 25, 1854, John Y. Mason Papers, Virginia Museum of History & Culture.

104. William L. Marcy to Pierre Soulé, August 16, 1854, in Manning, *Diplomatic Correspondence of the United States*, 11:193.

105. Klein, *President James Buchanan*, 240–41; Ettinger, *The Mission to Spain of Pierre Soulé*, 365–68.

106. James Buchanan, John Y. Mason, and Pierre Soulé to William L. Marcy, October 18, 1854, in Manning, *Diplomatic Correspondence of the United States*, 7:579–85.

107. Buchanan, Mason, and Soulé to Marcy, October 18, 1854, 7:584.

108. Buchanan, Mason, and Soulé to Marcy, October 18, 1854, 7:584.

109. "Telegraphic Dispatches," *Boston Daily Atlas*, November 17, 1854.

110. "The Meeting at Ostend," *North American and United States Gazette* (Phil-adelphia PA), December 7, 1854.

111. "The Ostend Conference—Attempt of the Cabinet to Suppress Inquiry," *New York Herald*, December 9, 1854.

112. "Manifesto of the Brigands," *New York Tribune*, March 7, 1855.

113. "The Buccaneering Embassy," *New York Tribune*, March 8, 1855.

114. Potter, *The Impending Crisis*, 192–93.

115. "From Our New York Correspondent," *Milwaukee Daily Sentinel*, March 13, 1855.

116. *Boston Daily Atlas*, March 9, 1855.

117. "To the Editors," *National Intelligencer*, March 13, 1855.

118. "The Soule Negotiations," *Fayetteville Observer* (NC), March 26, 1855.

119. "The Purchase of Cuba," *Louisville Journal*, January 20, 1855.

120. "The Purchase of Cuba."

121. "The Purchase of Cuba."

122. For a detailed examination of how humorists transformed the robber into a humorous character, see Burge, "Manifest Mirth," 285–86, 295–98.

123. Smith, *Thirty Years Out of the Senate*, 420.

124. Smith, *Thirty Years Out of the Senate*, 423.

125. Smith, *Thirty Years Out of the Senate*, 426.

126. Smith, *Thirty Years Out of the Senate*, 426.

127. "The Pierce Fire Burns Brightly," *Sauk County Standard* (Baraboo WI), October 6, 1852.

128. Franklin Pierce, "Proclamations," in Richardson, *A Compilation of the Messages and Papers of the Presidents, 1789–1907*, 5:271–72.

129. Pierce, "Proclamations," 5:272–73.

130. Garber, *The Gadsden Treaty*, 131.

131. "The Gadsden Treaty," *North American and United States Gazette* (Philadelphia PA), June 23, 1854.

132. For the argument that filibustering hindered U.S. expansion, see May, *Manifest Destiny's Underworld*, 247.

133. Lewis Cass did so in a speech in the Senate. See Cong. Globe, 32nd Cong., 2nd Sess. 140 (1853); but also Cong. Globe, 32nd Cong., 2nd Sess. 190.

134. William L. Marcy to L. B. Shepherd, Washington, April 15, 1855, William L. Marcy Papers, Library of Congress.

4. Stalling the Slave Power

1. Cong. Globe, 35th Cong., 2nd Sess. 543 (1859).

2. Cong. Globe, 35th Cong., 2nd Sess. 544. For studies of U.S. expansion that examine U.S. interest in Canada, see Shippee, *Canadian-American Relations, 1849–1874*; Warner, *The Idea of Continental Union*; Stuart, *United States Expansionism and British North America*; and Dagenais and Mauduit, *Revolutions across Borders*.

3. Sewell, *John P. Hale and the Politics of Abolition*, 153–64.

4. For the argument that manifest destiny became sectionalized after the passage of the Kansas-Nebraska Act, see May, *The Southern Dream of a Caribbean Empire*, 37.

5. For studies of southern empire, see McCardell, *The Idea of a Southern Nation*, 228–76; Oakes, *The Ruling Race*, 147–50; Fehrenbacher, *The Slaveholding Republic*, 91–118; Richards, *The Slave Power*, 115–16, 197–98; Guterl, *American Mediterranean*, 49–55; Bonner, *Mastering America*, 20–40; Quigley, *Shifting Grounds*, 52–63; Johnson, *River of Dark Dreams*, 15–16; Karp, *This Vast Southern Empire*; Waite, *West of Slavery*.

6. For the writing and implementation of the Kansas-Nebraska Act, see Malavasic, *The F Street Mess*; for an understanding of how this legislation influenced the careers of Lincoln and Douglas, see May, *Slavery, Race, and Conquest in the Tropics*, 105–10.

7. Childers, *The Failure of Popular Sovereignty*, 166.

8. For the Missouri Compromise, see Moore, *The Missouri Controversy*; Forbes, *The Missouri Compromise and Its Aftermath*; Van Atta, *Wolf by the Ears*; Hall, *Dividing the Union*.

9. Freehling, *The Road to Disunion: Secessionists at Bay*, 546–52; Potter, *The Impending Crisis*, 167–70.

10. Freehling, *The Road to Disunion: Secessionists Triumphant*, 62–63; Wilson, *Space, Time, and Freedom*, 172.

11. Gienapp, *The Origins of the Republican Party*, 75.

12. Gienapp, *The Origins of the Republican Party*, 89.

13. Gienapp, *The Origins of the Republican Party*, 90.

14. "Anti-Nebraska Congressional Address, to the People of the United States," *Boston Daily Atlas*, June 24, 1854.

15. "Anti-Nebraska Congressional Address."

16. For an overview of the slave power thesis, see Davis, *The Slave Power Conspiracy and the Paranoid Style*; Gara, "Slavery and the Slave Power," 5–18.

17. "The Voice of the People: Anti Nebraska Meeting of the Citizens of Addison County," *Middlebury Register* (VT), March 29, 1854.

18. Sinha, *The Slave's Cause*, 478–80.

19. "Manifest Destiny," *Frederick Douglass' Paper*, June 24, 1853; "The Crisis—What Can We Do?," *Frederick Douglass' Paper*, March 17, 1854; "The Cuban Question," *Frederick Douglass' Paper*, February 9, 1855.

20. The *National Era* had a somewhat positive view of expansion in the late 1840s and early 1850s, commenting as late as 1851, "The march of the American empire is onward; and annexation, by one means or another, inevitable." Senior [pseud.], "Fourth of July: 'Our Manifest Destiny' and Duty," *National Era*, July 10, 1851.

21. "Manifest Destiny," *National Era*, September 28, 1854, 154; "Conquest of Cuba—the First Demonstration," *National Era*, March 23, 1854, 46.

22. "Manifest Destiny in Central America," *National Era*, October 25, 1855, 170.

23. "Message of the President," *Liberator*, December 8, 1854, 194.

24. "Policy of the Nebraska Leaders," *New York Tribune*, May 15, 1854.

25. Appendix to Cong. Globe, 33rd Cong., 2nd Sess. 47 (1855).

26. Appendix to Cong. Globe, 33rd Cong., 2nd Sess. 47.

27. See also Appendix to Cong. Globe, 33rd Cong., 2nd Sess. 648.

28. "Southern Demands," *Ripley Bee* (OH), June 17, 1854.

29. "What Will the End Be?," *Fremont Weekly Journal*, June 30, 1854.

30. "County Politics," *Vermont Watchman and State Journal*, July 28, 1854.

31. "Oh! The President!," *Daily Scioto Gazette* (Chillicothe OH), June 25, 1855; "Doughfaces," *Albany Journal* (NY), quoted in *Daily Scioto Gazette* (Chillicothe OH), June 26, 1855.

32. Sallie Holley, "Letter from Miss Holley," *Liberator*, March 9, 1855, 40.

33. "The Anti-Slavery Movement," *Liberator*, August 10, 1855.

34. David Lee Child, "Kansas and Cuba," *Liberator*, April 13, 1855, 58.

35. See also, "General Intelligence," *Kansas Herald of Freedom*, May 12, 1855.

36. See Holt, *The Rise and Fall of the American Whig Party*, 951–60. For the argument that the Republicans were primarily dedicated to the principles of Free Soil and antislavery see Foner, *Free Soil, Free Labor, Free Men*, ix; and Anbinder, *Nativism and Slavery*, xiii. For the contrasting argument that the Republicans relied heavily upon nativism, temperance, and other ethnocultural issues to build their winning coalition, see Formisano, *The Birth of Mass Political Parties*, 8–12; Holt, *The Political Crisis of the 1850s*, 189–91; and Gienapp, *The Origins of the Republican Party*, 372.

37. Appendix to Cong. Globe, 33rd Cong., 2nd Sess. 252.

38. "Speech of Hon. Israel Washburn, of Maine," *Boston Daily Atlas*, November 2, 1855.

39. William Henry Seward, "The Advent of the Republican Party," in *The Works of William Henry Seward*, 4:225.

40. Seward, "The Advent of the Republican Party," 4:227.

41. Seward, "The Advent of the Republican Party," 4:286.

42. Scroggs, *Filibusters and Financiers*, 92, 108.

43. Rosengarten, *Freebooters Must Die!*, 1–2.

44. Johnson, *River of Dark Dreams*, 381–82.

45. For a history of similar invasions, see Stout, *Schemers and Dreamers*, 17–33.

46. Brown, *Agents of Manifest Destiny*, 194–95.

47. As it had with López, the Whig press labelled Walker a robber. See "Rollo Junior," *North American and United States Gazette* (Philadelphia PA), January 5, 1854; "The Marauders in Mexico," *National Intelligencer*, January 27, 1854; "The Buccaneers in Lower California," *Fayetteville Observer* (NC), March 2, 1854; "The Freebooters in Lower California," *National Intelligencer*, April 11, 1854.

48. Scroggs, *Filibusters and Financiers*, 65.

49. Brown, *Agents of Manifest Destiny*, 261.

50. Gobat, *Empire by Invitation*, 68–69.

51. Brown, *Agents of Manifest Destiny*, 297.

52. Brown, *Agents of Manifest Destiny*, 302.

53. Scroggs, *Filibusters and Financiers*, 165.

54. Nichols, *Franklin Pierce*, 460–62.

55. May, *Manifest Destiny's Underworld*, 74.

56. "Gen. Walker's Successes—Glorious Prospects of 'Manifest Destiny' in Central America," *New York Herald*, June 3, 1856.

57. "Sympathy for General Walker," *New York Herald*, May 10, 1856.

58. "The Nicaragua Meeting in New York," *National Intelligencer*, May 16, 1856.

59. "Chronicle of the Month: Foreign," *United States Democratic Review*, June 1856, 513.

60. "Nicaragua," *New York Tribune*, November 29, 1855.

61. "Nicaragua."

62. "Shall We Have a War?," *Boston Atlas*, May 22, 1856.

63. Sumner, *The Crime against Kansas*.

64. Etcheson, *Bleeding Kansas*, 100–105.

65. "The Nicaragua Question," *New York Tribune*, May 7, 1856; "Nicaragua—French Insolence," *New York Tribune*, May 9, 1856; "Walker's Government Recognized," *New York Tribune*, May 15, 1856; "The Kansas Letters," *New York Tribune*, May 19, 1856. See, for instance, the editorials in the *New York Tribune*, May 26, 1856, for articles on Kansas and Nicaragua running side by side.

66. See "Democratic Platform of 1856," in Porter, *National Party Platforms*, 45.

67. "Democratic Platform of 1856," 46.

68. "Democratic Platform of 1856," 46.

69. "Democratic Platform of 1856," 46.

70. Gienapp, *The Origins of the Republican Party*, 307–16.

71. Because of his role in leading exploring parties into the West, Frémont has often been identified as a believer in manifest destiny (when manifest destiny is defined as the acquisition of the Pacific Coast). See, for example, Menard, *Sight Unseen*, 184–85; Chaffin, *Pathfinder*, x–xi; Inskeep, *Imperfect Union*, xxii.

72. "Republican Platform of 1856," in Porter, *National Party Platforms*, 49.

73. "Buchanan Also Eats Dirt," *Bangor Daily Whig and Courier*, May 22, 1856.

74. "The 'Respectable' Candidate," *Boston Atlas*, June 10, 1856.

75. "Secret Movement of the Slave Power," *Bangor Daily Whig and Courier*, July 21, 1856; "Buchanan on Slavery—a Record without Blemish," *Boston Atlas*, July 22, 1856.

76. "Buchanan and Fillibuster Conspiracy," *Cleveland Herald*, October 7, 1856.

77. "Buchanan a Dead Plank in a Rotten Platform," *Vermont Watchman and State Journal*, July 4, 1856.

78. "The Three Parties for the Presidency and the Three Platforms," *New York Herald*, June 22, 1856.

79. *New York Tribune*, June 9, 1856.

80. "A Buchanier Indeed," *Fremont Journal*, October 31, 1856.

81. "Nursery Rhymes for Young Fremonters," *Milwaukee Daily Sentinel*, August 25, 1856.

82. "The First Slavery Shriek—a Buchanier's Eyes Wide Open," *Cleveland Herald*, September 13, 1856; J. R. S. Doolittle, "Another Buchanier Cured," *Boston Atlas*, September 15, 1856.

83. Appendix to Cong. Globe, 34th Cong., 1st Sess. 1069 (1856).

84. See also Appendix to Cong. Globe, 34th Cong., 1st Sess. 1195; Appendix to Cong. Globe, 34th Cong., 1st Sess. 640; Appendix to Cong. Globe, 34th Cong., 1st Sess. 1079.

85. "This Side and That Side," *Bangor Daily Whig and Courier*, August 19, 1856.

86. "Which Will Ye Serve?," *Boston Daily Atlas*, November 1, 1856.

87. "A Glance at the Future," *Boston Daily Atlas*, October 23, 1856.

88. Baker, *James Buchanan*, 33–36; Binder, *James Buchanan and the American Empire*, 274.

89. *Richmond Whig*, November 21, 1856.

90. Klein, *President James Buchanan*, 317–27.

91. Brown, *Agents of Manifest Destiny*, 403–5.

92. See Olliff, *Reforma Mexico and the United States*, 5–8.

93. Burnett, *The Pen Makes a Good Sword*, 83.

94. Lewis Cass to John Forsyth, July 17, 1857, in Manning, *Diplomatic Correspondence of the United States*, 9:235.

95. Cass to Forsyth, July 17, 1857, 9:235.

96. "Draft of Proposed Boundary Treaty," in Manning, *Diplomatic Correspondence of the United States*, 9:236–39.

97. Belohlavek, "In Defense of Doughface Diplomacy," 120–24.

98. James Buchanan, "Second Annual Message," in Richardson, *A Compilation of the Messages and Papers of the Presidents*, 5:511.

99. Buchanan, "Second Annual Message," 5:512.

100. Buchanan, "Second Annual Message," 5:514.

101. Senate Journal, 35th Cong., 2nd Sess., 342 (1859).

102. "The Blood Red Hand," *New Hampshire Statesman*, March 6, 1858.

103. Appendix to Cong. Globe, 35th Cong., 1st Sess. 68 (1858).

104. Appendix to Cong. Globe, 35th Cong., 1st Sess. 174 (1858).

105. Cong. Globe, 35th Cong., 2nd Sess. 706; Cong. Globe, 35th Cong., 2nd Sess. 502.

106. Cong. Globe, 35th Cong., 2nd Sess. 543.

107. Appendix to Cong. Globe, 35th Cong., 2nd Sess. 195 (1859).

108. Ponce, "As Dead as Julius Caesar,'" 345.

109. Ponce, "As Dead as Julius Caesar,'" 345.

110. See "The McLane Mexican Treaty," *New York Times*, January 17, 1860.

111. "Editorial Correspondence," *Lansing State Republican* (MI), February 28, 1860.

112. "The *New York Times*," *Vermont Phoenix*, June 9, 1860.

113. "The Mexican Treaty in Congress," *New York Times*, February 8, 1860.

114. "Anti-Slavery Festival," *Liberator*, February 19, 1858.

115. "Anti-Slavery Festival."

116. "Anti-Slavery Festival."

117. Cong. Globe, 36th Cong., 1st Sess. 383 (1860).

118. Appendix to Cong. Globe, 29th Cong., 2nd Sess. 217.

119. "Republican Meeting at Xenia: Speech of Hon. Thos. Corwin," *Cincinnati Commercial*, quoted in *Tiffin Weekly Tribune* (OH), July 20, 1859.

5. Controlling the Continent

1. John L. O'Sullivan to William H. Seward, "Sixty Years Hence," *New York Herald*, November 1, 1860.

2. Sampson, *John L. O'Sullivan and His Times*, 241.

3. *Press* (Philadelphia PA), quoted in "The Mexican Question," *Pioneer and Democrat* (St. Paul MN), February 10, 1860.

4. "The Defeat of the Nicaraguan and Mexican Treaties," *Pioneer and Democrat* (St. Paul MN), March 30, 1860.

5. "Mexico," *Register* (Monroe LA), April 12, 1860.

6. "Mexico to Be Invaded: Our Manifest Destiny," *Louisville Courier*, March 7, 1860.

7. "The Illinois National Democracy," *Democrat and News* (Davenport IA), January 13, 1860.

8. "The Diplomacy of the Sword," *United States' Democratic Review*, October 1859, 362.

9. Cong. Globe, 36th Cong., 1st Sess. 1244.

10. May, *Slavery, Race, and Conquest in the Tropics*, 159–64.

11. "Speech of the Hon. Stephen A. Douglas, at the Meeting in the Odd Fellows' Hall, New Orleans, on Monday Evening, the 6th December," *New Orleans Delta*, quoted in the *Missouri Republican*, December 18, 1858.

12. "Senator Douglas in New York," *Boston Daily Advertiser*, January 3, 1859.

13. "Manifest Destiny," *Memphis Daily Appeal*, April 4, 1860.

14. McPherson, *Battle Cry of Freedom*, 215–16.

15. Walther, *William Lowndes Yancey*, 243–44.

16. Sinha, *The Counter-Revolution of Slavery*, 202.

17. Halstead, *Caucuses of 1860*, 89–91.

18. Halstead, *Caucuses of 1860*, 210–13, 217–23; Huston, "The 1860 Southern Sojourns of Stephen A. Douglas," 29–67.

19. "Democratic Platform of 1860," in Porter, *National Party Platforms*, 53.

20. "Democratic (Breckinridge Faction) Platform of 1860," in Porter, *National Party Platforms*, 54.

21. Green, *Lincoln and the Election of 1860*, 55–62.

22. Egerton, *Years of Meteors*, 141.

23. Halstead, *Caucuses of 1860*, 146–48.

24. Donald, *Lincoln*, 121–26.

25. Guelzo, *Abraham Lincoln*, 228.

26. Abraham Lincoln, "Second Lecture on Discoveries and Inventions," in *The Collected Works of Abraham Lincoln*, 3:357.

27. For a detailed analysis on Lincoln's views on expansion, see May, *Slavery, Race, and Conquest in the Tropics*, 3–6.

28. Fry, *Lincoln, Seward, and US Foreign Relations in the Civil War Era*, 37–39.

29. William Henry Seward, "Political Equality: The National Idea," in *The Works of William Henry Seward*, 4:331–32.

30. Seward, "Political Equality," 333.

31. William Henry Seward, "The Policy of the Fathers of the Republic," in *The Works of William Henry Seward*, 4:397–409.

32. Seward, "The Policy of the Fathers of the Republic," 4:406.

33. "The Great Republican Programme of Annexation for the Extinction of Southern Slavery," *New York Herald*, September 20, 1860.

34. "Seward's New Phase of Manifest Destiny—Mexico in the Foreground," *New York Herald*, September 21, 1860.

35. Appendix to Cong. Globe, 36th Cong., 1st Sess. 388 (1860).

36. Appendix to Cong. Globe, 36th Cong., 1st Sess. 389.

37. "Political Death of Stephen A. Douglas," *Cass County Republican* (Dowagiac MI), June 28, 1860; "The Last Struggle of Democracy," *Holmes County Republican* (Millersburg OH), July 5, 1860; "Keep It before the People," *Tiffin Weekly Tribune* (OH), September 28, 1860.

38. For Schurz's role in the election of 1860, see Trefousse, *Carl Schurz*, 94.

39. Schurz, "Slavery at War with the Moral Sentiment," in *The Campaign of 1860*, 151.

40. "To-Day," *New York Tribune*, October 13, 1860.

41. "The 'Little Dodger' Dodges: Afraid to Show His Hand!," *Tiffin Weekly Tribune* (OH), September 28, 1860.

42. "Douglas Men!," *Times* (Bellows Falls VT), November 2, 1860.

43. Schurz, "Douglasism Exposed and Republicanism Vindicated," in *The Campaign of 1860*, 252.

44. Green, *Lincoln and the Election of 1860*, 105–6.

45. Egerton, *Years of Meteors*, 210.

46. Sinha, *The Counter-Revolution of Slavery*, 244.

47. Dew, *Apostles of Disunion*, 4–5.

48. Thomas, *The Confederate Nation*, 66; Rable, *The Confederate Republic*, 53–61.

49. For a detailed analysis of Confederate dreams of empire, see Brettle, *Colossal Ambitions*. For an understanding of Confederate plans in the Southwest, see Frazier, *Blood and Treasure*, 12–20; Masich, *Civil War in the Southwest Borderlands*, 110; Kiser, *Coast-to-Coast Empire*, 163–81; Nelson, *The Three-Cornered War*, 5–14.

50. Lowndes, "From the Capital of the Confederacy," *Daily Sun* (Columbus GA), March 14, 1861.

51. "Farewell Speech of Hon. A. H. Stephens," in *Alexander H. Stephens, in Public and Private*, 645.

52. For Stephens's changing views on expansion, see Schott, *Alexander H. Stephens of Georgia*, 156, 174, 269–70.

53. Lowndes, "From the Capital of the Confederacy," *Daily Sun* (Columbus GA), March 14, 1861.

54. Brettle, *Colossal Ambitions*, 22–25.

55. "Fato Profugus," *Montgomery Weekly Post* (AL), March 20, 1861.

56. "Fato Profugus."

57. See, for example, May, "The Irony of Confederate Diplomacy," 74.

58. "Demise of Manifest Destiny," *Richmond Dispatch*, December 14, 1861.

59. It bears mentioning that neither side defined the struggle over the West as a battle over manifest destiny. As they had throughout the nineteenth century, both northerners and southerners continued to define manifest destiny as the idea that a

single nation would dominate the continent of North America. Thus, expansionist southerners rarely talked of fulfilling manifest destiny. They often spoke of obtaining a southern empire.

60. Duffield, *The God of Our Fathers*, 24–25.

61. Lord, *A Sermon on the Causes and Remedy of the National Troubles*, 14.

62. Throughout the war, ministers employed manifest destiny within a traditional jeremiad. For the use of the jeremiad during the Civil War, see Stout, *Upon the Altar of the Nation*, 38; and Rable, *God's Almost Chosen Peoples*, 400–401.

63. R. M. Hatfield, "The Mexican War," *Independent*, October 17, 1861.

64. Fiske, *A Sermon on the Present National Troubles*, 17–18.

65. S., "Manifest Destiny," *Hydraulic Press* (North San Juan CA), April 13, 1861.

66. William H. Seward to Abraham Lincoln, "Memorandum: Some Thoughts for the President's Consideration," April 1, 1861, Lincoln Papers, Library of Congress.

67. See also Sowle, "A Reappraisal of Seward's Memorandum," 234–39.

68. "The Two Great Confederacies—Manifest Destiny of the North and of the South," *New York Herald*, January 25, 1861; and "The Southern Revolution—a Southern Confederacy—the Folly of Coercion," *New York Herald*, January 26, 1861.

69. "Opening of the Campaign—the Beginning of a New and More Glorious Epoch in the Domestic and Foreign Affairs of the United States," *New York Herald*, May 25, 1861.

70. "What Is to Be Done with the Army When the Rebellion Is Crushed," *New York Herald*, December 23, 1861.

71. Sainlaude, *France and the American Civil War*, 111–12.

72. Doyle, *The Cause of All Nations*, 124–25.

73. Jones, *Blue and Gray Diplomacy*, 129–30.

74. "A Warning to France," *Frank Leslie's Illustrated Newspaper*, July 5, 1862.

75. "Louis Napoleon in Mexico—European Intervention in America," *Daily Evening Bulletin* (San Francisco), June 13, 1862.

76. "The Signs of the Times," *New York Herald*, June 6, 1863.

77. "European Influence," *Daily Picayune*, April 6, 1862.

78. "Matamoras," *Charleston Mercury*, September 24, 1863.

79. "The United States and Mexico," *Richmond Dispatch*, September 5, 1863.

80. "The Gravest Political Error," *North American and United States Gazette* (Philadelphia PA), January 30, 1863.

81. "Has the South Been Wronged?," *North American and United States Gazette* (Philadelphia PA), March 5, 1863; see also "The Territories—Slavery—the Supreme Court—Past Compromises—Our Empire—the Policy and Necessities of the North," *North American and United States Gazette* (Philadelphia PA), August 27, 1863.

82. "Speech of the Hon. Montgomery Blair at the Mass Meeting in Cleveland, Wednesday, May 20, 1863," *Cleveland Herald*, May 21, 1863.

83. "Henry Vincent on the American Crisis," *Liberator*, April 4, 1862.

84. "The Democratic Party," *New York World*, quoted in the *Weekly Democrat* (Plymouth IN), March 26, 1863.

85. For Vallandigham's opposition to Lincoln throughout the Civil War, see Mackey, *Opposing Lincoln*.

86. Appendix to Cong. Globe, 37th Cong., 3rd. Sess. 55 (1863).

87. Horace Greeley, "Dark and Bright Hours," *Independent*, May 14, 1863.

88. Gillett, *Thanksgiving Sermon*, 9.

89. "The Coming Fast-Day," *Independent*, July 28, 1864.

90. For a detailed examination of the creative ways that Confederates demonized northerners during the conflict, see Rable, *Damn Yankees!*

91. "The Monroe Doctrine," *Richmond Dispatch*, April 19, 1864.

92. "French Policy in America," *Richmond Dispatch*, July 27, 1864.

93. *Richmond Dispatch*, July 27, 1864.

94. For a similar critique, see "Hope On—Hope Ever," *Daily Morning News* (Savannah GA), June 14, 1864.

95. "Republican Platform of 1864," in Porter, *National Party Platforms*, 62–63.

96. "Democratic Platform of 1864," in Porter, *National Party Platforms*, 59–60.

97. "The American Empire," *Republican* (Chicago IL), reprinted in the *East Saginaw Courier* (MI), June 21, 1865.

98. "Andrew Johnson a War Democrat—Our Foreign Policy under His Rule," *New York Herald*, April 23, 1865.

99. "Andrew Johnson a War Democrat."

100. See also "The New Foreign Policy of the United States—a Grand Congress of Nations," *New York Herald*, May 9, 1865; and "Louis Napoleon's Mexican Scheme and the 'Manifest Destiny' of the Monroe Doctrine," *New York Herald*, February 1, 1865.

101. "Speech of Col. Tate," *Republican Banner* (Nashville TN), November 5, 1865.

102. Of course, some decided to abandon the United States altogether rather than live under a "northern" government. See Wahlstrom, *The Southern Exodus to Mexico*; Wolnisty, *A Different Manifest Destiny*.

103. "Mexico—Her Position and Prospects," *New Orleans Times*, December 19, 1865.

104. "Solution of the Mexican Difficulty—Manifest Destiny," *Daily Picayune*, July 13, 1866.

105. "Manifest Destiny," *Daily Phoenix* (Columbia SC), November 30, 1865.

106. Cong. Globe, 38th Cong., 2nd Sess. 287 (1865).

6. Worthless Real Estate

1. "Manifest Destiny," *Daily Phoenix* (Columbia SC), June 30, 1867.

2. "Manifest Destiny," *Daily Phoenix* (Columbia SC), June 30, 1867.

3. Holbo, *Tarnished Expansion*, 90.

4. Students of U.S. foreign policy have tended to focus on Seward's accomplishments and have frequently dubbed him a "visionary" who laid the groundwork for the United States' burgeoning commercial empire. See LaFeber, *The New Empire*, 25; Van Deusen, *William Henry Seward*, 549; Paolino, *The Foundations of the American Empire*, x; Stahr, *Seward*.

5. Sexton, *Debtor Diplomacy*, 83, 203–4.

6. Jensen, *The Alaska Purchase*, 60–61.

7. Farrar, *The Annexation of Russian America to the United States*, 37.

8. Farrar, *The Annexation of Russian America to the United States*, 55.

9. For an invaluable recent analysis of the public debate on the treaty, see Hill, "The Myth of Seward's Folly," 43–64.

10. Bailey, "Why the United States Purchased Alaska," 47–48.

11. Bailey, "Why the United States Purchased Alaska," 48.

12. Jones, *Blue and Gray Diplomacy*, 205.

13. Bailey, "Why the United States Purchased Alaska," 49.

14. Hill, "Imperial Stepping Stone," 85–88; Shenton, *Robert John Walker*, 211–13.

15. For Republican support of annexation, see Smith, *The Republican Expansionists of the Early Reconstruction Era*.

16. Sumner, *Speech of Hon. Charles Sumner*, 12.

17. Sumner, *Speech of Hon. Charles Sumner*, 13.

18. Sumner, *Speech of Hon. Charles Sumner*, 13.

19. Pletcher, *The Diplomacy of Involvement*, 36–41.

20. "The Old Regime and the New—Our Manifest Destiny," *New York Herald*, April 17, 1867.

21. "The Old Regime and the New."

22. *New York World*, quoted in "The North Pole Question," *Milwaukee Daily Sentinel*, April 6, 1867; Dixon, "Russian America," *Boston Daily Advertiser*, April 15, 1867.

23. *Washington Chronicle*, quoted in in "Our New Northwestern Territory," *Titusville Herald* (PA), April 15, 1867.

24. "The Cession of Russian America," *Brooklyn Daily Eagle*, April 1, 1867.

25. *Alexandria Gazette*, April 8, 1867.

26. *Keowee Courier* (Pickens SC), May 4, 1867.

27. *New York Tribune*, April 29, 1867.

28. "Walrussia," *New Orleans Times*, July 30, 1867.

29. "Walrussia," *Milwaukee Daily Sentinel*, July 13, 1867.

30. "Natives of Walrussia," *New Orleans Times*, June 15, 1867; "Gold in Walrussia," *Bangor Daily Whig and Courier*, July 24, 1867.

31. "Presidential Journeyings," *New York Tribune*, May 14, 1867; *New York Tribune*, March 27, 1868.

32. *Cheyenne Leader*, October 3, 1867.

33. *Louisville Journal*, August 19, 1867.

34. "The Russian Treaty," *Freedom's Champion* (Atchison KS), April 18, 1867.

35. "Walrussia," *Albion, a Journal of News, Politics and Literature*, June 1, 1867.

36. "Alaska," *Milwaukee Daily Sentinel*, June 30, 1868.

37. "The Resurrection of a Poor Old Man," *Muscatine Weekly Journal* (IA), April 19, 1867.

38. "The Resurrection of a Poor Old Man."

39. *New York Herald*, April 12, 1867, 6.

40. "To Persons in Embarrassed Conditions," *New York Herald*, April 12, 1867, 6.

41. Crouthamel, *Bennett's New York Herald*, 135–41.

42. For a satire of Alaska in poetry, see Francis Bret Harte, "An Arctic Vision," *Daily Evening Bulletin* (San Francisco), April 8, 1867.

43. His letters were reprinted in book form in Stanton, *Corry O'Lanus*.

44. Stanton, *Corry O'Lanus*, 56.

45. Stanton, *Corry O'Lanus*, 59.

46. Harrison, *The Man Who Made Nasby*, 101.

47. Harrison, *The Man Who Made Nasby*, 101.

48. Locke, *The Struggles, Social, Financial, and Political, of Petroleum V. Nasby*, 416.

49. Locke, *The Struggles, Social, Financial, and Political, of Petroleum V. Nasby*, 419.

50. "Territorial Extension," *Milwaukee Daily Sentinel*, April 24, 1867.

51. "Territorial Extension."

52. Welch, "American Public Opinion and the Purchase of Russian America," 481–94.

53. "What Shall We Do with It?," *Frank Leslie's Illustrated Newspaper*, April 27, 1867; "Aliaska," *Frank Leslie's Illustrated Newspaper*, June 6, 1868.

54. For evidence that the treaty was somewhat popular within the broader public, see Hill, "The Myth of Seward's Folly," 63–64.

55. Stahr, *Seward*, 454–55.

56. Paolino, *The Foundations of the American Empire*, 120–24. Paolino argued that Seward did not desire a coaling station so much as he wanted to secure commercial supremacy.

57. Tansill, *The Purchase of the Danish West Indies*, 54–55.

58. "Telegrams," *Salt Lake Daily Telegraph*, November 20, 1867.

59. Parton, *The Danish Islands*, 32.

60. "Terrible Earthquakes at St. Thomas," *Ripley Bee* (OH), December 11, 1867; "Graphic Account of the Earthquake at St. Thomas," *Albion*, January 4, 1868.

61. Tansill, *The Purchase of the Danish West Indies*, 82.

62. News of the purchase did not reach the United States until November 1867, and it took until December before the public began to discuss the terms in earnest. See "Purchase of the Danish West Indies," *North American and United States Gazette* (Philadelphia PA), November 7, 1867; "The News," *Milwaukee Daily Sentinel*, November 16, 1867; "Our New Possessions," *Weekly Miners' Register* (Central City CO), November 26, 1867.

63. "Our Last Bargain," *Milwaukee Daily Sentinel*, December 6, 1867.

64. David D. Porter to William H. Seward, November 6, 1867, in *Compilation of Reports of the Committee on Foreign Relations, United States Senate, 1789–1901*, 8:200–201.

65. David D. Porter to William H. Seward, November 6, 1867, 8:202.

66. "Porter's Pastoral," *New York Daily Tribune*, December 14, 1867.

67. "Porter's Pastoral."

68. "Porter's Pastoral."

69. "Omens," *Frank Leslie's Illustrated Newspaper*, December 28, 1867.

70. "A Series of Calamities," *Daily Evening Bulletin* (San Francisco), December 7, 1867.

71. "From Fortress Monroe," *National Intelligencer*, December 13, 1867.

72. "Death of Rear Admiral Palmer," *North American and United States Gazette* (Philadelphia PA), December 18 1867; "Deaths of Admiral Palmer and Captain Burroughs from Yellow Fever—Their Remains Brought to New York," *National Intelligencer*, December 18, 1867.

73. "The Island and Harbor of St. Thomas," *Frank Leslie's Illustrated Newspaper*, January 25, 1868.

74. "Thad Stevens Intractable—Mr. Seward's Real Estate Operations," *National Intelligencer*, November 22, 1867; "Seward's Real Estate Operations," *Hinds County Gazette*, November 29, 1867.

75. "Seward's Real Estate Agency," *Freedom's Champion* (Atchison KS), January 2, 1868.

76. "More Real Estate Operations," *Vermont Chronicle*, January 11, 1868: "Secretary Seward is still at the work of buying or leasing islands, archipelagoes, bays, harbors, earthquakes, tornadoes and icebergs."

77. "The St. Thomas Purchase," *Bangor Daily Whig and Courier*, December 11, 1867.

78. "Another Mission," *Freedom's Champion* (Atchison KS), February 6, 1868.

79. "Letter from Washington," *Kansas Chief* (White Cloud), February 6, 1868.

80. See "Earthquakes," *New York Observer and Chronicle*, December 26, 1867. This paper criticized its fellow newspapers for making jokes about earthquakes, which it deemed serious events.

81. "Sound Doctrine," *Lowell Daily Citizen and News* (MA), December 23, 1867.

82. "Abuse of the Treaty Making Power," *Frank Leslie's Illustrated Newspaper*, August 8, 1868.

83. "More Room," *Woodstock Sentinel* (IL), December 19, 1867.

84. "The National Finances," *Waukegan Weekly Gazette* (IL), November 23, 1867.

85. *Brooklyn Daily Eagle*, September 14, 1867.

86. "Seward's Diplomacy," *New Orleans Crescent*, December 27, 1867.

87. "Abuse of the Treaty Making Power."

88. Mark Twain, "Information Wanted," *New York Tribune*, December 18, 1867.

89. Twain, "Information Wanted."

90. Twain, "Information Wanted."

91. Americans clearly understood the intent of Twain's satire. A paper in Pennsylvania ran Twain's story under the heading "Mr. Seward's Real Estate Transactions." See "Mr. Seward's Real Estate Transactions," *Daily Evening Express* (Lancaster PA), December 28, 1867.

92. F. B. H., "St. Thomas: A Geographical Survey," *Daily Evening Bulletin* (San Francisco), April 25, 1868.

93. Locke, *The Struggles, Social, Financial, and Political, of Petroleum V. Nasby*, 568.

94. Cong., Globe 40th Cong., 2nd Sess. Part II. 1221 (1868).

95. Cong., Globe 40th Cong., 2nd Sess. Part II. 1221.

96. Cong., Globe 40th Cong., 2nd Sess. Part II. 401 (1868).

97. Cong., Globe 40th Cong., 2nd Sess. Part V. 493 (1868).

98. Cong., Globe 40th Cong., 2nd Sess. Part V. 159.

99. *Boston Daily Advertiser*, January 2, 1868.

100. "More Territorial Acquisitions," *Chicago Tribune*, November 8, 1867.

101. Tansill, *The Purchase of the Danish West Indies*, 108.

102. Donald, *Charles Sumner and the Rights of Man*, 354–55.

103. Paolino, *The Foundations of the American Empire*, 118–21.

104. Seward, *Seward at Washington*.

105. Seward, *Seward at Washington*, 371.

106. "The Annexation of San Domingo," *Galaxy: A Magazine of Entertaining Reading* 11, no. 3 (March 1871): 410.

107. This is not to argue that the environmental critique of manifest destiny was the only reason that expansionism stalled after the Civil War. For a detailed analysis of the role that political scandals and the charge of corruption played in the halting of manifest destiny, see Holbo, *Tarnished Expansion*, 89–103.

7. Destiny's Demise

1. Appendix to Cong. Globe, 41st Cong., 1st Sess. 21 (1869).

2. Critics of expansion voiced their opposition to Mexican annexation throughout the 1850s. See, for example, Appendix to Cong. Globe, 32nd Cong., 2nd Sess. 270; Appendix to Cong. Globe, 34th Cong., 1st Sess. 114; Cong. Globe, 35th Cong., 2nd Sess. 1184; "What Are We to Do with Mexico?," *Charleston Mercury*, July 10, 1858.

3. "The Russian Treaty," *Freedom's Champion* (Atchison City ks), April 18, 1867.

4. Cong. Globe, 40th Cong., 1st Sess. 519 (1867).

5. Cong. Globe, 40th Cong., 1st Sess. 521.

6. G. E. Pond, "Russian America," *Galaxy: A Magazine of Entertaining Reading*, May 1, 1867, 171.

7. "The Greasian Question," *New Orleans Crescent*, December 25, 1868.

8. "A Valuable Possession," *Daily Courier* (Louisville ky), May 17, 1867.

9. Such critiques were somewhat effective. See "Letter from Mr. Collins to Secretary Seward," *Daily Evening Bulletin* (San Francisco), May 7, 1867.

10. "A Valuable Possession."

11. "A Valuable Possession."

12. "Our Polar Regions," *Bangor Daily Whig and Courier*, May 1, 1867.

13. Stanton, *Corry O'Lanus*, 57.

14. Stanton, *Corry O'Lanus*, 58.

15. Stanton, *Corry O'Lanus*, 58.

16. Summers, *The Ordeal of the Reunion*, 142.

17. "Democratic Platform of 1868," in Porter, *National Party Platforms*, 64.

18. "Republican Platform of 1868," in Porter, *National Party Platforms*, 70.

19. "The New Policy toward Mexico," *Cleveland Herald*, August 26, 1868.

20. "Manifest Destiny," *Cheyenne Leader*, September 3, 1868.

21. "Mexico—the African," *Richmond Dispatch*, August 10, 1868. See also "Mexico: Seward Reported to Have Bought Senora and Sinaloa," *New York Herald*, September 15, 1868; "Mexico and America," *New York Times*, October 9, 1868.

22. "Manifest Destiny," *Oakland Transcript*, quoted in *Trinity Journal* (Weaverville CA), October 3, 1868.

23. "Our Foreign Policy," *Round Table: A Saturday Review of Politics, Finance, Literature, Society and Art*, January 18, 1868, 36.

24. "Grant's Intentions; the President in the Future—His Model Men; Wholesale Annexation Likely to Be the Policy of the Administration," *New York World*, quoted in *Nashville Union and American*, April 18, 1869.

25. Mott, *American Journalism*, 351. For an overview of the press's hostile relationship to Grant, see Summers, *The Press Gang*, 172–95.

26. "Our Foreign Relations and General Grant's Foreign Policy—a Glorious Opportunity," *New York Herald*.

27. "Acquisition," *Montana Post* (Helena), December 18, 1868.

28. "Congress and the Cuban Question," *Courier* (Charleston SC), April 19, 1869.

29. J. Medill, "An Ocean Bound Republic," *Cleveland Herald*, December 4, 1868.

30. "Territorial Acquisition," *Evening Telegraph* (Philadelphia PA), July 13, 1869.

31. Welles, *Naboth's Vineyard*, 150–54.

32. Welles, *Naboth's Vineyard*, 332–33.

33. Nevins, *Hamilton Fish*, 126–28.

34. White, *American Ulysses*, 508.

35. Love, *Race over Empire*, 36–37.

36. Nelson, *Almost a Territory*, 79.

37. Bunting, *Ulysses S. Grant*, 104–5. Before sending the treaty to the Senate, Grant held a meeting with Charles Sumner. For details, see Hesseltine, *Ulysses S. Grant*, 200; Donald, *Charles Sumner and the Rights of Man*, 435–37.

38. Slap, *The Doom of Reconstruction*, 117–19.

39. Grant, "Memorandum," in *The Papers of Ulysses S. Grant*, 20:74–76. The most detailed analysis of the memorandum and of Grant's foreign policy plans is found in Semmes, "Exporting Reconstruction," 37–42.

40. "Annexation Policy of the United States," *New York Herald*, January 28, 1870.

41. "Seward on Manifest Destiny," *New York Herald*, May 15, 1870.

42. "The Dominican Annexation Treaty—General Grant's Policy," *New York Herald*, June 2, 1870.

43. "San Domingo," *Sentinel*, June 10, 1870.

44. "The Foreign Policy of the Administration," *Brooklyn Daily Eagle*, June 3, 1870.

45. *Memphis Daily Appeal*, July 12, 1870.

46. "A Rose-Colored View of Domingo," *Daily Commonwealth* (Topeka KS), May 15, 1870.

47. Cong. Globe, 41st Cong., 2nd Sess. Part II. 1187 (1870).

48. "Speeches of Senator Schurz against Ratification, and of Senator Carpenter and Cole in Its Favor—the Time for Ratification to Be Extended," *New York Tribune*, March 29, 1870.

49. "Speeches of Senator Schurz against Ratification, and of Senator Carpenter and Cole in Its Favor."

50. See also speech of John A. Logan, who called the Dominicans a "naked and half-savage people." Cong. Globe, 41st Cong., 2nd Sess. Part IV. 3628 (1870).

51. Senate Executive Journal, 41st Cong. 2nd Sess. 502–3 (1870). See also Brands, *The Man Who Saved the Union*, 458–59.

52. "Rejection of the St. Domingo Treaty," *New York Herald*, July 1, 1870.

53. "Defeat of the San Domingo Treaty," *Chicago Tribune*, July 1, 1870.

54. "The Value of Grant's Influence," *Nashville Union and American*, July 1, 1870.

55. "Rejection of the San Domingo Treaty," *Spirit of Jefferson* (Charles Town wv), July 5, 1870.

56. "Political Apostacy," *Milwaukee Sentinel*, July 2, 1870.

57. *New York Tribune*, July 1, 1870; for a similar view see "The San Domingo Treaty," *Vermont Chronicle*, July 9, 1870.

58. Calhoun, *The Presidency of Ulysses S. Grant*, 257–61.

59. Summers, *The Ordeal of the Reunion*, 225.

60. Motley had angered Grant previously by his refusal to carry out his diplomatic instructions, but the timing of his recall led many to suspect that it was owing to his friendship with Sumner. See "Why Mr. Motley Was Recalled," *Bangor Daily Whig and Courier*, July 20, 1870.

61. *Report of the Commission of Inquiry to Santo Domingo*, 1–3; see Blight, *Frederick Douglass*, 538–39.

62. "'Manifest Destiny,'" *Harrisburg Telegraph* (pa), March 20, 1871.

63. "Manifest Destiny," *Fort Scott Monitor* (ks), quoted in the *Anti-Monopolist* (Parsons ks), January 12, 1871.

64. "Manifest Destiny," *Daily Pantagraph* (Bloomington il), February 28, 1871; "Annexation of San Domingo," *Evening State Journal* (Philadelphia pa), March 9, 1871; "Oration: Delivered at Oregon on the 4th of July, 1871," *Holt County Sentinel* (Oregon mo), July 14, 1871.

65. William Lloyd Garrison, "American Swagger and 'Manifest Destiny,'" *Independent*, April 27, 1871.

66. For the life of Donn Piatt, see Bridges, *Donn Piatt*.

67. "The Grant Despotism: How the Administration Defies the Popular Will," *Republican Banner* (Nashville tn), January 10, 1871.

68. "Negro Barbarism and Suffrage," *Georgia Weekly Telegraph and Georgia Journal & Messenger*, April 11, 1871.

69. "Santo Domingo," *Frank Leslie's Illustrated Newspaper*, January 15, 1870.

70. "Santo Domingo—Executive Usurpations," *Frank Leslie's Illustrated Newspaper*, February 25, 1871.

71. "For Us There Are Three Insurmountable Objections to Annexation," *Frank Leslie's Illustrated Newspaper*, March 18, 1871.

72. "A Million of Savages," *Frank Leslie's Illustrated Newspaper*, March 4, 1871.

73. Cong. Globe, 41st Cong., 3rd Sess. Part I. 799 (1871).

74. Cong. Globe, 41st Cong., 3rd Sess. Part I. 387.

75. Cong. Globe, 41st Cong., 3rd Sess. Part I. 408. For the role of lobbyists in the Santo Domingo treaty, see May, "Lobbyists for Commercial Empire," 407–10.

76. Cong. Globe, 41st Cong., 3rd Sess. Part I. 412.

77. Cong. Globe, 41st Cong., 3rd Sess. Part I. 412.

78. Cong. Globe, 41st Cong., 3rd Sess. Part III. 33 (1871).

79. Cong. Globe, 41st Cong., 3rd Sess. Part III. 30.

80. Morrill, *Annexation of Santo Domingo*, 8.

81. Morrill, *Annexation of Santo Domingo*, 8.

82. "Latest from El Dorado," *Harper's Weekly*, March 11, 1871, 211. For the magazine's opposition to annexation, see "St. Domingo and St. Thomas," *Harper's Weekly*, April 16, 1870, 242; "An 'Inspired' Meeting," *Harper's Weekly*, May 28, 1870, 339.

83. Marc and Louvrier, "Character Sketches in San Domingo and Hayti," *Harper's Weekly*, March 18, 1871, 249.

84. "San Domingo," *Harper's Weekly*, February 4, 1871, 103; "Dr. Howe and San Domingo," *Harper's Weekly*, September 16, 1871.

85. "Grant's First Valentine," *Frank Leslie's Budget of Fun*, March 1, 1871, 1.

86. "The Santo Domingo Muddle," *Frank Leslie's Budget of Fun*, March 1, 1871.

87. Calhoun, *The Presidency of Ulysses S. Grant*, 392–93.

88. "Republican Platform of 1872," in Porter, *National Party Platforms*, 82.

89. "Democratic Platform of 1872," in Porter, *National Party Platforms*, 73.

90. "General Grant and His American Policy—Not Annexation, but a League of Independent Nations," *New York Herald*, November 23, 1872. The article was a response to "The Cry for More Territory," *Chicago Tribune*, November 19, 1872.

91. See "Seward on Manifest Destiny."

92. "General Grant and His American Policy."

93. "General Grant and His American Policy."

94. "The Sandwich and Fiji Islands," *New York Herald*, January 6, 1873; "The Great Isthmian Canal—One of the Practical Schemes of General Grant's Administration," *New York Herald*, May 28, 1873.

95. "How to Conquer Mexico," *New Orleans Bulletin*, December 8, 1875.

96. "Our Manifest Destiny," *Washington Post*, August 9, 1883.

97. "The Cuban Trouble," *Saint Paul Globe* (MN), August 30, 1887. See also "A Century's Growth: Territory Acquired by the United States since the Louisiana Purchase," *Toledo Blade* (OH), quoted in *Wichita Beacon* (KS), August 24, 1887.

98. *Dayton Herald* (OH), October 2, 1894.

99. "Canadian Annexation: Senator Ingalls' Views on This Important Subject: The Whole of America One Continental Republic," *St. Joseph Gazette-Herald* (MO), January 30, 1887.

100. "The Way Out," *State Record* (Topeka ᴋꜱ), September 28, 1899.

101. "'Manifest Destiny,'" *Virginia-Pilot* (Norfolk ᴠᴀ), January 9, 1900.

102. "Don't Hurry Up 'Manifest Destiny,'" *Washington Post*, February 12, 1906.

103. For an excellent study of how racism continued to limit U.S. expansion after Grant left office, see Love, *Race over Empire*, 80–135.

104. Grant, "Memorandum," 20:74–76.

Epilogue

1. "Basic American History Questions Everyone Should Know," *Baltimore Sun*, November 27, 1988.

2. "Mayor Wood on Manifest Destiny," *Baltimore Sun*, January 11, 1856.

3. "Mr. Fillmore and the Acquisition of Territory," *Baltimore Sun*, May 8, 1854.

4. "The Centre of the Republic," *Baltimore Sun*, June 23, 1870.

5. "The Future Population," *Baltimore Sun*, April 10, 1875.

6. "America's 'Manifest Destiny,'" *Baltimore Sun*, April 24, 1857.

7. "American Jingoism," *Baltimore Sun*, February 1, 1887.

8. "The Annexation of Canada," *Baltimore Sun*, March 26, 1889; Conservative Republican, "Where Are We At?," *Baltimore Sun*, November 12, 1898; "Northern Mexico: Important Rumored Negotiations," *Baltimore Sun*, July 21, 1874; "Progress Southward," *Baltimore Sun*, May 12, 1877.

9. For opposition, see "Against Imperialism: Speech of President Jordan, of Leland Stanford University, at the Omaha Exposition," *Baltimore Sun*, October 28, 1898; "Evils of Annexation: Mr. McEnery Says Territorial Expansion Will Surely Lead to Foreign Complications," *Baltimore Sun*, June 24, 1898. For proponents, see "Majority Should Rule: Mr. Lodge Defends His Annexation Amendments to War Revenue Bill," *Baltimore Sun*, June 1, 1898; "The President's Position," *Baltimore Sun*, September 14, 1898; "Living Questions: Subjects That the People and the Press of the Country Are Discussing; the Policy of Cecil Rhodes," *Baltimore Sun*, March 9, 1899.

10. "Mexico's 'Manifest Destiny,'" *Baltimore Sun*, January 2, 1910; "The Brawl at Santiago Not an Argument for Annexation," *Baltimore Sun*, May 3, 1907; "Canada May Join U.S., British Told: Possibility of Annexation Broached in London," *Baltimore Sun*, May 16, 1925.

11. "Foreign Opinion on the Annexation of Cuba," *Baltimore Sun*, October 14, 1906; "Our Victory in Nicaragua," *Baltimore Sun*, July 19, 1927; "Our Imperialistic Policy in the Panama Canal Zone," *Baltimore Sun*, January 7, 1910; "Dewey Would Keep the Philippines," September 23, 1907; "Haitians Fear Uncle Sam Wants to Adopt Another Black Baby," *Baltimore Sun*, December 6, 1908; "An Impracticable Dream," *Baltimore Sun*, May 15, 1902.

12. "Basic American History Questions."

13. H. L. Mencken, "Manifest Destiny," *Chicago Daily Tribune*, October 23, 1927.

14. "American Progress," *Crofutt's Western World* 3, no. 4 (April 1873): 49. The image and accompanying article were reprinted in Crofutt, *Crofutt's Trans-Continental Tourist*, 157.

15. Coen, "David's 'Sabine Women,'" 67–76.

16. Coen, "David's 'Sabine Women,'" 73.

17. Sweeney, *The Columbus of the Woods*, 65.

18. From 1995 to 2015, Gast's image appeared on Stephanson, *Manifest Destiny*; Weeks, *Building the Continental Empire*; Madsen, *American Exceptionalism*; Hudson, *Mistress of Manifest Destiny*; Heidler and Heidler, *Manifest Destiny*; Greenberg, *Manifest Manhood*; Greenberg, *Manifest Destiny and American Territorial Expansion*; Chaffin, *Met His Every Goal?*

19. "Description of Our Oil Chromo Entitled American Progress!," *Crofutt's Western World* 3, no. 4 (April 1873): 63. Western Americana Collection, Beinecke Rare Book and Manuscript Library, Yale University.

20. "Annexation on a Grand Scale," *Tribune* (Jefferson City MO), quoted in the *New Orleans Republican*, March 16, 1873.

21. "Manifest Destiny," *Inter-Ocean* (Chicago IL), July 27, 1872; "Manifest Destiny—Mexico," *New Orleans Republican*, May 25, 1873; "Manifest Destiny," *New North-West* (Deer Lodge MT), August 8, 1874; "Northern Mexico," *Rutland Daily Herald* (VT), July 22, 1874.

22. *Chicago Tribune*, April 1, 1872.

23. Holt, "Looking at American History through Art," 189; Reichard, "How Do Students Understand the History of the American West?," 211.

24. Fish, *The Rise of the Common Man*, 315; Burns, *The American Idea of Mission*, 32; Tuveson, *Redeemer Nation*, 91; Horsman, *Race and Manifest Destiny*, 219.

25. Harvey, *American Geographics*, 6. See also Greenberg, *Manifest Manhood*, 1.

26. "Annexation," *United States Magazine, and Democratic Review* 17, no. 85 (July/August 1845): 6; "Our Mission—Diplomacy and Navy," *Democratic Review* 31, no. 1 (July 1852): 38; "The Monroe Doctrine versus the Clayton and Bulwer Treaty: An Expose," *United States Review* 1, no. 3 (March 1853): 199; "The Message: Political Considerations Suggested by the President's Message of December, 1852," *United States Review*, 1, no. 2 (February 1853): 103; "Cuba! Philosophy of the Ostende Correspondence," *United States Review*, June 1855, 449–50; "Continental Policy of the United States—the Acquisition of Cuba," *United States' Democratic Review*, April 1859, 2.

27. John L. O'Sullivan to William H. Seward, "Sixty Years Hence," *New York Herald*, November 1, 1860.

28. "Telegraphic Summary," *New York Herald*, January 25, 1848; "Important News from Mexico," *New York Herald*, October 31, 1848; "The Emigration to California—the Prospects of the New State," *New York Herald*, March 10, 1851; "The Consular System of the United States—What Is It?—What Should It Be?," *New York Herald*, August 18, 1853.

29. "Mr. Clay's Speech—Again," *Independent Monitor* (Tuscaloosa AL), December 9, 1847; "Manifest Destiny," *Weekly Courier and Journal* (Natchez MS), January 5, 1848.

30. Harvey, *American Geographics*, 6. See also, Greenberg, *Manifest Manhood*, 1. Greenberg's very first footnote mentioned that she was capitalizing the phrase. Her source was Harvey.

31. Guardino, *The Dead March*, 328.

32. See Rauch, *American Interest in Cuba*, 81–100.

33. Wilson, *Space, Time, and Freedom*, 107–8, 211–14; Rauch, *American Interest in Cuba*, 101; Greenberg, *Manifest Manhood*, 275–80; Howe, *What Hath God Wrought*, 706.

34. LaFeber, *The New Empire*, 61. For the argument that Seward was a commercial rather than a territorial expansionist, see Paolino. *The Foundations of American Empire*, 25–41. This view has been widely accepted. See Nugent, *Habits of Empire*, 244; Fry, *Lincoln, Seward, and US Foreign Relations in the Civil War Era*, 168–69.

35. Plesur, *America's Outward Thrust*, 26; Campbell, *The Transformation of American Foreign Relations*, 1–13.

36. The threat of filibustering had worked for the United States in its previous dealings with Spain. See Owsley and Smith, *Filibusters and Expansionists*, 181–83.

37. This is in no way meant to argue that Native American opposition to U.S. expansion was ineffective or unimportant. As this study focuses on opposition to manifest destiny from within the United States, future studies will need to analyze how Spanish, Mexican, British, and Indigenous resistance limited specific iterations of U.S. empire.

38. Leahy, *President without a Party*, 332–38.

39. For an understanding of the reasons why Democrats believed in expansion, see especially Graebner, *Empire on the Pacific*; and Hietala, *Manifest Design*. Both of these authors demonstrated that expansionists had specific motivations for acquiring the Pacific Coast. Not coincidentally, both authors encouraged historians to abandon their reliance upon manifest destiny.

BIBLIOGRAPHY

Archives/Manuscript Materials

Beinecke Rare Book and Manuscript Library, Yale University, New Haven CT.

Connecticut Historical Society, Hartford CT.

Kentucky Historical Society, Frankfort KY.

Library of Congress, Washington DC.

Massachusetts Historical Society, Boston MA.

New Hampshire Historical Society, Concord NH.

Rauner Special Collections Library, Dartmouth College, Hanover NH.

Southern Historical Collection, Wilson Library, University of North Carolina, Chapel Hill NC.

Virginia Museum of History & Culture (formerly Virginia Historical Society), Richmond VA.

Published Works

Adams, Charles. *Adventures of My Cousin Smooth; Or, the Little Quibbles of Great Governments*. New York: Miller, Orton, & Mulligan, 1855.

Adams, Ephraim Douglass. *The Power of Ideals in American History*. New Haven CT: Yale University Press, 1913.

Adams, Francis Colburn. *The Life and Adventures of Maj. Roger Sherman Potter: Together with an Accurate and Exceedingly Interesting Account of His Great Achievements in Politics, Diplomacy, and War—All of Which Are Here Recorded Out of Sheer Love for the Martial Spirit of This Truly Ambitious Nation*. New York: Stanford & Delisser, 1858.

Allen, Thomas M. *A Republic in Time: Temporality and Social Imagination in Nineteenth-Century America*. Chapel Hill: University of North Carolina Press, 2008.

Anbinder, Tyler. *Nativism and Slavery: The Northern Know Nothings and the Politics of the 1850s*. New York: Oxford University Press, 1992.

Bailey, Thomas A. "Why the United States Purchased Alaska." *Pacific Historical Review* 3, no. 1 (March 1934): 39–49.

Baker, Anne. *Heartless Immensity: Literature, Culture, and Geography in Antebellum America*. Ann Arbor: University of Michigan Press, 2005.

Baker, Jean H. *James Buchanan*. New York: Times Books, 2004.

Bauer, K. Jack. *Zachary Taylor: Soldier, Planter, Statesman of the Old Southwest*. Baton Rouge: Louisiana State University Press, 1985.

Beisner, Robert L. *From the Old Diplomacy to the New, 1865–1900*. 2nd ed. Arlington Heights IL: Harlan Davison, 1986.

Belohlavek, John M. *Broken Glass: Caleb Cushing and the Shattering of the Union*. Kent OH: Kent State University Press, 2005.

———. "In Defense of Doughface Diplomacy: A Reevaluation of the Foreign Policy of James Buchanan." In *James Buchanan and the Coming of the Civil War*, edited by John W. Quist and Michael J. Birkner, 111–33. Gainesville: University Press of Florida, 2013.

Bemis, Samuel Flagg. *A Diplomatic History of the United States*. 5th ed. New York: Holt, Rinehart and Winston, 1965.

Bercovitch, Sacvan. *The American Jeremiad*. Madison: University of Wisconsin Press, 1978.

———. *The Puritan Origins of the American Self*. New Haven CT: Yale University Press, 1975.

———. *The Rites of Assent: Transformations in the Symbolic Construction of America*. New York: Routledge, 1993.

Binder, Frederick Moore. *James Buchanan and the American Empire*. Selinsgrove PA: Susquehanna University Press, 1994.

Blackhawk, Ned. *Violence over the Land: Indians and Empires in the Early American West*. Cambridge MA: Harvard University Press, 2006.

Blaine, James G. *Twenty Years of Congress: From Lincoln to Garfield, with a Review of the Events Which Led to the Political Revolution of 1860*. Norwich CT: Henry Bill, 1884.

Blair, Walter, and Hamlin Hill. *America's Humor: From Poor Richard to Doonesbury*. New York: Oxford University Press, 1978.

Blight, David W. *Frederick Douglass: Prophet of Freedom*. New York: Simon & Schuster, 2018.

Blue, Frederick J. *The Free Soilers: Third Party Politics, 1848–54*. Urbana: University of Illinois Press, 1973.

Bonner, Robert E. *Mastering America: Southern Slaveholders and the Crisis of American Nationhood*. Cambridge UK: Cambridge University Press, 2009.

Boucher, Chauncey S. "In Re That Aggressive Slaveocracy." *Mississippi Valley Historical Review* 8, no. 1–2 (June–September 1921): 13–79.

Braman, Milton P. *The Mexican War: A Discourse Delivered on the Annual Fast, 1847*. Danvers MA: Courier Office, 1847.

Brands, H. W. *The Man Who Saved the Union: Ulysses Grant in War and Peace*. New York: Doubleday, 2012.

Brettle, Adrian. *Colossal Ambitions: Confederate Planning for a Post–Civil War World*. Charlottesville: University of Virginia Press, 2020.

Bridges, Peter. *Donn Piatt: Gadfly of the Gilded Age*. Kent OH: Kent State University Press, 2012.

A Brief Review of the Career, Character and Campaigns of Zachary Taylor. Washington DC: J. & G. S. Gideon, 1848.

Brooks, Corey M. *Liberty Power: Antislavery Third Parties and the Transformation of American Politics*. Chicago: University of Chicago Press, 2016.

Brown, Charles H. *Agents of Manifest Destiny: The Lives and Times of the Filibusters*. Chapel Hill: University of North Carolina Press, 1980.

Browne, Charles Farrar. *Artemus Ward in London and Other Papers*. New York: G. W. Carleton, 1867.

Bryan, Jimmy L., Jr. *The American Elsewhere: Adventure and Manliness in the Age of Expansion*. Lawrence: University Press of Kansas, 2017.

———. "'Everybody Needs Some Elbow Room': Culture and Contradiction in the Study of US Expansion." In *Inventing Destiny: Cultural Explorations of US Expansion*, edited by Jimmy L. Bryan Jr., 1–21. Lawrence: University Press of Kansas, 2019.

Buchanan, James. *The Works of James Buchanan, Comprising His Speeches, State Papers, and Private Correspondence*. Edited by John Bassett Moore. 12 vols. Philadelphia: J. B. Lippincott, 1908–11.

Buck, Christopher. *Religious Myths and Visions of America: How Minority Faiths Redefined America's World Role*. Westport CT: Praeger, 2009.

Bunting, Josiah, III. *Ulysses S. Grant*. New York: Henry Holt, 2004.

Buntline, Ned. *The Mysteries and Miseries of New Orleans*. New York: Akarman and Ormsby, 1851.

Burge, Daniel J. "Manifest Mirth: The Humorous Critique of Manifest Destiny, 1846–1858." *Western Historical Quarterly* 47, no. 3 (Autumn 2016): 283–302.

———. "Stealing Naboth's Vineyard: The Religious Critique of Expansion, 1830–1855." In *Inventing Destiny: Cultural Explorations of US Expansion*, edited by Jimmy L. Bryan Jr., 40–55. Lawrence: University Press of Kansas, 2019.

Burnett, Lonnie A. *The Pen Makes a Good Sword: John Forsyth of the Mobile Register*. Tuscaloosa: University of Alabama Press, 2006.

Burns, Edward McNall. *The American Idea of Mission: Concepts of National Purpose and Destiny*. New Brunswick NJ: Rutgers University Press, 1957.

Calhoun, Charles W. *The Presidency of Ulysses S. Grant*. Lawrence: University Press of Kansas, 2017.

The Campaign of 1860. Albany NY: Weed, Parsons, 1860.

Campbell, Charles S. *The Transformation of American Foreign Relations, 1865–1900*. New York: Harper & Row, 1976.

Carwardine, Richard J. *Evangelicals and Politics in Antebellum America*. New Haven CT: Yale University Press, 1993.

Caughfield, Adrienne. *True Women and Westward Expansion.* College Station: Texas A&M University Press, 2005.

Chaffin, Tom. *Fatal Glory: Narciso López and the First Clandestine U.S. War against Cuba.* Charlottesville: University of Virginia Press, 1996.

———. *Met His Every Goal? James K. Polk and the Legends of Manifest Destiny.* Knoxville: University of Tennessee Press, 2014.

———. *Pathfinder: John Charles Frémont and the Course of American Empire.* 2002. Reprint, Norman: University of Oklahoma Press, 2014.

Channing, William Henry. *The Civil War in America: Or, the Slaveholders' Conspiracy. An Address.* Liverpool UK: W. Vaughan, 1861.

Childers, Christopher. *The Failure of Popular Sovereignty: Slavery, Manifest Destiny, and the Radicalization of Southern Politics.* Lawrence: University Press of Kansas, 2012.

Clark, Dan E. "Manifest Destiny and the Pacific." *Pacific Historical Review* 1, no. 1 (March 1932): 1–17.

Clay, Henry. *Henry Clay's Advice to His Countrymen: The Speech of Henry Clay, and Resolutions Adopted at a Mass Meeting.* New York: H. R. Robinson, 1847.

Coen, Rena N. "David's 'Sabine Women' in the Wild West." *Great Plains Quarterly* 2, no. 2 (Spring 1982): 67–76.

Compilation of Reports of the Committee on Foreign Relations, United States Senate, 1789–1901. 8 vols. Washington DC: Government Printing Office, 1901.

Congleton, Betty Carolyn. "Contenders for the Whig Nomination in 1848 and the Editorial Policy of George D. Prentice." *Register of the Kentucky Historical Society* 67, no. 2 (April 1969): 119–33.

———. "George D. Prentice: Nineteenth Century Southern Editor." *Register of the Kentucky Historical Society* 65, no. 2 (April 1967): 94–119.

Cooper, William J., Jr. *Jefferson Davis, American.* New York: Vintage, 2001.

———. *The South and the Politics of Slavery, 1828–1856.* Baton Rouge: Louisiana State University Press, 1978.

Crofutt, George A. *Crofutt's Trans-Continental Tourist.* New York: George A. Crofutt, 1874.

Crouthamel, James L. *Bennett's New York Herald and the Rise of the Popular Press.* Syracuse NY: Syracuse University Press, 1989.

Curry, Herbert F., Jr. "British Honduras: From Public Meeting to Crown Colony." *The Americas* 13, no. 1 (July 1956): 31–42.

Curti, M. E. "Young America." *American Historical Review* 32, no. 1 (October 1926): 34–55.

Dagenais, Maxime, and Julien Mauduit, eds. *Revolutions across Borders: Jacksonian America and the Canadian Rebellion.* Montreal: McGill-Queen's University Press, 2019.

Davis, David Brion. *The Slave Power Conspiracy and the Paranoid Style.* Baton Rouge: Louisiana State University Press, 1969.

de la Cova, Antonio Rafael. *Cuban Confederate Colonel: The Life of Ambrosio José Gonzales.* Columbia: University of South Carolina Press, 2003.

———. "The Kentucky Regiment That Invaded Cuba in 1850." *Register of the Kentucky Historical Society* 105, no. 4 (Autumn 2007): 571–615.

———. "The Taylor Administration versus Mississippi Sovereignty: The Round Island Expedition of 1849." *Journal of Mississippi History* 52, no. 4 (Winter 2000): 294–327.

DeLay, Brian. *War of a Thousand Deserts: Indian Raids and the U.S.-Mexican War.* New Haven CT: Yale University Press, 2008.

DeVoto, Bernard. *The Year of Decision: 1846.* Boston: Little, Brown, 1943.

Dew, Charles R. *Apostles of Disunion: Southern Secession Commissioners and the Causes of the Civil War.* Charlottesville: University of Virginia Press, 2001.

Dodd, William E. *Expansion and Conflict.* Cambridge MA: Riverside, 1915.

Donald, David. *Charles Sumner and the Rights of Man.* New York: Alfred A. Knopf, 1970.

———. *Lincoln.* New York: Simon & Schuster, 1996.

Dow, Jr. [Elbridge Gerry Paige]. *Dow's Patent Sermons.* 1st series. Philadelphia: T. B. Peterson and Brothers, 1856.

Downs, Gregory P. *The Second American Revolution: The Civil War–Era Struggle over Cuba and the Rebirth of the American Republic.* Chapel Hill: University of North Carolina Press, 2019.

Doyle, Don. *The Cause of All Nations: An International History of the Civil War.* New York: Basic Books, 2015.

Drinnon, Richard. *Facing West: The Metaphysics of Indian Hating and Empire Building.* New York: Schocken, 1980.

Duffield, George, Jr. *The God of Our Fathers. An Historical Sermon, Preached in the Coates' Street Presbyterian Church, Philadelphia, on Fast Day, January 4, 1861.* Philadelphia: T. B. Pugh, 1861.

Earle, Jonathan H. *Jacksonian Antislavery and the Politics of Free Soil, 1824–1854.* Chapel Hill: University of North Carolina Press, 2004.

Egerton, Douglas R. *Years of Meteors: Stephen Douglas, Abraham Lincoln, and the Election That Brought on the Civil War.* New York: Bloomsbury, 2010.

Eisenhower, John S. D. *Zachary Taylor.* New York: Henry Holt, 2008.

Etcheson, Nicole. *Bleeding Kansas: Contested Liberty in the Civil War Era.* Lawrence: University Press of Kansas, 2004.

Ettinger, Amos Aschbach. *The Mission to Spain of Pierre Soulé, 1853–1855: A Study in the Cuban Diplomacy of the United States.* New Haven CT: Yale University Press, 1932.

Eyal, Yonatan. *The Young America Movement and the Transformation of the Democratic Party, 1828–1861.* Cambridge UK: Cambridge University Press, 2007.

Farrar, Victor J. *The Annexation of Russian America to the United States.* Washington DC: W. F. Roberts, 1937.

Fehrenbacher, Don E. *The Slaveholding Republic: An Account of the United States Government's Relations to Slavery.* New York: Oxford University Press, 2001.

Fish, Carl Russell. *The Rise of the Common Man, 1830–1850*. 1927. Reprint, New York: Macmillan, 1969.

Fiske, John O. *A Sermon on the Present National Troubles, Delivered in the Winter Street Church, January 4, 1861, the Day of the National Fast*. Bath ME: Daily Times Office, 1861.

Flint, H. M. *Life of Stephen A. Douglas: To Which Are Added His Speeches and Reports*. Philadelphia: John E. Potter, 1865.

Foner, Eric. *Free Soil, Free Labor, Free Men: The Ideology of the Republican Party before the Civil War*. New York: Oxford University Press, 1970.

Forbes, Robert Pierce. *The Missouri Compromise and Its Aftermath: Slavery and the Meaning of America*. Chapel Hill: University of North Carolina Press, 2007.

Formisano, Ronald P. *The Birth of Mass Political Parties: Michigan, 1827–1861*. Princeton NJ: Princeton University Press, 1971.

Franklin, John Hope. *The Militant South, 1800–1861*. 1956. Reprint, Urbana: University of Illinois Press, 2002.

Frazier, Donald S. *Blood and Treasure: Confederate Empire in the Southwest*. College Station: Texas A&M University Press, 1995.

Freehling, William W. *The Road to Disunion: Secessionists at Bay, 1776–1854*. New York: Oxford University Press, 1990.

———. *The Road to Disunion: Secessionists Triumphant, 1854–1861*. New York: Oxford University Press, 2007.

Freeman, Joanne B. *The Field of Blood: Violence in Congress and the Road to the Civil War*. New York: Picador, 2018.

Fresonke, Kris, *West of Emerson: The Design of Manifest Destiny*. Berkeley: University of California Press, 2003.

Fry, Joseph. *Lincoln, Seward, and US Foreign Relations in the Civil War Era*. Lexington: University Press of Kentucky, 2019.

Fuller, John D. *The Movement for the Acquisition of All Mexico, 1846–1848*. Baltimore: Johns Hopkins University Press, 1936.

Gara, Larry. "Slavery and the Slave Power: A Crucial Distinction." *Civil War History* 15, no. 1 (March 1969): 5–18.

Garber, Paul Neff. *The Gadsden Treaty*. 1923. Reprint, Gloucester MA: Peter Smith, 1959.

Gienapp, William E. *The Origins of the Republican Party, 1852–1856*. New York: Oxford University Press, 1987.

Gillett, Ezra H. *Thanksgiving Sermon, Preached in the Presbyterian Church at Harlem, November 27, 1862*. New York: A. J. Brady, 1863.

Gobat, Michel. *Empire by Invitation: William Walker and Manifest Destiny in Central America*. Cambridge MA: Harvard University Press, 2018.

Gomez, Adam. "Deus Vult: John L. O'Sullivan, Manifest Destiny, and American Democratic Messianism." *American Political Thought* 1, no. 2 (September 2012): 236–62.

Graebner, Norman A. *Empire on the Pacific: A Study in American Continental Expansion*. New York: Ronald, 1955.

Grant, Ulysses S. *The Papers of Ulysses S. Grant*. Edited by John T. Simon and John F. Marszalek. 31 vols. Carbondale: Southern Illinois University Press, 1967–2009.

Green, Michael S. *Lincoln and the Election of 1860*. Carbondale: Southern Illinois University Press, 2011.

Greenberg, Amy S. *Lady First: The World of First Lady Sarah Polk*. New York: Alfred A. Knopf, 2019.

———. *Manifest Destiny and American Territorial Expansion: A Brief History with Documents*. 2nd ed. Boston: Bedford/St. Martin's, 2018.

———. *Manifest Manhood and the Antebellum American Empire*. Cambridge UK: Cambridge University Press, 2005.

———. *A Wicked War: Polk, Clay, Lincoln, and the 1846 U.S. Invasion of Mexico*. New York: Alfred A. Knopf, 2012.

Griswold del Castillo, Richard. *The Treaty of Guadalupe Hidalgo: A Legacy of Conflict*. Norman: University of Oklahoma Press, 1990.

Grunewald, Donald. "The Anglo-Guatemalan Dispute over British Honduras." *Caribbean Studies* 5, no. 2 (July 1965): 17–44.

Guardino, Peter F. *The Dead March: A History of the Mexican-American War*. Cambridge MA: Harvard University Press, 2017.

Guelzo, Allen C. *Abraham Lincoln: Redeemer President*. Grand Rapids MI: William B. Eerdmans, 1999.

Guterl, Matthew Pratt. *American Mediterranean: Southern Slaveholders in the Age of Emancipation*. Cambridge MA: Harvard University Press, 2008.

Guyatt, Nicholas. *Providence and the Invention of the United States, 1607–1876*. Cambridge UK: Cambridge University Press, 2007.

Hahn, Steven. *A Nation without Borders: The United States and Its World in an Age of Civil Wars, 1830–1910*. New York: Viking, 2016.

Hall, Matthew W. *Dividing the Union: Jesse Burgess Thomas and the Making of the Missouri Compromise*. Carbondale: Southern Illinois University Press, 2016.

Halstead, Murat. *Caucuses of 1860*. Columbus OH: Follett, Foster, 1860.

Hamilton, Holman. *Prologue to Conflict: The Crisis and Compromise of 1850*. 1964. Reprint, Lexington: University Press of Kentucky, 2005.

———. *Zachary Taylor: Soldier in the White House*. Indianapolis IN: Bobbs-Merrill, 1951.

Harrison, John M. *The Man Who Made Nasby, David Ross Locke*. Chapel Hill: University of North Carolina Press, 1969.

Harvey, Bruce A. *American Geographics: U.S. National Narratives and the Representation of the Non-European World, 1830–1865*. Palo Alto CA: Stanford University Press, 2001.

Haynes, Sam W. *Unfinished Revolution: The Early American Republic in a British World*. Charlottesville: University of Virginia Press, 2010.

Heidler, David S., and Jeanne T. Heidler. *Manifest Destiny*. Westport CT: Greenwood, 2003.

Herring, George C. *From Colony to Superpower: U.S. Foreign Relations since 1776*. New York: Oxford University Press, 2008.

Hesseltine, William B. *Ulysses S. Grant: Politician*. 1937. Reprint, New York: Frederick Ungar, 1957.

Hietala, Thomas R. *Manifest Design: Anxious Aggrandizement in Late Jacksonian America*. Ithaca NY: Cornell University Press, 1985.

Hill, Michael A. "Imperial Stepping Stone: Bridging Continental and Overseas Empire in Alaska." *Diplomatic History* 44, no. 1 (January 2020): 76–101.

———. "The Myth of Seward's Folly." *Western Historical Quarterly* 50, no. 1 (Spring 2019): 43–64.

Hine, Robert V., John Mack Faragher, and Jon T. Coleman. *The American West: A New Interpretive History*. 2nd ed. New Haven CT: Yale University Press, 2017.

Holbo, Paul S. *Tarnished Expansion: The Alaska Scandal, the Press, and Congress, 1867–1871*. Knoxville: University of Tennessee Press, 1983.

Holt, Jeff. "Looking at American History through Art." *History Teacher* 31, no. 2 (February 1998): 181–92.

Holt, Michael F. *Franklin Pierce*. New York: Times Books, 2010.

———. *The Political Crisis of the 1850s*. 1978. Reprint, New York: W. W. Norton, 1983.

———. *The Rise and Fall of the American Whig Party*. New York: Oxford, 1999.

Horsman, Reginald. *Race and Manifest Destiny: The Origins of American Racial Anglo-Saxonism*. Cambridge MA: Harvard University Press, 1981.

Howe, Daniel Walker. *The Political Culture of the American Whigs*. New York: Oxford University Press, 1979.

———. *What Hath God Wrought: The Transformation of America, 1815–1848*. New York: Oxford University Press, 2007.

Howe, William Wirt. *The Pasha Papers, Epistles of Mohammed Pasha, Rear Admiral of the Turkish Navy, Written from New York to His Friend Abel Ben Hassen*. New York: Scribner, 1858.

Hubbell, George A. *Sermon for the Times: Delivered in the Town Hall of Meriden, Conn., February 17, and March 3, 1861*. New Haven CT: J. H. Benham, 1861.

Hudson, Linda S. *Mistress of Manifest Destiny: A Biography of Jane McManus Storm Cazneau, 1807–1878*. Austin: Texas State Historical Association, 2001.

Huston, James L. "The 1860 Southern Sojourns of Stephen A. Douglas and the Irrepressible Separation." In *The Election of 1860 Reconsidered*, edited by A. James Fuller, 29–67. Kent OH: Kent State University Press, 2013.

Inskeep, Steve. *Imperfect Union: How Jessie and John Frémont Mapped the West, Invented Celebrity, and Helped Cause the Civil War*. New York: Penguin, 2020.

Isenberg, Andrew C., and Thomas Richards Jr. "Alternative Wests: Rethinking Manifest Destiny." *Pacific Historical Review* 86, no. 1 (2017): 4–17.

Jensen, Ronald J. *The Alaska Purchase and Russian-American Relations*. Seattle: University of Washington Press, 1975.

Johannsen, Robert W. "The Meaning of Manifest Destiny." In *Manifest Destiny and Empire: American Antebellum Expansionism*, edited by Sam W. Haynes and Christopher Morris, 7–20. College Station: Texas A&M University Press, 1997.

———. *Stephen A. Douglas*. Urbana: University of Illinois Press, 1973.

————. *To the Halls of the Montezumas: The Mexican War in the American Imagination*. New York: Oxford University Press, 1985.

Johnson, Walter. *River of Dark Dreams: Slavery and Empire in the Cotton Kingdom*. Cambridge MA: Harvard University Press, 2013.

Jones, Howard. *Blue and Gray Diplomacy: A History of Union and Confederate Foreign Relations*. Chapel Hill: University of North Carolina Press, 2010.

Jones, Thomas B. "Henry Clay and Continental Expansion, 1820–1844." *Register of the Kentucky Historical Society* 73, no. 3 (July 1975): 241–62.

Kaplan, Amy. *The Anarchy of Empire in the Making of U.S. Culture*. Cambridge MA: Harvard University Press, 2002.

————. "Manifest Domesticity." *American Literature* 70, no. 3 (September 1998): 581–606.

Karp, Matthew. *This Vast Southern Empire: Slaveholders at the Helm of American Foreign Policy*. Cambridge MA: Harvard University Press, 2016.

Kastor, Peter J. *William Clark's World: Describing America in an Age of Unknowns*. New Haven CT: Yale University Press, 2011.

Keehn, David C. *Knights of the Golden Circle: Secret Empire, Southern Secession, Civil War*. Baton Rouge: Louisiana State University Press, 2013.

Kerrigan, William Thomas. "'Young America!': Romantic Nationalism in Literature and Politics, 1843–1861." PhD dissertation, University of Michigan, 1997.

Kimball, Richard Burleigh. *Cuba, and the Cubans, Comprising a History of the Island of Cuba, Its Present Social, Political, and Domestic Condition; Also, Its Relation to England and the United States*. New York: Samuel Hueston, 1850.

Kiser, William S. *Coast-to-Coast Empire: Manifest Destiny and the New Mexico Borderlands*. Norman: University of Oklahoma Press, 2018.

Klein, Philip Shriver. *President James Buchanan*. 1962. Reprint, Norwalk CT: Easton, 1987.

Klotter, James. *Henry Clay: The Man Who Would Be President*. New York: Oxford University Press, 2018.

Klunder, Willard Carl. *Lewis Cass and the Politics of Moderation*. Kent OH: Kent State University Press, 1996.

LaFeber, Walter. *The New Empire: An Interpretation of American Expansion, 1860–1898*. Ithaca NY: Cornell University Press, 1963.

Lander, Ernest M., Jr. *Reluctant Imperialists: Calhoun, the South Carolinians, and the Mexican War*. Baton Rouge: Louisiana State University Press, 1980.

Landis, Michael Todd. *Northern Men with Southern Loyalties: The Democratic Party and the Sectional Crisis*. Ithaca NY: Cornell University Press, 2014.

Langley, Lester D. "The Whigs and the López Expeditions to Cuba, 1849–1851: A Chapter in Frustrating Diplomacy." *Revista de Historia de América*, no. 71 (January–June 1971): 9–22.

Leahy, Christopher J. *President without a Party: The Life of John Tyler*. Baton Rouge: Louisiana State University Press, 2020.

Leeds, S. P. *A Discourse Delivered on the National Fast, Sept. 26, 1861, in the Congregational Church at Dartmouth College.* Windsor vt: Bishop & Tracy, 1861.

LeMenager, Stephanie. *Manifest and Other Destinies: Territorial Fictions of the Nineteenth-Century United States.* Lincoln: University of Nebraska Press, 2004.

Leonard, Thomas M. *James K. Polk: A Clear and Unquestioned Destiny.* Wilmington de: Scholarly Resources, 2001.

"Letters of Bancroft and Buchanan on the Clayton-Bulwer Treaty, 1849, 1850." *American Historical Review* 5, no.1 (October 1899): 95–102.

Ley, Douglas Arthur. "Expansionists All? Southern Senators and American Foreign Policy, 1841–1860." PhD dissertation, University of Wisconsin, 1990.

Lightfoot, Gregg Thomas. "Manifesting Destiny on Cuban Shores: Narciso López, Cuban Annexation and the Path of American Empire, 1800–1859." PhD dissertation, Cornell University, 2015.

Limerick, Patricia Nelson. *The Legacy of Conquest: The Unbroken Past of the American West.* New York: W. W. Norton, 1987.

Lincoln, Abraham. *The Collected Works of Abraham Lincoln.* Edited by Roy Basler. 8 vols. New Brunswick nj: Rutgers University Press, 1953.

Locke, David Ross. *The Struggles, Social, Financial, and Political, of Petroleum V. Nasby.* Boston: Lee and Shepard, 1888.

Lord, William H. *A Sermon on the Causes and Remedy of the National Troubles, Preached at Montpelier, Vt., April 4th, 1861.* Montpelier vt: E. P. Walton, 1861.

Love, Eric T. L. *Race over Empire: Racism and U.S. Imperialism, 1865–1900.* Chapel Hill: University of North Carolina Press, 2004.

Lundberg, James M. *Horace Greeley: Print, Politics, and the Failure of American Nationhood.* Baltimore: Johns Hopkins University Press, 2019.

Mackey, Thomas C. *Opposing Lincoln: Clement L. Vallandigham, Presidential Power, and the Legal Battle over Dissent in Wartime.* Lawrence: University Press of Kansas, 2020.

Madsen, Deborah L. *American Exceptionalism.* Edinburgh UK: Edinburgh University Press, 1998.

Magnuson, Lynnea Ruth. "In the Service of Columbia: Gendered Politics and Manifest Destiny Expansion." PhD dissertation, University of Illinois, 2001.

Maizlish, Stephen E. *A Strife of Tongues: The Compromise of 1850 and the Ideological Foundations of the American Civil War.* Charlottesville: University of Virginia Press, 2018.

Malanson, Jeffrey J. *Addressing America: George Washington's Farewell and the Making of National Culture, Politics, and Diplomacy, 1796–1852.* Kent oh: Kent State University Press, 2015.

Malavasic, Alice Elizabeth. *The F Street Mess: How Southern Senators Rewrote the Kansas-Nebraska Act.* Chapel Hill: University of North Carolina Press, 2017.

Manning, William R., ed. *Diplomatic Correspondence of the United States: Inter-American Affairs, 1831–1860.* 12 vols. Washington dc: Carnegie Endowment for International Peace, 1932–39.

Masich, Andrew Edward. *Civil War in the Southwest Borderlands, 1861–1867*. Norman: University of Oklahoma Press, 2017.

May, Robert E. "Dixie's Martial Image: A Continuing Historiographical Enigma." *Historian* 40, no. 2 (February 1978): 51–64.

————. "The Irony of Confederate Diplomacy: Visions of Empire, the Monroe Doctrine, and the Quest for Nationhood." *Journal of Southern History* 83, no. 1 (February 2017): 69–106.

————. *John A. Quitman: Old South Crusader*. Baton Rouge: Louisiana State University Press, 1985.

————. "Lobbyists for Commercial Empire: Jane Cazneau, William Cazneau, and U.S. Caribbean Policy, 1846–1878." *Pacific Historical Review* 48, no. 3 (August 1979): 383–412.

————. *Manifest Destiny's Underworld: Filibustering in Antebellum America*. Chapel Hill: University of North Carolina Press, 2002.

————. *Slavery, Race, and Conquest in the Tropics: Lincoln, Douglas, and the Future of Latin America*. Cambridge UK: Cambridge University Press, 2013.

————. *The Southern Dream of a Caribbean Empire, 1854–1861*. 1973. Reprint, Gainesville: University Press of Florida, 2002.

McCaffrey, James M. *Army of Manifest Destiny: The American Soldier in the Mexican War, 1846–1848*. New York: New York University Press, 1992.

McCardell, John. *The Idea of a Southern Nation: Southern Nationalists and Southern Nationalism, 1830–1860*. New York: W. W. Norton, 1979.

McDonough, Matthew Davitian. "Manifestly Uncertain Destiny: The Debate over American Expansionism, 1803–1848." PhD dissertation, Kansas State University, 2011.

McDougall, Walter A. *Promised Land, Crusader State*. Boston: Houghton Mifflin, 1997.

McPherson, James. *Battle Cry of Freedom: The Civil War Era*. New York: Oxford University Press, 1988.

Menard, Andrew. *Sight Unseen: How Frémont's First Expedition Changed the American Landscape*. Lincoln NE: Bison, 2012.

Merk, Frederick. *The Monroe Doctrine and American Expansionism: 1843–1849*. With Lois Bannister Merk. New York: Alfred A. Knopf, 1966.

————. *The Oregon Question: Essays in Anglo-American Diplomacy and Politics*. Cambridge MA: Harvard University Press, 1967.

Merk, Frederick, and Lois Bannister Merk. *Manifest Destiny and Mission in American History*. 1963. Reprint, Cambridge MA: Harvard University Press, 1995.

Miller, Hunter, ed. *Treaties and Other International Acts of the United States of America*. 8 vols. Washington DC: Government Printing Office, 1931–48.

Miller, Robert J. *Native America, Discovered and Conquered: Thomas Jefferson, Lewis and Clark, and Manifest Destiny*. Lincoln: University of Nebraska Press, 2008.

Moore, Glover. *The Missouri Controversy, 1819–1821*. Lexington: University Press of Kentucky, 1953.

Morrill, Justin S. *Annexation of Santo Domingo: Speech of Hon. Justin S. Morrill, of Vermont, Delivered in the Senate of the United States, April 7, 1871.* Washington: F. & J. Rives & George A. Bailey, 1871.

Morrison, Chaplain. *Democratic Politics and Sectionalism: The Wilmot Proviso Controversy.* Chapel Hill: University of North Carolina Press, 1967.

Morrison, Michael A. *Slavery and the American West: The Eclipse of Manifest Destiny and the Coming of the Civil War.* Chapel Hill: University of North Carolina Press, 1997.

Morton, Oliver T. *The Southern Empire.* Cambridge MA: Riverside, 1892.

Mott, Frank Luther. *American Journalism: A History of Newspapers in the United States through 260 Years: 1690 to 1950.* Rev. ed. New York: Macmillan, 1950.

Nelson, Megan Kate. *The Three-Cornered War: The Union, the Confederacy, and Native Peoples in the Fight for the West.* New York: Scribner, 2020.

Nelson, William Javier. *Almost a Territory: America's Attempt to Annex the Dominican Republic.* Newark: University of Delaware Press, 1990.

Nevins, Allan. *Hamilton Fish: The Inner History of the Grant Administration.* New York: Dodd, Mead, 1937.

———. *Ordeal of the Union: Fruits of Manifest Destiny, 1847–1852.* New York: Charles Scribner's Sons, 1947.

Nichols, Roy Franklin. *Franklin Pierce: Young Hickory of the Granite Hills.* 1931. Reprint, Newton CT: American Political Biography, 2007.

Nugent, Walter. *Habits of Empire: A History of American Expansion.* New York: Vintage, 2009.

Oakes, James. *The Ruling Race: A History of American Slaveholders.* New York: Alfred A. Knopf, 1982.

Olliff, Donathon C. *Reforma Mexico and the United States: A Search for Alternatives to Annexation, 1854–1861.* Tuscaloosa: University of Alabama Press, 1981.

Owen, Tom. *The Taylor Anecdote Book: Anecdotes and Letters of Zachary Taylor and the Mexican War.* New York: D. Appleton, 1848.

Owsley, Frank L., and Gene A. Smith. *Filibusters and Expansionists: Jeffersonian Manifest Destiny, 1800–1821.* Tuscaloosa: University of Alabama Press, 1997.

Paolino, Ernest N. *The Foundations of the American Empire: William Henry Seward and U.S. Foreign Policy.* Ithaca NY: Cornell University Press, 1973.

Parker, Theodore. *A Sermon of the Mexican War: Preached at the Melodeon, on Sunday, June 25th, 1848.* Boston: Coolidge & Wiley, 1848.

Parton, James. *The Danish Islands: Are We Bound in Honor to Pay for Them?* Boston: Fields, Osgood, 1869.

Pearson, Joseph W. *The Whigs' America: Middle-Class Political Thought in the Age of Jackson and Clay.* Lexington: University Press of Kentucky, 2020.

Pierce, Jason E. *Making the White Man's West: Whiteness and the Creation of the American West.* Boulder: University of Colorado Press, 2016.

Pinheiro, John C. *Missionaries of Republicanism: A Religious History of the Mexican-American War.* New York: Oxford University Press, 2014.

Plesur, Milton. *America's Outward Thrust: Approaches to Foreign Affairs, 1865–1890*. DeKalb: Northern Illinois University Press, 1971.

Pletcher, David M. *The Diplomacy of Annexation: Texas, Oregon, and the Mexican War*. Columbia: University of Missouri Press, 1973.

———. *The Diplomacy of Involvement: American Economic Expansion across the Pacific, 1784–1900*. Columbia: University of Missouri Press, 2001.

Ponce, Pearl T. "'As Dead as Julius Caesar': The Rejection of the McLane-Ocampo Treaty." *Civil War History* 53, no. 4 (December 2007): 342–78.

Poore, Ben: Perley. *Life of Gen. Zachary Taylor, the Whig Candidate for the Presidency*. Boston: Stacy, Richardson, 1848.

Porter, Kirk H, comp. *A Compilation of the Messages and Papers of the Presidents, 1789–1897*. Washington DC: Government Printing Office, 1898.

———. *National Party Platforms*. New York: Macmillan, 1924.

Potter, David M. *The Impending Crisis, 1848–1861*. New York: Harper & Row, 1976.

Pratt, Julius. "John L. O'Sullivan and Manifest Destiny." *New York History* 14, no. 3 (July 1933): 213–34.

———. "The Origin of 'Manifest Destiny.'" *American Historical Review* 32, no. 4 (July 1927): 795–98.

Quigley, Paul. *Shifting Grounds: Nationalism and the American South, 1848–1865*. New York: Oxford University Press, 2012.

Rable, George C. *The Confederate Republic: A Revolution against Politics*. Chapel Hill: University of North Carolina Press, 1994.

———. *Damn Yankees! Demonization and Defiance in the Confederate South*. Baton Rouge: Louisiana State University Press, 2015.

———. *God's Almost Chosen Peoples: A Religious History of the American Civil War*. Chapel Hill: University of North Carolina Press, 2010.

Rauch, Basil. *American Interest in Cuba: 1848–1855*. 1948. Reprint, New York: Octagon, 1974.

Rayback, Joseph G. *Free Soil: The Election of 1848*. Lexington: University Press of Kentucky, 1970.

———. *Millard Fillmore: Biography of a President*. 1959. Reprint, Newton CT: American Political Biography, 1992.

———. "Who Wrote the Allison Letters: A Study in Historical Detection." *Mississippi Valley Historical Review* 36, no. 1 (June 1949): 51–72.

Reichard, David A. "How Do Students Understand the History of the American West? An Argument for the Scholarship of Teaching and Learning." *Western Historical Quarterly* 37, no. 2 (Summer 2006): 207–14.

Report of the Commission of Inquiry to Santo Domingo. Washington DC: Government Printing Office, 1871.

Reséndez, Andrés. *Changing National Identities at the Frontier: Texas and New Mexico, 1800–1850*. Cambridge UK: Cambridge University Press, 2005.

Reynolds, David. *America, Empire of Liberty: A New History of the United States*. New York: Basic Books, 2009.

Richards, Leonard L. *The Slave Power: The Free North and Southern Domination, 1780–1860*. Baton Rouge: Louisiana State University Press, 2000.

Richards, Thomas, Jr. *Breakaway Americas: The Unmanifest Future of the Jacksonian United States*. Baltimore: Johns Hopkins University Press, 2020.

Richardson, James D., ed. *A Compilation of the Messages and Papers of the Presidents, 1789–1907*. 11 vols. New York: Bureau of National Literature and Art, 1908.

Riepma, Siert F. "Young America: A Study in American Nationalism before the Civil War." PhD dissertation, Western Reserve University, 1939.

Ritchie, Donald A. *Press Gallery: Congress and the Washington Correspondents*. Cambridge MA: Harvard University Press, 1991.

Rodríguez, Sarah K. M. "'Children of the Great Mexican Family': Anglo-American Immigration to Texas and the Making of the American Empire, 1820–1861." PhD dissertation, University of Pennsylvania, 2015.

———. "'The Greatest Nation on Earth': The Politics and Patriotism of the First Anglo American Immigrants to Mexican Texas, 1820–1824." *Pacific Historical Review* 86, no. 1 (February 2017): 50–83.

Roosevelt, Theodore. *Life of Thomas Hart Benton*. Cambridge MA: Riverside, 1887.

Rose, E. M. P. *The Poetry of Locofocoism; Or, Modern Democracy and Cassism Unmasked*. Wellsburg VA: J. A. Metcalf, 1848.

Rosengarten, Frederic, Jr. *Freebooters Must Die! The Life and Death of William Walker, the Most Notorious Filibuster of the Nineteenth Century*. Wayne PA: Haverford House, 1976.

Rourke, Constance. *American Humor: A Study of the National Character*. 1931. Reprint. New York: New York Review of Books, 2004.

Rowe, John Carlos. *Literary Culture and U.S. Imperialism: From the Revolution to World War II*. New York: Oxford University Press, 2000.

Sainlaude, Stève. *France and the American Civil War: A Diplomatic History*. Translated by Jessica Edwards. Chapel Hill: University of North Carolina Press, 2019.

Sampson. Robert. *John L. O'Sullivan and His Times*. Kent OH: Kent State University Press, 2003.

Sanford, Miles. "The True Elements of National Greatness and Prosperity." In *The American Pulpit: A Collection of Sermons on Important Subjects, by Living Ministers, of the Various Evangelical Denominations in America*, edited by Reverend J. D. Bridge, 295–307. Worcester MA: Samuel Chism, 1848.

Schlesinger, Arthur M., Jr. *The Age of Jackson*. Boston: Little, Brown, 1945.

Schott, Thomas E. *Alexander H. Stephens of Georgia: A Biography*. Baton Rouge: Louisiana State University Press, 1988.

Schroeder, John H. "Major Jack Downing and American Expansionism: Seba Smith's Political Satire, 1847–1856." *New England Quarterly* 50, no. 2 (June 1977): 214–23.

———. *Mr. Polk's War: American Opposition and Dissent, 1846–1848*. Madison: University of Wisconsin Press, 1973.

Scribe, Seraiah [pseud]. *Chronicles of the Fire-Eaters of the Tribe of Mississippi*. Brandon MS: Republican Office, 1853.

Scroogs, William O. *Filibusters and Financiers: The Story of William Walker and His Associates*. New York: MacMillan, 1916.

Semmes, Ryan Patrick. "Exporting Reconstruction: Civilization, Citizenship, and Republicanism during the Grant Administration, 1869–1877." PhD dissertation, Mississippi State University, 2020.

Seward, Frederick W. *Seward at Washington, as Senator and Secretary of State: A Memoir of His Life, with Selections from His Letters, 1861–1872*. New York: Derby and Miller, 1891.

Seward, William Henry. *The Works of William Henry Seward*. Edited by George E. Baker. 5 vols. Boston: Houghton Mifflin, 1884.

Sewell, Richard H. *Ballots for Freedom: Antislavery Politics in the United States, 1837–1860*. New York: Oxford University Press, 1976.

———. *John P. Hale and the Politics of Abolition*. Cambridge MA: Harvard University Press, 1965.

Sexton, Jay. *Debtor Diplomacy: Finance and American Foreign Relations in the Civil War Era, 1837–1873*. New York: Oxford University Press, 2005.

———. *The Monroe Doctrine: Empire and Nation in Nineteenth-Century America*. New York: Hill & Wang, 2011.

Shenton, James P. *Robert John Walker: A Politician from Jackson to Lincoln*. New York: Columbia University Press, 1961.

Shippee, Lester Burrell. *Canadian-American Relations, 1849–1874*. New Haven CT: Yale University Press, 1939.

Shire, Laurel Clark. *The Threshold of Manifest Destiny: Gender and National Expansion in Florida*. Philadelphia: University of Pennsylvania Press, 2016.

Silbey, Joel H. *Party over Section: The Rough and Ready Presidential Election of 1848*. Lawrence: University Press of Kansas, 2009.

———. *Storm over Texas: The Annexation Controversy and the Road to Civil War*. New York: Oxford University Press, 2005.

Sinha, Manisha. *The Counter-Revolution of Slavery: Politics and Ideology in Antebellum South Carolina*. Chapel Hill: University of North Carolina Press, 2000.

———. *The Slave's Cause: A History of Abolition*. New Haven CT: Yale University Press, 2016.

A Sketch of the Life and Public Services of General Zachary Taylor, The People's Candidate for the Presidency, with Considerations in Favor of His Election. Washington DC: J. T. Towers, 1848.

Slap, Andrew L. *The Doom of Reconstruction: The Liberal Republicans in the Civil War Era*. New York: Fordham University Press, 2006.

Slotkin, Richard. *The Fatal Environment: The Myth of the Frontier in the Age of Industrialization, 1800–1890*. New York: Atheneum, 1985.

———. *Regeneration through Violence: The Mythology of the American Frontier, 1600–1860*. Middletown CT: Wesleyan University Press, 1973.

Smith, Elbert B. *The Presidencies of Zachary Taylor and Millard Fillmore*. Lawrence: University Press of Kansas, 1988.

Smith, Joe Patterson. *The Republican Expansionists of the Early Reconstruction Era.* Chicago: University of Chicago Libraries, 1933.

Smith, Seba. *My Thirty Years out of the Senate.* New York: Derby and Jackson, 1860.

Southern Chivalry: The Adventures of G. Whillikens, C.S.A. Knight of the Golden Circle; and of Guinea Pete, His Negro Squire. Philadelphia, 1861.

Sowle, Patrick. "A Reappraisal of Seward's Memorandum of April 1, 1861, to Lincoln." *Journal of Southern History* 33, no. 2 (May 1967): 234–39.

Spalding, Matthew, and Patrick J. Garrity. *A Sacred Union of Citizens: George Washington's Farewell Address and the American Character.* Lanham MD: Rowman & Littlefield, 1996.

Spencer, Donald S. *Louis Kossuth and Young America: A Study of Sectionalism and Foreign Policy.* Columbia: University of Missouri Press, 1977.

Spencer, Ivor Debenham. *The Victor and the Spoils: A Life of William L. Marcy.* Providence RI: Brown University Press, 1959.

Sproat, John G. *"The Best Men": Liberal Reformers in the Gilded Age.* Chicago: University of Chicago Press, 1968.

Stahr, Walter. *Seward: Lincoln's Indispensable Man.* New York: Simon & Schuster, 2012.

Stanton, John. *Corry O'Lanus: His Views and Experiences.* New York: G. W. Carleton, 1867.

Stegmaier, Mark J. *Texas, New Mexico, and the Compromise of 1850: Boundary Dispute and Sectional Crisis.* Kent OH: Kent State University Press, 1996.

Stephanson, Anders. *Manifest Destiny: American Expansion and the Empire of Right.* New York: Hill and Wang, 1995.

Stephens, Alexander H. *Alexander H. Stephens, in Public and Private, with Letters and Speeches, before, during, and since the War.* Edited by Henry Cleveland. Philadelphia: National Publishing Company, 1866.

Stewart, Gordon T. *The American Response to Canada since 1776.* East Lansing: Michigan State University Press, 1992.

Stewart, James Brewer. *Holy Warriors: The Abolitionists and American Slavery.* New York: Hill and Wang, 1976.

St. John, Rachel. "Contingent Continent: Spatial and Geographic Arguments in the Shaping of the Nineteenth-Century United States." *Pacific Historical Review* 86, no. 1 (2017): 18–49.

———. "The Unpredictable America of William Gwin: Expansion, Secession, and the Unstable Borders of Nineteenth-Century America." *Journal of the Civil War Era* 6, no. 1 (March 2016): 56–84.

Stout, Harry S. *Upon the Altar of the Nation: A Moral History of the American Civil War.* New York: Viking, 2006.

Stout, Joseph A., Jr. *Schemers and Dreamers: Filibustering in Mexico, 1848–1921.* Fort Worth: Texas Christian University Press, 2002.

Streeby, Shelley. *American Sensations: Class, Empire, and the Production of Popular Culture.* Berkeley: University of California Press, 2002.

Stuart, Reginald C. *United States Expansionism and British North America*. Chapel Hill: University of North Carolina Press, 1988.

Summers, Mark Wahlgren. *The Ordeal of the Reunion: A New History of Reconstruction*. Chapel Hill: University of North Carolina Press, 2014.

———. *The Press Gang, Newspapers and Politics, 1865–1878*. Chapel Hill: University of North Carolina Press, 1994.

Sumner, Charles. *The Crime against Kansas*. Boston: John P. Jewett, 1856.

———. *Naboth's Vineyard: Speech of Hon. Charles Sumner of Massachusetts, on the Proposed Annexion of "The Island of San Domingo," Delivered in the Senate of the United States, December 21, 1870*. Washington: F. & J. Rives & Geo. A. Bailey, 1870.

———. *Speech of Hon. Charles Sumner, of Massachusetts, on the Cession of Russian America to the United States*. Washington DC: Congressional Globe Office, 1867.

Sundquist, Eric J. *Empire and Slavery in American Literature, 1820–1865*. Jackson: University Press of Mississippi, 1995.

Sweeney, J. Gray. *The Columbus of the Woods: Daniel Boone and the Typology of Manifest Destiny*. St. Louis: Washington University Gallery of Art, 1992.

Tansill, Charles C. *The Canadian Reciprocity Treaty of 1854*. Baltimore: Johns Hopkins Press, 1922.

———. *The Purchase of the Danish West Indies*. Baltimore: Johns Hopkins Press, 1932.

———. *The United States and Santo Domingo, 1798–1873: A Chapter in Caribbean Diplomacy*. Baltimore: Johns Hopkins Press, 1938.

Thomas, Emory M. *The Confederate Nation, 1861–1865*. New York: Harper, 1979.

Torget, Andrew. *Seeds of Empire: Cotton, Slavery, and the Transformation of the Texas Borderlands*. Chapel Hill: University of North Carolina Press, 2015.

Travis, Ira Dudley. *The History of the Clayton-Bulwer Treaty*. Ann Arbor: Michigan Political Science Association, 1900.

Trefousse, Hans L. *Carl Schurz: A Biography*. Knoxville: University of Tennessee Press, 1982.

Tucker, Ann L. *Newest Born of Nations: European Nationalist Movements and the Making of the Confederacy*. Charlottesville: University of Virginia Press, 2020.

Turner, Frederick Jackson. "The Problem of the West." *Atlantic Monthly* 78, no. 467 (September 1896): 289–97.

———. *The United States, 1830–1850*. 1935. Reprint, New York: W. W. Norton, 1963.

Tuveson, Ernest Lee. *Redeemer Nation: The Idea of America's Millennial Role*. 1968. Reprint, Chicago: Midway Reprint, 1980.

Van Alstyne, Richard W. "British Diplomacy and the Clayton-Bulwer Treaty." *Journal of Modern History* 11, no. 2 (June 1939): 149–83.

Van Atta, John R. *Wolf by the Ears: The Missouri Crisis, 1819–1821*. Baltimore: Johns Hopkins University Press, 2015.

Van Deusen, Glyndon G. *William Henry Seward*. New York: Oxford University Press, 1967.

Varg, Paul A. *Foreign Policies of the Founding Fathers*. Reprint, 1963. Baltimore: Penguin, 1972.

Vilá, Herminio Portell. *Narciso López y su época*, vol. 1. Habana [Havana], Cuba: Cultural, S.A., 1930.

Wahlstrom, Todd W. *The Southern Exodus to Mexico: Migration across the Borderlands after the American Civil War*. Lincoln: University of Nebraska Press, 2015.

Waite, Kevin. *West of Slavery: The Southern Dream of a Transcontinental Empire*. Chapel Hill: University of North Carolina Press, 2021.

Walters, Ronald G. *The Antislavery Appeal: American Abolitionism after 1830*. Baltimore: Johns Hopkins University Press, 1976.

Walther, Eric H. *William Lowndes Yancey: The Coming of the Civil War*. Chapel Hill: University of North Carolina Press, 2006.

Warner, Donald F. *The Idea of Continental Union: Agitation for the Annexation of Canada to the United States, 1849–1893*. Lexington: University Press of Kentucky, 1960.

Webster, Daniel. *Mr. Webster's Speech at Marshfield, Mass. Delivered September 1, 1848, and His Speech on the Oregon Bill, Delivered in the United States Senate, August 12, 1848*. Boston: T. R. Marvin, 1848.

_____. *The Papers of Daniel Webster: Correspondence*. Edited by Charles M. Wiltse, Wendy B. Tilghman, Harold D. Moser, David G. Allen, and Michael J. Birkner. 7 vols. Hanover NH: University Press of New England, 1974–86.

Weeks, William Earl. *Building the Continental Empire: American Expansion from the Revolution to the Civil War*. Chicago: Ivan R. Dee, 1996.

———. *The New Cambridge History of America Foreign Relations*, vol. 1: *Dimensions of the Early American Empire, 1754–1865*. Cambridge UK: Cambridge University Press, 2013.

Weinberg, Albert K. *Manifest Destiny: A Study of Nationalist Expansionism in American History*. 1935. Reprint, Chicago: Quadrangle Paperback, 1963.

Welch, Richard E., Jr. "American Public Opinion and the Purchase of Russian America." *American Slavic and East European Review* 17, no. 4 (December 1958): 481–94.

Welles, Sumner. *Naboth's Vineyard: The Dominican Republic, 1844–1924*. 1928. Reprint, Washington DC: Savile, 1966.

White, Ronald C. *American Ulysses: A Life of Ulysses S. Grant*. New York: Random House, 2016.

Widmer, Edward. *Young America: The Flowering of Democracy in New York City*. New York: Oxford University Press, 1999.

Wilentz, Sean. *The Rise of American Democracy: Jefferson to Lincoln*. New York: W. W. Norton, 2005.

Williams, Mary Wilhelmine. *Anglo-American Isthmian Diplomacy, 1815–1915*. 1916. Reprint, Gloucester MA: Peter Smith, 1965.

Wilsey, John D. *American Exceptionalism and Civil Religion: Reassessing the History of an Idea*. Downers Grove IL: IVP Academic, 2015.

Wilson, Major L. *Space, Time, and Freedom: The Quest for Nationality and the Irrepressible Conflict*. Westport CT: Greenwood, 1974.

Winter, Aaron McLean. "The Laughing Dove: Satire in 19th-Century U.S. Anti-War Rhetoric." PhD dissertation, University of California, Irvine, 2008.

Wire, Richard Arden. "John M. Clayton and the Search for Order: A Study in Whig Politics and Diplomacy." PhD dissertation, University of Maryland, 1971.

Wolnisty, Claire R. *A Different Manifest Destiny: U.S. Southern Identity and Citizenship in Nineteenth-Century South America*. Lincoln: University of Nebraska Press, 2020.

Woodworth, Steven E. *Manifest Destinies: America's Westward Expansion and the Road to the Civil War*. New York: Alfred A. Knopf, 2010.

Wyman, Mary Alice. *Two American Pioneers: Seba Smith and Elizabeth Oakes Smith*. New York: Columbia University Press, 1927.

INDEX

118–19, 125, 130; and manifest destiny, 20, 110, 119–20, 122–23; origins of, 117–18

Copenhagen, Denmark, 139

Corry O'Lanus (character). *See* Stanton, John

Corwin, Thomas, 34–35, 107

Costa Rica, 60, 102

Courier-Journal, 1–2

Cox, Samuel Sullivan, 111–12, 165

Crofutt, George, 173–75, *174*

Crofutt's Western World, 173

Crusades, 26–27

Cuba: compared to Dominican Republic, 152, 167–68, 170; Confederate plans for, 20, 110, 117–18; and failure of manifest destiny, 2, 3–5, 7, 16, 18–19, 21–22, *42*, 64, 120, 128, 171–73, 175, 177–78, 180; filibustering for, 65–69, 70–72, 75–78, 82–86, 109, 120; slave power and, 89–94, 97–102, 104, 106–7, 115–17, 123–24; as undesirable, 17, 50–52, 57, 75–76, 115, 158, 163; U.S. desire to purchase, 69–70, 72, 73, 79–81, 87–88, 102–3, 111–12, 113, 126–27, 138, 143, 149, 156, 157–59, 162, 169

Cushing, Caleb, 79, 106

Danish West Indies: sale of, 139, 147–48; as undesirable, 130, 140–47, 158, 177, 178; U.S. desire for, 20, *142*, 148, 175

David, Jacques-Louis, 173

Davis, Jefferson, 61, 79, 117

Dayton, William L., 37–38

Declaration of Independence, 171

Democratic Party: divisions within, 38, 44, 61–64, 65–66, 73–76, 85, 112–13; and filibustering, 67–69, 71–72, 77–79, 94–96; opposition to manifest destiny by, 152, 155, 164–65, 169; in popular culture, 40–43, 52–56, 83–84, 135–37; and slave power, 90–91, 97–101, 102–7, 114, 115–16; support for manifest destiny by, 1, 3, 8, 18, 39, 45, 47–48, 82, 109–12, 120, 124, 126, 131, 156, 173

Democratic Review: annexation of Mexico discussed in, 24–25, 44; capitalization of manifest destiny in, 176; Clayton-Bulwer Treaty denounced in, 64; definition of manifest destiny in, 3–4, 5; influence of, 11, 14; rise of Young America and, 73; support for filibustering in, 69, 71, 96

deserts, 24, 36–37, 133, 149

Dickinson, Daniel, 61, 189n126

diplomacy: Democratic Party and, 58, 79, 84, 85, 94, 97–98, 103, 111, 116; Republican Party and, 139, 146; Whig Party and, 58. *See also* foreign policy

Dominican Republic, 17, 21, 22, 151–52, 158, 172. *See also* Santo Domingo

Dominicans: compared to Cubans, 152, 167, 170; U.S. racial stereotypes of, 21, 151–52, 159–60, 161, 163–66, 168–69, 212n50

doughfaces, 45, 92, 115, 148

Douglas, Stephen: as believer in manifest destiny, 6, 22, 64, *74*, 75–76, 112–13, 126, 148, 177, 179; and Clayton-Bulwer Treaty, 61, 64; and Compromise of 1850, 66; death of, 169; and Kansas-Nebraska Act, 88; as presidential candidate, 115, 116, 117; and Treaty of Guadalupe Hidalgo, 43, 44, 61; and Young America, 73–74, 79

Douglass, Frederick, 162

Dow, Jr. (character). *See* Paige, Elbridge Gerry

Downs, Solomon, 63

Duffield, George, Jr., 119

earthquakes: and Danish West Indies, 20, 130, 140, 141, 179; jokes about, 139, 140, 143, 145, 146–47, 148, 149, 177, 209n76

Egypt, 27

Emerson, Ralph Waldo, 11

empire: Confederate plans for, 117–18; Great Britain as rival, 3; internal opposition to U.S., 3, 13–14, 15–17, 22–23, 27–28, 40, 149, 176–77, 178–80; Napoléon III and French, 121–22; Spain as rival, 59–60; support for U.S., 4, 24, 96, 112, 115, 124, 126, 127, 156–57, 173–74

enslavers: and expansion, 19, 88, 90–92, 93, 94, 100, 104, 114, 123, 129; as politicians, 56, 66, *101*. *See also* slaveholders; slavery

environment: as reason to oppose expansion, 20, 35–37, 129–30, 138–39, 148, 149, 210n107; as reason to support expansion, 140, 158–59, 188n87. *See also* climate

Europe: and the Crusades, 26; as impediment to U.S. empire, 120, 121–22, 125–26, 130, 132, 142, 148, 158–59; U.S. intervention in, 18, 41, 42

Democratic, 75; 1856 Democratic, 97, 98–99, *100*, *101*, 102; 1856 Republican, 97–98; 1860 northern Democratic, 113; 1860 southern Democratic, 113; 1864 Democratic, 126, 169; 1864 Republican, 125–26; 1868 Democratic, 155; 1868 Republican, 155; 1872 Democratic, 167–68; 1872 Republican, 167

patriotism, 30, 49, 71, 111

peace: George Washington and, 29, 47, 56; religion and, 26, 28; Republican Party and, 167; Whig Party and, 18, 49, 50, 52, 57

Pearce, James, 38

Petroleum V. Nasby (character). *See* Locke, David Ross

Philadelphia PA, 72, 97

Philippines, 172

Piatt, Donn, 163

Pierce, Franklin: background of, 74–75; failures of, 18–19, 21, 84–86, 111, 177; and filibustering, 65, 77–78, 82–84, 196n89; and Kansas-Nebraska Act, 87–88, 90; and Nicaragua, 95, 96; and Ostend Manifesto, 80, 81–82; as presidential candidate, 75–76, 101; and slave power, 91–92, 98; and Young America, 75, 79

pirates, 69, 143. *See also* robber doctrine

polar bears: and Alaska, 20, 130, 133, 155; jokes about, *134*, *137*, 138, 140, 144, 145, 146–47, 148, 152

Polk, James K.: Democratic support of, 24–25, 45, 84; failures of, 21, 177, 179–80; significance of, 2–3, 8; Whig critique of, 29–31, 33, 36, 40–43, 47, 52–53, 58, 59, 64, 75

Pollock, James, 38

Poore, Ben: Perley, 49, 190n24

popular sovereignty, 128

Porter, David D., 140

Portland Courier, 39–40

Pratt, Julius W., 8

Prentice, George D., 29–31, 43–44, 75, 82–83

presidential proclamations, 67, 70–72, 85

prophets, 23, 28

protectorate, 103, 104, 105, 111

Puerto Rico, 91, 156, 172

Puritanism, 10, 119

Quebec, Canada, 131

race: as hindrance to U.S. expansion, 32, 37–39, 152–55, 157–58, 159–62, 163–67; as motivation for Confederate expansion, 117, 118; as motivation for U.S. expansion, 4–5, 13, 25, 43; in popular culture, 41–43, *153*, *154*, 155, 166–67. *See also* Anglo-Saxons

Raleigh Register, and North-Carolina Gazette, 27

Rayback, Joseph, 56, 191n52

Republican Party: divisions within, 19, 105, 115, 146–47, 148–49, 158, 161–62, 165–66, 177, 179; and filibustering, 95–96, 98–99; foreign policy of, 125–26, 169, 177–78; and manifest destiny, 6, 20–21, 93, 109–10, 112, 113–14, 131, 151, 170; and McLane-Ocampo Treaty, 104–5; origins of, 87, 92–93; and Ostend Manifesto, 97–98, 99–100; and slave power, 19, 87–88, 93–107, 115–17, 177

Reséndez, Andrés, 14

Reynolds, David, 2

Rhode Island, 173

Richards, Thomas, Jr., 15–16, 17

Richmond Dispatch, 118–19, 123, 125, 156

Richmond Whig, 27, 31, 32, 44, 69, 102

Rivas, Patricio, 95, 96

robber doctrine: definition of, 65–66; effectiveness of, 84–86; and filibustering, 18, 67–69, 70, 71, 77, 129; and manifest destiny, 31, 44, 88; Ostend Manifesto and, 80–83; U.S.-Mexican War and, 17, 24, 31–32

Rodríguez, Sarah K. M., 14–15

Rome, 27, 29, 30, 118

Roosevelt, Theodore, 6–7

Root, Joseph, 31–32

Round Island MS, 66–67

Russia, 120, 129, 130–31, 133, 135, 152

Russian Alaska, 136, 138. *See also* Alaska

Russian America, 114, 133. *See also* Alaska

Sack of Lawrence, 96–97

Samaná Bay, 158

Sanders, George N., 73–74, 83

San Diego CA, 36

Sandwich Islands, 55, 91, 92. *See also* Hawaii

Sanford, Miles, 28

San Francisco CA, 36–37